ROME AND THE VATICAN
GUIDE 4 PILGRIMS

"This book is at the top of my list as one of the most comprehensive Catholic travel guides to Rome. I especially love the stunning images, interesting facts about the saints and our Catholic faith, as well as all of the travel tips included in this book. I am taking this book with me on all 4 of my pilgrimages to Rome this year."
Teresa Tomeo
Catholic Radio & Television Host
Pilgrimage Leader to Rome & The Vatican for over 10 Years

"If you take one book to Rome, take this one! If you want one book to help you through Rome and the Vatican, this is it. Loaded with information from a spiritual and historical point of view. Especially excellent for Catholic pilgrims. Full of pictures, facts, detailed and pertinent information. It is in my pack on every trip."
Steve Ray
Catholic Convert, Apologist and Pilgrimage Leader

ROME
AND THE
VATICAN
GUIDE 4 PILGRIMS

KENNETH E. NOWELL
ELIZABETH H. NOWELL

VERO HOUSE PUBLISHING

THE AURELIAN WALL
275 AD

ROME AND THE VATICAN
GUIDE 4 PILGRIMS

Kenneth E. Nowell &
Elizabeth H. Nowell
Copyright © 2013 - 2016 Kenneth E. Nowell

For information, contact:
Vero House Publishing, Corp.
750 Fortrunella Cir. SW
Vero Beach, FL 32968
Email: admin@VeroHousePublishing.com

Printed in the United States of America.

PAPERBACK
ISBN: 978-0-9886539-8-6

HARDBACK
ISBN: 978-0-9886539-7-9

Library of Congress Control Number:
2016902951

Originally published December 9, 2013,
Feast of the Immaculate Conception.
This book contains minor revisions from 2016.

www.VeroHousePublishing.com
www.Guide4Pilgrims.com

DEDICATED:

TO ROME'S CREATIVE
PAINTERS, SCULPTORS,
ARCHITECTS AND CRAFTSMEN;

MORE IMPORTANTLY,
TO THE CLERGY, SAINTS AND MARTYRS
WHO INSPIRED THEM;

MOST IMPORTANTLY,
TO THE GREATEST CREATOR
WHO INSPIRED THEM ALL.

CONTENTS

PART ONE:
Orientation to Rome
and to this Guide

DOME OF THE PANTHEON
AKA SANTA MARIA AD MARTYRES
126 AD

"THE BLOOD OF MARTYRS
IS THE SEED OF THE CHURCH."
TERTULLIAN
2ND CENTURY

HISTORY 4 PILGRIMS

The Via Sacra ("Sacred Road") dates from the 5th century BC. It was used as a parade route into the Forum, where Roman conquerors displayed the spoils of war from around the world, as citizens cheered. These "triumphs" were extravagantly staged and directed through the Triumphal Arch of Titus (81 AD). Often, the procession included newfound slaves, conquered kings in chains, as well as exotic animals, never before seen. Many of them eventually would end their days on the arena of the nearby Colosseum,.

AUTHORS' PREFACE

Dear Readers,

We are pleased to present this visually stimulating, faith-based guide to Rome's unique Christian history. In it, you will discover surprising details on sites and subjects rarely found in other travel books. That is because during our explorations of the art, architecture, history and faith of Rome and the Vatican, we sought what engages and inspires Christian pilgrims, not just tourists.

The unparalleled human drama of Rome spans more than twenty-five centuries. Most of that time, for a variety of reasons, the Eternal City demanded the world's attention. Even while alternating between the extremes of faith and decadence, triumph and downfall, Renaissance and plunder, Rome was a force like no other in the development of Western civilization. Because of that, Rome is often called *caput mundi* – capital of the world. It is a title the Eternal City has earned.

But while most tourists are fascinated by the violent imperial history of Rome, or the artistic beauty of Renaissance Rome, they and their guides often miss a more important story. Even before Rome destroyed Jerusalem's Temple in 70 AD, Saints Peter and Paul had arrived here, spreading the Gospel and establishing the foundation of the Church. Because of their sacrifices, and those of countless other saints and martyrs, our Christian heritage was nurtured and preserved.

That extraordinary legacy continues to this day.

So, even as we venerate the heroic virtue of early saints and martyrs, we still wonder at the grand but decaying remnants of imperial Rome. We admire Rome's countless masterpieces of art and are elevated by its amazing range of architectural and engineering excellence. Nevertheless, we are most moved when we reflect on the indomitable Spirit of Christian Rome in its churches. There, we are reminded that from Christ to His Roman martyrs our faith was preserved in blood.

We should not fail to mention, however, a few issues regarding the book itself. First, we have attempted to list correct times at each site for opening and closing. Especially in Italy, however, hours of operation are subject to personal discretion. So, before risking a major inconvenience, apply the old adage: trust but verify. Second, throughout this book, names are often listed in both Italian and English, but to prevent unnecessary duplication, we opt for the Italian version most of the time.

Finally, when traveling to Rome, carry along your favorite guidebook for dining, entertainment and travel information that this *Guide 4 Pilgrims* may not include. But with this book in hand, prepare to see what most tourists miss. Prepare to appreciate what most Christians never learn. Prepare to elevate your faith to a new level.

That is our prayer: May God bless you with an unforgettable Spirit-filled journey as you explore Rome and the Vatican through this book. If Christ's legacy in the Eternal City elevates your faith half as much as it has ours, you will be blessed indeed.

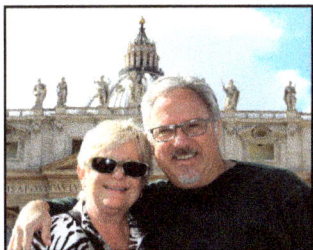

Buon Viaggio!

Kenneth and
Elizabeth Nowell

Meals:

In breakfast shops, many Italians stand at the bar (*al banco*) because prices are higher if you sit at a table (*à tavola*). So, if you prefer to sit, claim a table before ordering, and pay the price. Most Italians grab breakfast (*calazione*) on the run. A typical breakfast for them is a bold shot of *espresso*, along with a pastry or croissant-like roll (*briosce or cornetto*). Order *cafe' Americano* if you want your coffee home-style. *Cappuccino* is popular, also, but you may receive an odd look if you order it later in the day. Italians only drink *cappuccino* for a day-starter.

Lunch (*pranzo*) is generally the most substantial meal of the day and is eaten between 12:30 and 3. Many meals start with appetizers (*antipasti*) of cured meats, cheeses or marinated vegetables. The first main plate (*primo piatto*) might include pasta, rice, soup or pizza. The second plate (*secundo piatto*) would include a meat, sometimes along with a side dish (*contorno*) consisting of a vegetable, salad or potatoes. The meal is usually finished off with dessert (*dolci*), that include fruit or sweets, and coffee. Italians drink bottled water with their meals, which comes either plain (*naturale*) or sparkling (*minerale*). Of course, wine is also popular. Full five-course meals are reserved for special occassions. So, Italians generally mix and match two or three options on most days. Keep in mind that a single plate will not represent a very satisfying meal.

Dinner (*cena*) is usually eaten between 7:30 or 8, to 11 PM. The selections will be similar to what is offered at lunch, but Italians eat a lighter dinner. For Americans who tend to eat less lunch, go ahead and indulge!

Many restaurants close on Mondays and at least two weeks in August.

Restaurants

A source of confusion, for Americans, is the variety of types of restaurants in Italy. Of course, you will find the occassional McDonalds. But, when in Rome, eat like the Romans!

- A *ristorante* offers finer dining and an upscale atmosphere. Consequently, prices tend toward the high end.
- A *trattoria* is, traditionally, a more relaxed atmosphere with home-style Italian food like *Nonna* made. As these have become more popular, however, some have fancied themselves "*chic*" enough to charge *ristorante* prices.
- An *osteria* is similar to an American coffee shop, except they serve wine by the glass. They offer short menus of simple homemade specialties in an atmosphere that is relaxed enough to invite card playing.
- A *tavola calda* ("hot table") is a stand-up buffet where you can choose as little or as much as your appetite dictates. Some even offer the luxury of seats!

As always, seek out wherever the locals eat. A restaurant that is packed with families means the food is not only good but reasonably priced. In our experience, the hotel desk clerk may not be the best guide. His recommendation may be biased or even compensated.

Other Eating Options

Abundant coffee shops offer a variety of pastries and sandwiches (*panini*) along with pizza. Grocery stores (*alimentari*) and markets (*mercati*) furnish food and drink that you can enjoy in your hotel room or at a countryside picnic. But keep in mind that Rome recently began ticketing tourists who picnic in trafficked areas. If you are eating, keep moving, or find a secluded spot. Finally, in Rome, to top it all off, there is nothing tastier than a scoop of high-quality *gelato*. It is creamier and more smoothly flavored than American ice cream. Our favorite flavor is pistachio.

Tipping

At restaurants, a *pane e coperto* charge – usually 1 to 3€ per person – is often added to the tab. The name implies it is a charge for bread, but it is actually a seating charge, whether you want the bread or not. A service charge (tip) is usually included in your restaurant bill, but if you are unsure, ask: *È incluso il servizio?* (ay een-cloo-soh eel sair-vee-tsoh?). If not included, leave 5% to 10% tip, depending on the quality of the restaurant.

Tourist Menu

In Rome, many restaurants cater to travelers from around the world. So, tourist menus are popular. Usually, a sign is posted outside (in English) specifying a basic three-course meal, often in the range of 12 to 15€. The tourist menu will not feature the best of Italian food, but it can be enjoyable. When finished, to request the bill, ask: *Il conto, per favore* (eel con-toh, por fah-vohr-ay).

Orientation: Accommodations

Typically, tourist hotel rooms are clean, comfortable and reasonably priced. But they may lack some American-style amenities. Keep in mind that you won't need every hotel convenience when the Eternal City awaits at your doorstep. Still, here are a few examples of the differences:

- Bath tubs are rare and showers, small to tiny.
- Beds are usually twin size, and a "double bed" is two twins, pushed together.
- Bath wash cloths, generally, are not available. (See tip, below.)
- Hotels offer satellite television, but usually with few English-speaking channels. Still, Italian TV can be quite amusing (sometimes for unintended reasons, as shown, right).

An example of Italian TV.

Hotel practices also differ, a bit:

- Usually, you will be asked to drop your key at the front desk whenever the room is left empy. Many hotels offer room safes for valuables. When in doubt, play it safe.
- Tile floors are common. Rooms are rarely carpeted.
- Ice machines are practically nonexistent and ice, all over Europe, is far less available than in America.
- Elevators can be tiny, and you may have to carry luggage up stairs in some hotels. (See tip, below.)
- In the summer months, some hotels assess an extra charge for each day the room air conditioner is used. We have also encountered room air conditioners that freeze up if left on all day. For night-time comfort, you may leave the window open. But city traffic noise can be annoying.
- Also, a daily hotel tax has been initiated in Rome. Expect to pay an extra 2€ per person, per day, even if you were not forewarned. In nicer hotels, the tax can escalate to 6€ per person, per day. (These charges, however, should be explained to you at check in.)
- A modest but sufficient, self-serve breakfast is usually offered for free at tourist hotels. Generally, it includes a nice collection of pastries, oatmeal, yogurt, cereals, milk, coffees and fruit drinks. Cheeses and cold cuts also may be available. A small tip (perhaps, 1€, each day) will be appreciated by the kitchen staff who also clean the tables.

Italian hotels are graded by a five-star rating system. Even some one-star hotels, may be perfectly adequate for short stays, as we found on an overnight trip to Florence. They might simply lack amenities, like in-room telephones, air conditioning, internet access and televisions. However, before reserving, it is best to seek out reviews, like those offered at TripAdvisor.com. If in doubt, stick to three stars and above. The one pictured at the left was 3.5 stars and comfortably spacious.

Tips 4 Pilgrims

- Stock up on disposable hand towels before leaving America. You are not likely to find wash cloths in Rome. (In America, you can buy them, 8 to a pack, at Dollar stores.)
- One word of advice regarding renting a car or scooter in Rome: Don't.
- In choosing a hotel, convenient access to public transportation is important. So, since Termini Station offers it all: metro, taxis, busses – including convenient rail connections to the airport and other cities in Italy – the authors prefer hotels in the vicinity of Termini.
- To avoid a strenuous check-in, verify that your hotel has an elevator. Keep in mind that the ground floor in Roman hotels is labelled "0". So, their second floor rooms, by our reckoning, are on the third floor. Many elevators fit little more than one person and a large suitcase.

TIPS 4 PILRIMS

In Rome, all modes of transportation lead to Termini Station (*Stazione Termini*.) Newcomers to Rome would be wise to arrange hotel accomodations within walking distance to this hub, so that every other form of transportation will be convenient during their stay.

TRAIN

Two trains connect Fiumicino Airport (aka Leonardo da Vinci Airport) to Rome. The Leonardo Express runs every half hour to Termini Station. The ride lasts about 30 minutes and costs under 10€. The other train runs more frequently and services Trastevere, Ostiense and Tiburtina. Its cost is under 5€. Tickets can be purchased in vending machines or at ticket shops near the boarding platform.

To find the airport's boarding platforms, follow the *Treni* signs from the airport baggage claim area. It is a bit of a walk from there. After reaching the train station nearest your hotel, taxis will be plentiful, or you may be able to walk to your hotel.

METRO

Rome's subway is called *Metropolitana*, or metro, and consists of two main lines: *Linea A* (red) and *Linea B* (blue). A third line is shceduled for 2018. Both existing lines intersect at Termini Station (*Stazione Termini*), Rome's transportation hub. Each metro boarding location is marked with a square red box, displaying a white "M." Metro maps are laid out like the ones in most major cities. (Just be sure to be on the platform that is headed in the right direction.) The metro service is efficient, reasonably priced and clean. But the historic nature of underground Rome has prevented it from being able to tunnel under the *centro storico*, or historic district. Still, most important tourist sites are within walking distance of a metro stop. When exiting the metro car, look for the *uscita* – "exit" – sign to find the way out.

TAXI

An abundance of convenient transportation options in Rome means that taxis are not needed very often – provided travelers have planned for other options in advance. (See pilgrim tips at bottom of page.) Tips are not expected, except for rounding up small change.

BUS AND TRAM

These are convenient and plentiful in Rome but, because of their abundance, sometimes a little overwhelming to track for beginners. Fortunately, bus and tram stops are well marked with designated routes. Still, be careful to board not only the correct bus number, but also it is headed in the right direction. At the massive bus station at Termini, an information kiosk is available for answering tourist questions, especially useful to determine which bus will be quickest to your destination.

TAXI TIPS 4 PILGRIMS

Use only the yellow or white licensed taxis. They should be picked up only at marked taxi stops. From Fiumicino Airport, the trip may take 50 minutes and cost 50€. (Trains are much cheaper.) Taxi drivers sometimes rudely refuse to give change, so always carry some coins and smaller bills.

"Hop on, hop off" sightseeing buses are very popular in Rome. The most popular ones are Roma Cristiana, Archeobus, and Trambus Open. For more information, check out the Resources chapter at the end of this guide.

TRANSPORTATION TIPS 4 PILGRIMS

For tourists, multi-day transportation passes are a good deal for navigating Rome's urban area. They can be used interchangeably on the metro, city buses, and trams. (Train tickets are usually purchased individually.) Immediately after arriving in Rome, seek out one of the shops that sells these tickets. (At train stations, vending machines are available but, there and elsewhere, newsstands, tobacconists, and other small shops sell them.) You can choose 1, 3 or 7 day passes. (These are calendar days, not 24 hours from time of purchase.) At the time of this writing, ticket prices are as follows:

- B.I.T. € 1.50. Standard ticket, valid for one metro ride or 75 minutes on all buses.
- B.I.G. € 6.00. Daily ticket, valid for unlimited metro, bus, and train travel within Rome.
- B.T.I. €16.50. Three-day ticket, valid for everything listed under the B.I.G ticket.
- C.I.S. €24.00. Weekly ticket, valid for everything listed under the B.I.G. ticket.
- Children under 10 travel for free.

When using Rome's transportation services – especially the trains – seek out and use the yellow electronic box that date-stamps tickets. (For trains they are at the station. On buses and trams, they are on board.) Inspectors infrequently check tickets, but can fine travelers who fail to comply. However, they tend to cut obvious tourists some slack.

VATICAN TRANSPORTATION
TIPS 4 PILGRIMS

Of course, every pilgrim in Rome has a plan to visit the Vatican. But since the metro veers wide of the Vatican, transportation issues are not as easy as one might expect. Here are popular ways to get there.

BY BUS:
- Bus 64 is the most popular Vatican bus, both for pilgrims and pickpockets. But don't let that discourage you. Just watch out for them. This bus can be boarded at many popular spots, including Termini station, Piazza Venezia, and Argentina.
- Bus 60 connects with Repubblica, the Spanish Steps, Piazza Venezia, and Argentina.
- Bus 40 is the express bus with limited stops. It connects with Termini station, Piazza Venezia, and Argentina.
- Buses 62 and 40 both have stops between the Castel Sant'Angelo and the Piazza San Pietro.
- Bus 64 stops just south of St. Peter's Piazza and Basilica.

BY METRO:
Take metro red line (A) to either the Ottaviano stop (closer to the basilica) or the Cipro stop (closer to Vatican Museum entrance). Still, in either case, you will have a 10 minute walk to your destination.

MAP OF METROPOLITANA
The metro runs approximately every 7 to10 minutes,
from 5:30am until 11.30pm every day (until 12:30am on Saturday night).

Buon giorno
bwon zhor-no
Hello (daytime greeting)

Buona sera
bwoh-nah seh-rah
Good evening

Buona notte
bwoh-nah noht-teh
Good night

Ciao
chow
Hi / Bye (informal)

Per favore
pehr fah-voh-reh
Please

Grazie (mille)
graht-zee-eh (mee-leh)
Thank you (very much)

Prego
preh-goh
You're welcome

Mi dispiace
mee dee-spyah-cheh
Sorry

Scusi
skoo-zee
Excuse me

Come sta?
koh-meh stah
How are you?

Sto bene.
stoh beh-neh
I am fine / well.

Sì / No
see / noh
Yes / No

Come si chiama?
koh-meh see kee-ah-mah
What's your name? (formal)

Mi chiamo...
mee kee-ah-mo
My name is...

Piacere
pee-ah-cheh-reh
Pleased (to meet you)

Signore, Signora, Signorina
seen-yoh-reh, seen-yoh-rah,
seen-yoh-reen-ah
Mister, Misses, Miss

Parla inglese?
par-lah een-gleh-zeh
Do you speak English?

Non parlo italiano / Parlo inglese.
non par-lo ee-tahl-ee-ah-no / par-
lo een-gleh-zeh
I don't speak Italian. / I speak
English.

Capisce?
kah-pee-sheh
Do you understand?

[Non] capisco.
[non] kah-pees-koh
I [don't] understand

Non so / Lo so
non soh / low soh
I don't know / I know

D'accordo.
dah-kohr-doh
Sure / OK

Come?
koh-meh?
What?

Come si dice [word]?
koh-meh see dee-cheh [word]?
How do you say [word]?

Dov'è [place]?
doh-veh [place]?
Where is [place]?

Ho freddo. / Ho caldo.
oh freh-doh / oh kal-doh
I'm cold. / I'm hot.

Congratulazioni!
kohn-grah-tsoo-lah-tsee-oh-nee
Congratulations!

Benvenuti!
behn-veh-noo-tee
Welcome!

Buona fortuna!
bwoh-nah for-too-nah
Good luck!

Va bene!
vah beh-neh
OK (that's good)!

Quanto costa?
kwan-toh coh-stah?
How much does this cost?

Scrive?
scree-veh?
Can you write that down for me?

QUESTION WORDS:
Chi? *kee?* Who?
Che cosa? *keh koh-sah?* What?
Perché? *pehr-keh?* Why?
Quando? *kwahn-doh?* When?
Dove? *doh-veh?* Where?
Quanto? *kwahn-toh?* How much?
Quale? *kwah-leh?* Which?

DAYS OF THE WEEK:
Lunedì *loo-neh-dee* Monday
Martedì *mahr-teh-dee* Tuesday
Mercoledì *mehr-koh-leh-dee* Wed.
Giovedì *zhoh-veh-dee* Thursday
Venerdì *veh-nehr-dee* Friday
Sabato *sah-bah-toh* Saturday
Domenica *doh-men-ee-kah* Sunday

Ieri *yer-ee* yesterday
Ieri sera *yer-ee seh-rah* last night
Oggi *ohd-jee* today
Domani *doh-mahn-ee* tomorrow

DIRECTIONS:
Destra *deh-strah* right
Sinistra *see-nee-strah* left
Diritto *dee-ree-toh* straight
Nord *nohrd* north
Sud *sood* south
Est *est* east
Ovest *oh-vest* west

NUMBERS:
zero *dzeh-roh* 0
uno *oo-noh* 1
due *doo-eh* 2
tre *treh* 3
quattro *kwaht-troh* 4
cinque *cheen-kweh* 5
sei *say* 6
sette *seht-teh* 7
otto *aw-toh* 8
nove *naw-vay* 9
dieci *dee-ay-chee* 10

Language Tips 4 Pilgrims

Italian is a phonetic language in which letters and letter combinations are usually pronounced the same. However, the Italian alphabet does not have the letters J, K, W, X, or Y. A little Italian can go a long way in Rome. If you ask, "*Dove* [name of a place, in English]?" You usually get directions. Want to know how much something costs? Just say, "*Quanto costa?*" If the answer is not understandable, ask "*Scrive?*" and they will write the cost down for you.

Italy's Off-Hours

Your daily pilgrimage must be scheduled around Italy's traditional off-hours. Much of Rome is closed on Sundays, but some restaurants and museums take Mondays off. In the central part of Rome, where the tourists wander – the *centro storico* – shop hours are more extended. Expect shops to open around 10 with churches opening hours earlier. Everywhere in Italy, however, do not be surprised to find a shop, here or there, that is closed, regardless of their posted hours.

Most sights close for *riposo* – the Italian version of *siesta* – from 1 to about 3:30 PM. For that reason, the walking tours in this *Guide 4 Pilgrims* are presented in half day excursions, with the rare sights that are open during the mid-day off-hours (*orario continuato*) noted as such. So, with a little schedule juggling, the Italian *riposo* will not slow you down.

The early afternoon break not only allows for leisurely enjoyment of the largest Italian meal each day, but also compensates for Italy's traditionally longer shop hours. Many businesses stay open until 7:30 PM. Except for the major basilicas, even most churches follow this afternoon tradition. After all, art thieves are plentiful in Italy. So, every church needs caretakers to keep an eye on whatever a thief might value.

National Holidays

January 1 (New Year's Day)
January 6 (The Epiphany)
Easter Monday
April 25 (Liberation Day)
May 1 (Labor Day)
June 2 (Republic Day)
August 15 (The Feast of the Assumption)
November 1 (All Saints' Day)
December 8 (Feast of the Immaculate Conception)
December 25 (Christmas)
December 26 (Feast of St. Stephen)

A Lot of Walking, with Obstacles

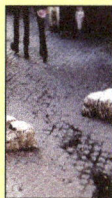

Bring comfy walking shoes, and watch your step!

Up-escalators are sometimes closed when you need them most. Only cross streets at crosswalks. Always use caution as some streets are narrow, with sidewalks missing.

Avoiding the Crowds

The Eternal City is a magnificent place to visit any time of year. But in terms of budget and convenience, some months are better than others. The high (crowded) season, for tourists, is June through August, when the days are very hot – in the 90s – but rainfall is rare and *gelato* is perfect! Beginning August 15, however, many Romans leave town for summer vacation. So, expect more sights and shops to be closed at that time. Prayerful Pilgrims can avoid the crowds by traveling during the fringe or slow seasons, especially shortly before or after religious holidays. Rain is more likely during the Roman winter, but often worth the tradeoff.

At major sites, like the Vatican museums, don't line up at the beginning of the day. Wait for the inexperienced tourists to exhaust themselves. Then, by afternoon, when they are headed home, you can enjoy the sights in relative isolation.

Rest Stops, Dress Codes

Roman public restrooms are rare and, sometimes, require entry through coin-operated turnstiles. (Usually 1€.) So, keep plenty of change in your pocket and always take advantage of restroom facilities whenever you patronize a restaurant.

St. Peter's Basilica posts its dress code in five languages, near the entrance. Shorts, above the knees, are not permitted and women will not be admitted with short skirts, bare midriffs, or sleeveless tops. Though not usually as strictly enforced, these restrictions are best respected at all places of worship in Rome.

Conversions (check for current currency rates.)

$1 US = .92€ (as of 1/16)	1 mile = 1.6 km	40° Farenheit = 4.4° Celsius
1€ = $1.09 US	1 km = .62 of a mile	90° Farenheit = 32.2° Celsius

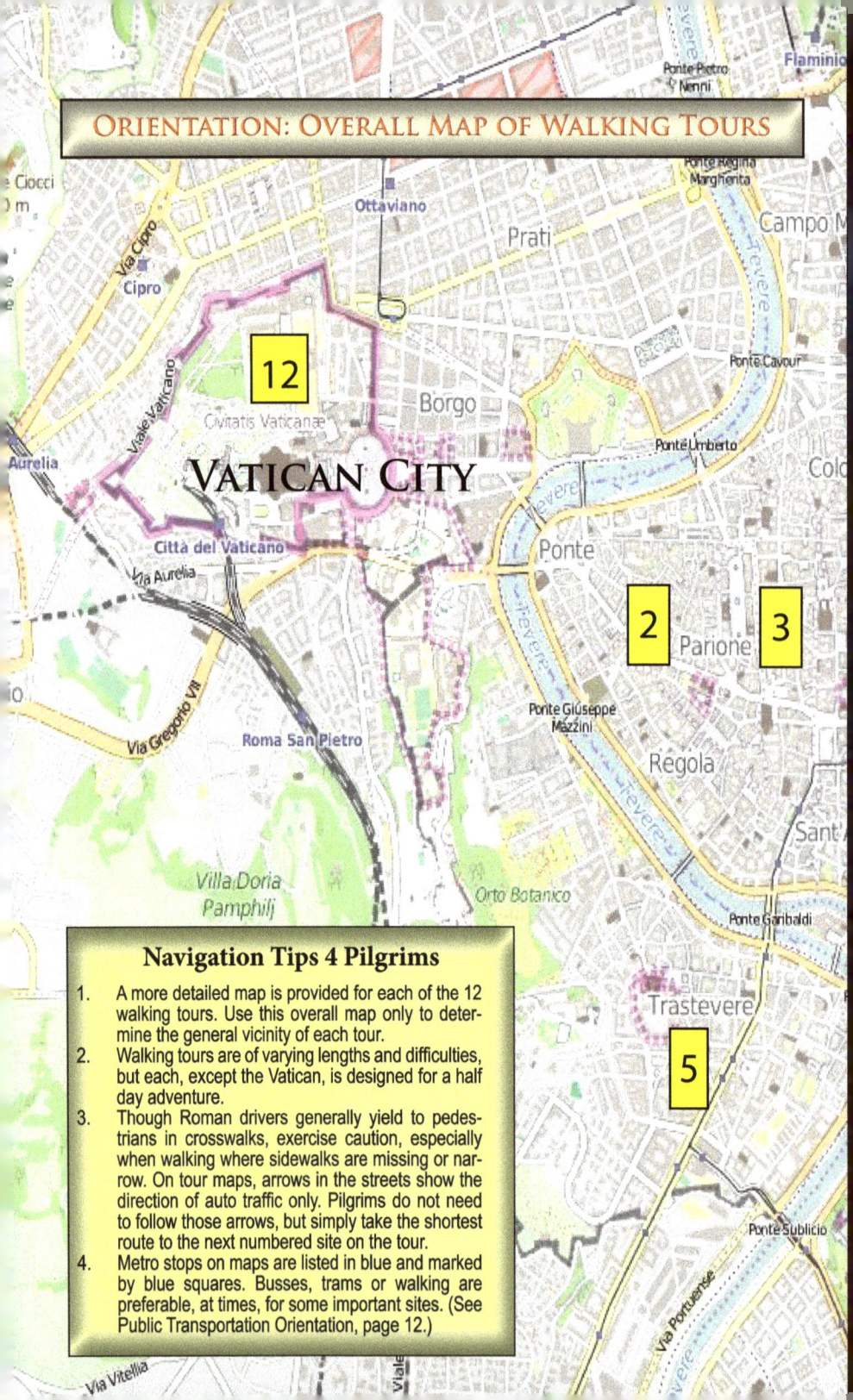

Ottaviano

Prati

Campo M

Cipro

Via Cipro

12

Borgo

Ponte Cavour

Civitatis Vaticanae

Ponte Umberto

Aurelia

Viale Vaticano

VATICAN CITY

Col

Città del Vaticano

Ponte

2

Parione

3

Via Aurelia

Via Gregorio VII

Roma San Pietro

Ponte Giuseppe Mazzini

Regola

Sant'

Villa Doria Pamphilj

Orto Botanico

Ponte Garibaldi

Navigation Tips 4 Pilgrims

1. A more detailed map is provided for each of the 12 walking tours. Use this overall map only to determine the general vicinity of each tour.
2. Walking tours are of varying lengths and difficulties, but each, except the Vatican, is designed for a half day adventure.
3. Though Roman drivers generally yield to pedestrians in crosswalks, exercise caution, especially when walking where sidewalks are missing or narrow. On tour maps, arrows in the streets show the direction of auto traffic only. Pilgrims do not need to follow those arrows, but simply take the shortest route to the next numbered site on the tour.
4. Metro stops on maps are listed in blue and marked by blue squares. Busses, trams or walking are preferable, at times, for some important sites. (See Public Transportation Orientation, page 12.)

Trastevere

5

Ponte Sublicio

Via Portuense

Via Vitellia

ROME

PART TWO:
MAJOR PLAYERS IN THE GREATEST HUMAN DRAMA

THE APOSTLES

COLOSSAL STATUES OF CHRIST'S APOSTLES
FLANK THE NAVE OF ST. JOHN LATERAN.
THEY ARE 15' TALL AND WERE
SCULPTED IN THE BERNINI SCHOOL,
PRIOR TO 1720.

SIMON PETER was just a fisherman from Bethsaida. Still, Christ named him the rock upon which His Church would be built and honored his leadership with the symbolic Keys to the Kingdom. Peter was blessed to witness the Transfiguration and the Agony in the Garden. But he wavered in his faith when walking to Christ on water, and denied Jesus three times after His arrest. The Lord even scolded Peter, once, with the command, "Away from me, Satan." Still, Peter was the first apostle to see Jesus after His resurrection (1 Cor. 15:4-5), and forgave his shortcomings. In the Bible, he is mentioned most and always first, among the apostles. He became the first Bishop of Rome and two of his epistles are included in the Bible. However, near the end of his life, Emperor Nero began a vicious persecution of Christians. He imprisoned Peter in the Mamertine (See p. 133) and, eventually, ordered his crucifixion. But when Peter insisted that he was not worthy to die in the manner of his Lord, the executioners complied by crucifying him, head down. He died within view of the obelisk that was later moved to mark the spot of his execution, in the middle of today's St. Peter's Square. Now, his bones rest directly under the altar of the greatest church in Christendom. Peter is the patron saint of fishermen, ship builders, longevity and the papacy.

ANDREW, a devoted disciple of John the Baptist, initially recognized Jesus as the Messiah and hastened to introduce Him to his brother, Simon (Peter). The two fishermen became the first apostles when Jesus invited them to join Him and become "fishers of men." On November 30, 60 AD, Andrew was scourged seven times, then hung on a diagonal structure, now commonly known as "St. Andrew's Cross." He was tied, rather than nailed down, in order to prolong his suffering. Andrew perseveringly preached from his cross for two days before expiring. That date is remembered as his Feast Day, both in the Latin and Greek Churches. His remains are liberally divided around Italy, Greece, Poland and Scotland. Andrew is the patron saint of fishermen, singers, unmarried women, and those suffering from gout or sore throats.

JAMES THE LESS

was also called the son of Alpheus and was related to Jesus through Mary. He is believed to have written the Book of James. He witnessed the Resurrection and was the first Bishop of Jerusalem, but was cast from the Temple and beaten to death. His body rests at *Santi Apostoli* in Rome. (See p. 63) James the Less is patron saint of pharmacists and hat makers.

JOHN, a teenage fisherman, became Jesus' 'Beloved Disciple.' He was the youngest, lived the longest and was the only apostle to die of natural causes. John witnessed the Transfiguration, the Agony in the Garden and was the sole apostle remaining at the foot of the Cross until Jesus' death. Honoring the Lord's last request before dying, John cared for Mary in Ephesus, as if she were his own mother, for the rest of her life. There, he wrote his Gospel and three epistles that remain in our Bible. Later, he returned to Rome and fell victim to Domitian's persecutions. He was imprisoned and then sentenced to death. Some legends claim that he was miraculously spared from poison and stoning. However, a stronger tradition is from ancient historian, Tertulian, who wrote that John was 'plunged, unhurt, into boiling oil.' One version of the account claims that it occurred in the Colosseum, and that the audience was converted to Christianity upon witnessing the miracle. However, a monument memorializes the site of the miracle, just inside Rome's Latin Gate. (See p. 123) Regardless of its location, the miracle forced the uncomfortable emperor to exercise his only remaining option: exiling the pesky evangelist to the Greek island of Patmos. There, he wrote the Book of Revelation in his waning years. John is patron saint of writers, booksellers, editors, engravers, publishers and theologians.

PHILIP was from Behtsaida, the hometown of Peter and Andrew. It is believed that he also spoke Greek. He is known to have helped distribute bread for the Feeding of the Five Thousand. In his travels, he primarily evangelized in Greece and Syria. In Hierapolis (Turkey), he was crucified or hung, head down, along with fellow apostle, Bartholomew. Because of Philip's unstoppable preaching, the crowd freed Bartholomew from his constraints. But Philip refused assistance, accepting his fate. After his death, the enemies of Christianity stoned him for good measure. His tomb is in the Roman church of *Santi Apostoli*. (See p. 63) Philip is patron saint of hatters and pastry chefs.

In addition to Paul, seven apostles are entombed around Rome: Peter, Bartholomew, James the Less, Jude, Philip, Simon and Matthias (replacing Judas).

BARTHOLOMEW associated with Nathanial and travelled with Philip, who was instrumental in saving his life. (See above) He witnessed Christ's Ascension and went on to evangelize in Ethiopia, Mesopotamia and India, where he left the Gospel of Matthew. In Armenia, however, after converting the king, the king's brother ordered his execution. Bartholomew was flayed alive and crucified, head down, but Armenia still became the world's first Christian country. His remains are found in a Roman church, on an island in the Tiber. (See p. 80) Bartholomew is the patron saint of those who suffer from nervous disorders.

JAMES THE GREATER was the son of Zebedee and the older brother of John. Along with Peter, the three simple fishermen became the triumvirate of the Lord's most trusted apostles. James witnessed the Transfiguration and the Agony in the Garden. He and John were nicknamed by Jesus, "Sons of Thunder," apparently because of their naturally passionate personalities. In what is believed to be the first apparition of the Virgin Mary, while still living, she appeared to James during his missionary travels in Zaragoza, Spain. There, he established the first church dedicated to the Blessed Mother. A column in the church of *Nuestra Señora del Pilr* is preserved, marking the spot where the Virgin appeared. James was the first apostle to be martyred. Herod Antipas ordered his beheading in Palestine. However, James' executioner converted at the last moment. So, he also met his fate alongside the apostle. James is the patron saint of hat makers, sufferers of rheumatoid arthritis, and laborers.

> The index finger of 'Doubting Thomas' is preserved and displayed at Santa Croce in Gerusalemme. (See p. 34)

THOMAS is most famously known as 'Doubting Thomas' for his short-lived skepticism regarding the reports of the Lord's resurrection. (He said he would not believe the miracle until he could thrust his finger into Christ's wounds.) Thomas was the only witness to the Assumption of Mary into heaven. He travelled widely, preaching the Gospel as far away as India. There, he met his martyrdom from spears and arrows. Thomas is the patron saint of architects, the blind, construction workers, doubters, and theologians.

> "Jesus went up on a mountainside and called to him those he wanted, and they came to him. He appointed twelve – designating them apostles – that they might be with him and that he might send them out to preach and to have authority to drive out demons."
> Mark 3:13-15

> "Again Jesus said, 'Peace be with you! As the Father has sent me, I am sending you.'"
> John 20:21

SIMON THE ZEALOT is also called Simon the Canaanite but, other than that, not much is known about him. Various traditions describe his martyrdom in different ways and places but a prominent one says that he was sawn in half in Persia. He may be the same person as Simeon of Jerusalem, also known as Simon 'the brother of Jesus' who could have been either a cousin or the son of Joseph from a previous marriage. His relics can be found in St. Peter's Basilica. Simon is the patron saint of those who work with lumber or leather.

PAUL was a diaspora Jew and Pharisee who became known as the Apostle of the Gentiles. He was born with the name Saul, in Tarsus - a bustling city in the Roman Empire. He was likely urbane and well-educated. Paul had been dedicated to the persecution of the early Christians and had cooperated in the killing of the proto-martyr Stephen. But after his miraculous conversion on the road to Damascus, he became comitted to Christ. His persistent faith made him the most influential of early Christian missionaries because his knowledge did not originate from the apostles, but through direct revelation from Jesus Christ. He travelled throughout Europe and Asia Minor. He was arrested, beaten and imprisoned many times, including in the Mamertine Prison. (See p. 133) Paul was executed in Rome at the site of today's *Tre Fontane* Abbey. At that time, Roman citizens were not allowed to be crucified, so he was given the lighter sentence of beheading. Tradition says that his head bounced three times, where fountains immediately sprung up – hence the name *Tre Fontane*, or Three Fountains. His body was transported about two miles away to be buried where the Basilica of San Paolo Fuori le Mura was later built. (See p. 168) There, in addition to his tomb, the chains of his imprisonment are also on display. Apart from Jesus, Himself, St. Paul became the most prominent personality of the New Testament with 14 of 27 Books attributed to him. Saint Paul is the patron of the City of London, authors, members of the press, publishers and writers.

JUDE is also known as Thaddeus. He was the brother of James the Less and probably a relative of Jesus. He preached in Mesopotamia and Persia and is the author of the Epistle Jude, one of the shortest books in the Bible, only one chapter long. Tradition holds he was martyred in Persia by being beaten to death with a club and then beheaded. His relics are in St. Peter's Basilica. Jude is famously known as the very effective patron saint of those in desperation or faced with seemingly hopeless situations.

MATTHIAS (not pictured) was chosen to replace Judas as one of the twelve. He witnessed the Baptism of Jesus. He was stoned in Jerusalem and then beheaded. His tomb is in the confessio of Rome's Santa Maria Maggiore supporting the reliquary that holds remnants of Jesus Christ's crib. (See p. 98)

MATTHEW was a tax collector, a profession that naturally incited resentments in taxpayers. When Jesus was asked to dine with him at his home, along with other tax collectors and 'sinners,' the Pharisees asked why he would do such a scandalous thing. Jesus answered, "I have not come to call the righteous, but sinners." Matthew witnessed the Ascension and became the the the author of the Gospel that bears his name. He met his martyrdom in Ethiopia, the result of a halberd stabbing. He is believed to have continued preaching until the execution. Matthew is the patron saint of accountants, bankers, bookkeepers, stockbrokers, and tax collectors.

THE APOSTLES

23

NERO
December 15, 37 to June 9, 68

Nero was the first emperor to direct a systematic persecution against Christians. He was thoroughly depraved, fancying himself a great singer, song writer and actor. To prove his talent, he chose to engage in sexual acts and murders, on stage.

In 64 AD, a great fire destroyed much of Rome. Many Romans suspected Nero started it because they knew he wanted to rebuild the city according to his own whims. So, to divert blame, Rome's mysterious community of Christians soon proved to be Nero's convenient scapegoat.

The emperor's barbarities included having animal skins sewn around Christians before throwing them to ravenous wild dogs. Others, he coated with waxy tar and dangled them, alive, from the trees of his gardens. Then they were set on fire, to light the night for his festivities.

Along with many other martyrs, he ordered the deaths of Saints Peter and Paul. However, Christians were not his only casualties. He also murdered many perceived adversaries, including his mother, stepbrother, and both of his spouses -- one of which was pregnant when he kicked her to death.

Eventually, after a reign of terror lasting 15 years, the Roman senate declared Nero a public enemy. When he received the message, the aspiring actor took his own life, lamenting, "What an artist dies within me!" He was just 30 years old.

Above: Some say this is the face of the Antichrist, described by St. John, because he was familiar with the emperor's heinous crimes and the letters in Nero's name equate with the number 666. Others, however, believe he was only a forerunner of the true Antichrist.

DOMITIAN
October 24, 51 to September 18, 96

In 81 AD, Domitian began another great persecution of Christians. He was the first emperor to declare himself "Lord and God." Yet, he murdered his own brother as well as a number of Roman senators. He also commanded the death of every descendant of David.

Domitian declared that no Christian would be tried under Roman law without first renouncing their religion. Failure to do so was a capital offense. Soon, Rome's every adversity became reason for Christian blame and revenge.

Timothy, the famous disciple of St. Paul, was clubbed to death during the persecutions of Domitian, and the emperor is said to have ordered St. John to be boiled in oil. (See p. 123) But when that execution miraculously failed, he banished the saint into exile on Patmos.

After a reign of 15 years, at the age of 44, Domitian was assassinated in a palace conspiracy, organized by his court officials. Happy senators then changed his title to "Damned Memory" and had his name and image erased from all public records.

More Christian persecutions were ordered by:
Trajan in 108;
Severus in 192;
Maximus in 235;
Valerian in 257;
Aurelian in 274.

MARCUS AURELIUS
April 26, 121 to March 17, 180

Perhaps the most disappointing of the Roman persecutors is Marcus Aurelius. Historians consider him the last of the "Five Good Emperors." He was a man of war but also an important stoic philosopher who wrote his *Meditations* with such worldly detachment that even modern Christians find great wisdom in his words. Yet, by 161 he was leading a terrible persecution.

Christians were scourged until their skin literally fell off. Some were devoured by wild beasts and, others, forced to walk with bare feet over all sorts of sharp, piercing objects. Those who refused to renounce their faith were clubbed to death, crushed or beheaded. St. Polycarp, bishop of Smyrna, was burned alive. Yet, many who witnessed these tortures found such serene courage in the saintly martyrs that they, themselves, converted to the faith.

Marcus Aurelius and his wife of 30 years raised 13 children. However, death haunted what he treasured most and only one son and four daughters outlived him. That deeply flawed son, Commodus, succeeded his father and led with such neurotic zeal that Rome was plunged into tumult.

DECIUS
ca. 201 to June 251

By 250, pagan temples of the Roman empire were in decline while, even in the shadows, Christianity thrived. Emperor Decius resented the trend, especially since his despised predecessor, Phillip, was rumored to have become Christian.

So, Decius issued an extraordinary imperial edict requiring that, 'for the safety of the empire,' every inhabitant must perform a religious sacrifice before a local magistrate. Predictably, the Christian bishops did not respond favorably. As defiance increased, it became clear that anyone who did not possess the required certificate of loyalty to the ancestral gods would risk torture and execution. Many Christians did not cooperate and were martyred, including Pope Fabian in 250. Then, a rising tide of anti-Christian resentment flooded the empire as pogroms, particularly in Alexandria and Carthage, decimated Christian communities.

Decius died on the battlefield just 18 months after his proclamation, but the law endured under his successor. For 16 years following the edict, the empire was ravaged by a severe plague, claiming as many as 5,000 lives a day. Romans named it "The Plague of Cyprian," after the Bishop of Carthage, where the persecutions had been among the worst.

DIOCLETIAN
December 22, 244 to December 3, 311

On February 23, 303, Roman pagans celebrated the *Terminalia*: a day to terminate Christianity. The persecution began in Nicomedia where Diocletian watched as a church was forcibly entered and its sacred books burned. Then the church was levelled.

An edict followed, directing the destruction of all Christian churches and books. In Christian Phyrgia, flames consumed the entire city, along with every inhabitant. For the following decade, countless saints were martyred, throughout the empire.

Then came Constantine.

THE PERSECUTORS

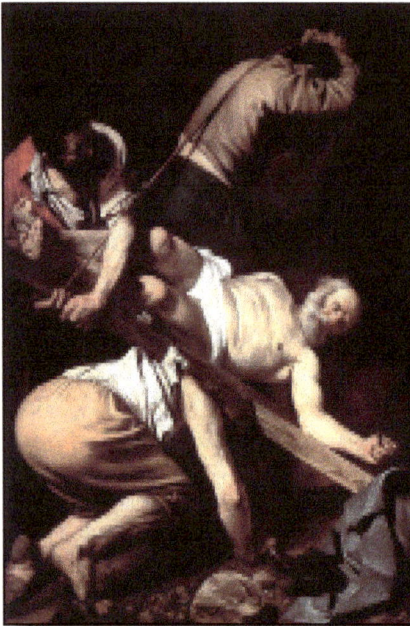

In 313, Emperor Constantine issued the Edict of Milan, a declaration of tolerance for the Christian faith. So, the Reign of Terror against Christians subsided, at least for a while. However, prior to that time, popes accepted their role knowing that the honor would earn them a death sentence. The following thirty one popes were martyred during the early years of Roman persecution:

Peter (67)	Urban I (230)
Linus (76)	Pontian (235)
Anacletus (92)	Anterus (236)
Clement (99)	Fabian (250)
Evaristus (108)	Cornelius (253)
Alexander I (119)	Lucius I (254)
Sixtus I (128)	Stephen I (257)
Telesphorus (138)	Sixtus II (258)
Hyginus (142)	Denis (268)
Pius I (154)	Felix I (274)
Anicetus (166)	Eutychian (283)
Soter (175)	Caius (296)
Eleuterius (189)	Marcellinus (304)
Victor (199)	Marcellus I (309)
Zephyrinus (217)	Eusebius (309).
Calixtus I (222)	

A partial listing of saints who have called Rome home, includes the following:

St. Agnes
St. Aloysius Gonzaga
St. Augustine
St. Benedict of Nursia
St. Benedict Joseph Labre
St. Bridget of Sweden
St. Camillus de Lellis
St. Charles of Sezze
St. Catherine of Sienna
St. Cecilia
St. Crispin of Viterbo
St. Dominic Guzman
St. Felix of Cantalice
St. Frances of Rome
St. Francis of Assisi
St. Gregory the Great
St. John-Baptist de Rossi
St. Ignatius Loyola
Sts. John and Paul
St. John Berchmans
St. John Bosco
St. John Calabytes
St. Madeleine Sophie Barat
St. Monica
St. Paola Frassinetti
St. Paul
St. Paul of the Cross
St. Philip Neri
St. Stanislaus Kostka
St. Vincent Pallotti

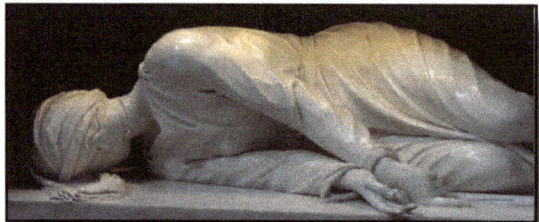

Above, Left: Caravaggio
Crucifixion of St. Peter,
Santa Maria del Popolo, Rome.

Above: Stefano Maderno
Martyrdom of Saint Cecilia
Church of St. Cecilia, Rome

Above: Jean-Leon Gerome - *The Christian Martyrs' Last Prayer*

GIAN LORENZO BERNINI'S
ECSTASY OF ST. TERESA,
SANTA MARIA DELLA VITTORIA

POPE JULIUS II
(Giuliano della Rovere)
Papacy: 1503 to 1513

Pope Julius was a man of ambition, both in matters of art and war. So, Italians nicknamed him "The Fearsome Pope" and "The Warrior Pope." By the time of his pontificate, the existing St. Peter's Basilica had deteriorated into a dangerous state of disrepair. Though its walls had entombed saints and previous pontiffs, Julius authorized its destruction and commissioned its rebuilding, grander than ever. Like a fierce taskmaster, he also drove Michelangelo to complete the the job he had tried to resist: painting the ceiling of the Sistine Chapel. The Roman Renaissance may never have happened without this pope. But, then again, perhaps the Protestant Reformation would not have occurred if not for this pope's insistence on funding and building the grandest church in Christendom.

POPE JOHN XII
(Octavianus)
Papacy: 955 to 964

The father of Pope John XII was a Roman patrician with the influential means to pave the path of his son's rise to papal power. But junior, at just 18 years of age, was not yet suited for a life of saintly self-sacrifice. Perhaps, he never would have been.

Though most of what we now know about the man was written by his enemies, it is clear he was not an appropriate candidate to lead Christ's Church on earth. He was accused, many times, of adultery, even with his own neice. Allegedly, he blinded his confessor, castrated and then murdered a subdeacon, and invoked demons and foreign gods.

His death is said to have been at the hands of a jealous husband whose wife had fallen under the charm of the playboy pontiff. If the stories are true, it seems a fitting ending.

IOANNES·XII·PP·ROMANVS

PAPAL TRIVIA 4 PILGRIMS

- From Peter to Francis, 266 popes have officially ruled the Catholic Church.
- In addition to defending the faith of a global Catholic community, the pope has numerous secular responsibilites. He is the Vatican's head of state, chief executive, legislature and judiciary. He is an absolute, though benevolent, monarch.
- The longest Conclave began in 1268. Cardinals took 2 years, 9 months and 2 days to elect Pope Gregory X.
- On March 22, 752, Pope Stephen II died, ending the shortest pontificate just four days after his election.
- John is the most popular – and unlucky – of papal names. However, even though there never was a Pope John XX, two men have carried the name John XXIII. The first, a schismatic pontiff, is not listed on the Vatican's official list. He was kicked out of office in 1415 for "notorious incest, adultery, defilement and homicide."
- In the first 15 centuries of Christianity, there were almost 40 antipopes who attempted to rule the Church in opposition to the official pontiff.
- Throughout the centuries, popes have risen from the following nationalities: Syrian, Greek, French, Spanish, Portuguese, English, Polish, Argentinian and, of course, Italian.

SERGIVS·III·PP·ROMANVS

POPE SERGIUS III
(Sergius)
Papacy: 904 to 911

History is controlled by the victors and, so, the enemies of Pope Sergius must have provided us with the dismal details of his papacy. Allegedly, he ordered the murders of Pope Leo V – his predecessor – as well as the death of the competing antipope, Christoper, who was imprisoned at the time. His mistress, Marozia, later became a famous Roman noblewoman, and the future Pope John XI is believed to have been their son.

But no one can deny that, most famously, he ordered the bizarre "Cadaver Synod" in which his deceased predecessor, Pope Formosus (right) was tried.

FORMOSVS ·I· PP· CORSICA

Sergius had the dead pope's body exhumed, dressed in papal vestments, and charged with usurping the papal throne. At the conclusion of the adjudication, the corpse of Formosus was found guilty and stripped of his pontifical garb. On the hand that he had offered papal blessings, the fingers were chopped off. Then his remains were dumped into the Tiber River. Historians tend to agree that, on the witness stand, Formosus did not offer a very convincing defense.

POPE ALEXANDER VI
(Rodrigo Borgia)
Papacy: 1492 to 1503

Historians suggest Alexander VI might have been the worst pope ever. His rise was helped by his uncle, Pope Calixtus III, who engineered Rodrigo's speedy ascent from bishop to cardinal to vice-chancellor. Along the way, Rodrigo managed to gain an enormous fortune and, by 1492, put that wealth to good use, allegedly, by bribing his way onto the throne. The ugly evidence suggests that his mistresses presented him with at least seven children, to whom he awarded handsome endowments from Church funds. However, he never seemed to have enough money. So, he fabricated charges against the wealthy, imprisoning and even having them murdered, in order to take their fortunes. His rule was not only unlawful but unGodly.

Upon Rodrigo's rise, a contemporary – the future Pope Leo X – worried: "Now we are in the power of a wolf, the most rapacious perhaps that this world has ever seen. And if we do not flee, he will inevitably devour us all."

THE LEGEND OF POPE JOAN
Alleged Papacy:9th or 11th Century

This tall tale has caused tongue-wagging for centuries: A resourceful woman rises through Church hierarchy while pretending to be a man. Then, after reaching the pinacle and ruling capably, she scandalizes the world by giving birth, on the street, during a papal procession. It all makes great gossip, but contemporary historians never mentioned the event. The story only surfaced centuries later, and modern historians cannot find a credible papal gap that could account for her papacy. Still, there are those who will claim: The lack of evidence only proves the Church's determination to hide the scandal!

VOLATILE GENIUS:
ROME'S GREAT ARTISTS AND ARCHITECTS

MICHELANGELO
(Michelangelo di Lodovico Buonarroti Simoni)
March 6, 1475 to February 18, 1564

Young Michelangelo exhibited such prodigious talent that, even as a pre-teen, he gained the attention of one of history's most important art patrons: Lorenzo de Medici. In Florence, Michangelo received unparalled artistic training, but also tangled with another promising student who broke his nose, disfiguring it for the rest of his life. In 1492, however, the 17 year old Michelangelo and his patron fled Florence when an excessively religious firebrand, Savonarola, began turning the population against the materialistic excesses of the Renaissance.

Still, Michelangelo was not deterred, establishing his reputation as a sculpting genius by the age of 24, with the completion of his unforgettable *Pietà*. For him, it was only the beginning.

Michelangelo's life defined the phrase "Renaissance Man," as a master of painting, sculpting and architecture. He was a driven genius, pushed by a demanding patron: Pope Julius II. Regularly laboring to the point of exhaustion, he claimed he did it all in the service of God and St. Peter. In 1535, artist Jacopino del Conte captured (above) a glimpse of the spent man at the age of 60. Though Michelangelo lived another productive 28 years, he was already exhibiting a reddened eye, hunched back and fatigued hand. He looks as if he is ready for a well-deserved rest.

RAPHAEL
(Raffaello Sanzio da Urbino)
April 6, 1483 to April 6, 1520

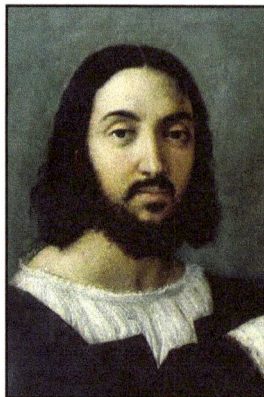

To Raphael, Michelangelo once quipped, "Painting is for sissies." But that criticism never slowed the brushwork of either master artist. Still, Raphael went on to prove his genius in more than one medium, including tapestry production that reached unprecedented excellence, making him a favorite on Vatican Hill.

The brilliant pair were driven to compete by Julius II, prompting Raphael to establish a workshop that employed as many as 50 pupils and assistants. But his industrious productivity was cut short. He died of a fever, some say, after a night of debauchery with his mistress. Raphael's last day was his 37th birthday. It was also Good Friday. Today, he is entombed at the Pantheon.

BORROMINI
(Francesco Borromini)
September 25, 1599 to august 2, 1667

Borromini was Bernini's contemporary and fierce competitor. But no matter how bright the adversary, he believed he understood architecture at a deeper structural level than masters of the visual arts. After all, he was the nephew and student of Carlo Maderno, architect of many of Rome's most famous churches.

Borromini became a leader in *baroque* architecture but, with patrons, his impulsive nature put him at a disadvantage against the smooth-talking Bernini. Consequently, he failed to accomplish what he had dreamed. So, reaching a low point, he wrote that he hoped to be buried in an unmarked tomb next to his famous uncle. Then he committed suicide. (See p. 51)

BERNINI
(Gian Lorenzo Bernini)
December 7, 1598 to November 28, 1680

Thirty four years after the death of Michelangelo, another Renaissance Man was born, for whom only one name is necessary. Bernini became not only a noted playwrite, stage designer and metalwork designer, but also a master architect, artist and sculptor. He is credited with creating the *baroque* style that captured dynamic action and movement in his subjects, unlike anything that had been seen before. This self-portrait is of Bernini in his mid-thirties.

Touring Rome with an observant eye will force one to conclude that he belongs among the greatest of art masters. In his twenties, he infused unprecedented emotion into his sculptures of *David, Apollo and Daphne,* and *The Rape of Persephone.* They can all be found at Rome's Villa Borghese.

At St. Peter's Basilica, the magnificently spiralling bronze *baldacchin* and monumental colonnade are both from his fertile imagination.

Cleverly, Bernini's moving *Ecstasy of St. Teresa* drew upon his stage design background. There, the intensity of the central subjects makes it easy to miss that marble spectators observe from box seats on the sides. This *baroque* masterpiece can be seen at the church of *Santa Maria della Vittoria* in Rome.

However, Bernini's subjects were not always so serious. At the *piazza* of *Santa Maria Sopra Minerva,* a baby elephant amuses viewers as he lugs a large obelisk through the square. Similarly, the Fountain of Four Rivers, in *Piazza Navonna,* presents some interesting characters for tourists to ponder. These are just a few of his many master works in Rome.

CARAVAGGIO
(Michelangelo Merisi da Caravaggio)
September 28, 1571 to July 18, 1610

The bad boy of the Renaissance was another Michelangelo, called Caravaggio. He was often criticized for cavorting with the undesirables of the street and using many of them for models. But even though his commissioned works were sometimes rejected because of the gritty realism they offered, he was undeniably a genius of light and shadow. His holy subjects might have filthy feet, or dirt under the fingernails, but they still inspired. Yet, even when his success blossomed, he courted trouble and was jailed several times.

When he arrived in Rome, in 1600, he quickly gained favor with art patrons. However, he still roamed the streets, seemingly seeking arguments and fist fights. In 1606, his brawling went too far, and an opponent did not survive. Caravaggio had to flee the city as a wanted killer. Still, for the next few years, he wandered about the Italian peninsula, fighting and being arrested. Ottavio Leoni's chalk portrait at the right seems to capture a bit of that angry spirit.

We will never know if his planned rehabilitation, in 1610, would have been successful. On the eve of returning to Rome, for a papal pardon, he died from a mysterious illness. Surprisingly, the master painter remained an obscure footnote in art history until the 20th century. Now, however, his talent is revered and his rehabilitation complete. Some even credit him as "The father of modern painting." Among his many striking works in Rome are: *The Crucifixion of St. Peter* and *The Conversion of St. Paul,* both at *Santa Maria del Popolo; David with the Head of Goliath* and *St. Jerome,* both at *Villa Borghese;* and *The Calling of St. Matthew* at *San Luigi dei Francese.*

PART THREE:
PILGRIM WALKING TOURS OF ROME

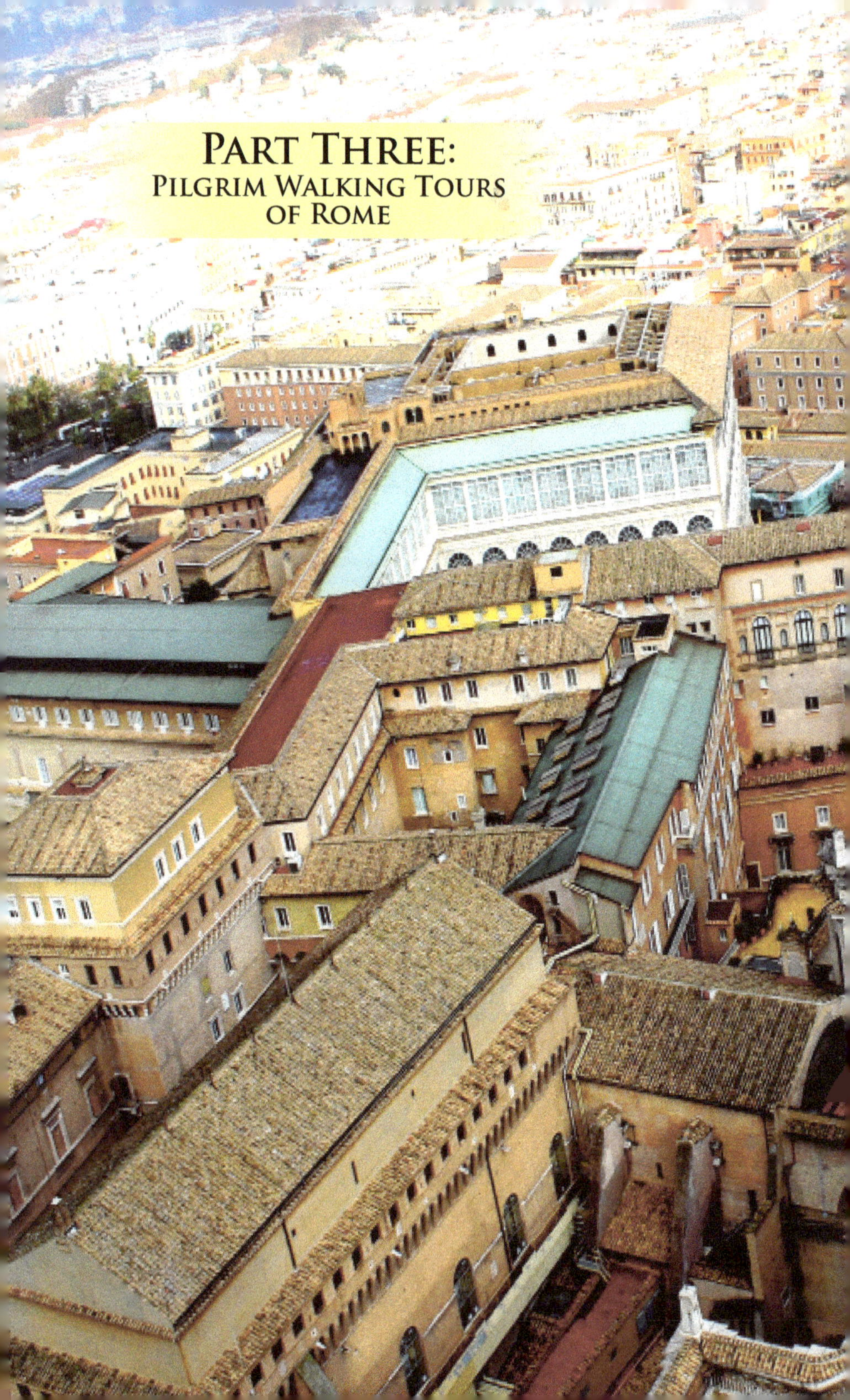

ROME AND VATICAN CITY,
VIEWED FROM
ST. PETER'S BASILICA DOME

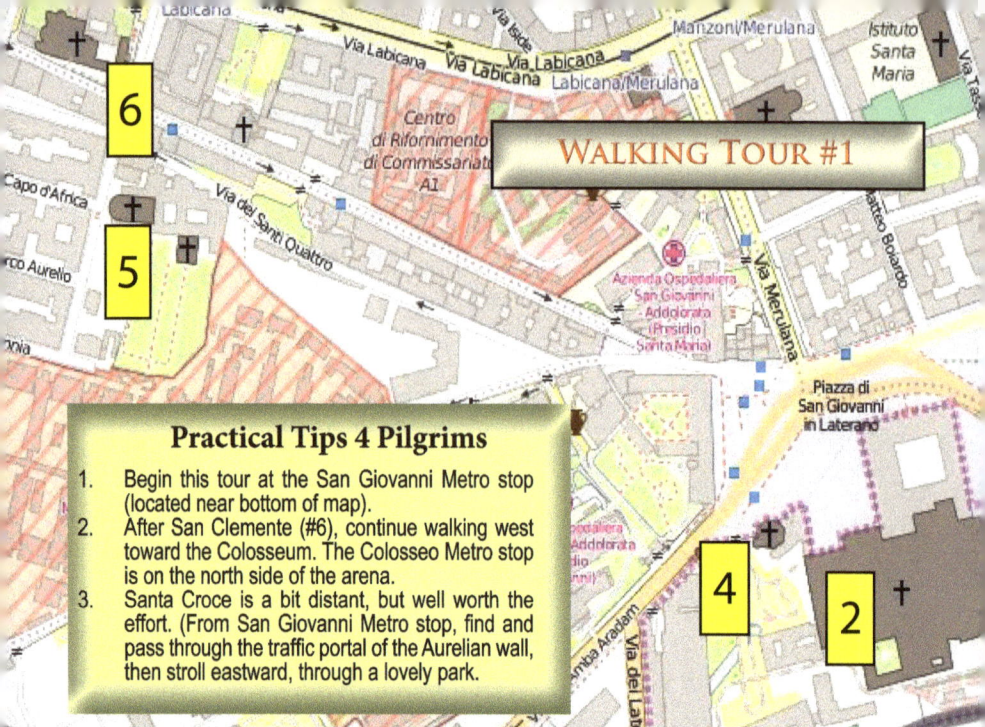

6

5

4

2

Practical Tips 4 Pilgrims

1. Begin this tour at the San Giovanni Metro stop (located near bottom of map).
2. After San Clemente (#6), continue walking west toward the Colosseum. The Colosseo Metro stop is on the north side of the arena.
3. Santa Croce is a bit distant, but well worth the effort. (From San Giovanni Metro stop, find and pass through the traffic portal of the Aurelian wall, then stroll eastward, through a lovely park.)

SANTA CROCE IN GERUSALEMME
HOLY CROSS OF JERUSALEM
DAILY: 6:00AM-12:30PM & 3:30-6:30PM (7:30 JUL.-SEPT.)

Six blocks from San Giovanni in Lateran is the basilica of Santa Croce. Its name includes "Gerusalemme" because of the holy relics from Jerusalem that are preserved here.

This is one of the first and most important of the churches established by Emperor Constantine. Influenced by his Christian mother, Helena, he proclaimed the Edict of Milan, in 313, a Roman declaration of tolerance of Christianity. This decisive turning point in Christian history allowed St. Helena to become a major force in the preservation of Christian relics and the establishment of Santa Croce.

She was zealous for the faith and, even though in her eighties and suffering from declining health, set sail for Jerusalem. There, with the power that only an emperor's mother can wield, she conducted a search and discovery mission the likes of which the world had never seen before.

Ironically, the anti-Christian efforts of Emperor Hadrian, two centuries earlier, made Helena's work easier. At that time, Hadrian had reached his limit with pesky Christians who regularly made pilgrimages to Golgotha where the ground had been soaked with their Savior's blood. Also, under that soil, Christ's executioners had buried the defiled instruments of execution, including the infamous cross, nails and crown of thorns.

So, Hadrian planned to confound Christian efforts to memorialize their history by building two large pagan temples over the site. The misguided effort, however, did not erase the memory of the execution, as intended. Instead, it identified the precise location of Christ's sacrificial relics, preserving them in the dry sands of Jerusalem until the dawn of a new Christian era.

Walking Tour 1 near
San Giovanni in Laterano

1. Santa Croce in Gerusalemme
2. San Giovanni in Laterano
3. Scala Santa
4. Battistero Lateranense
5. Santi Quattro Coronati
6. San Clemente

© OpenStreetMap contributors

SANTA CROCE RELICS

The Chapel of Relics holds Pilate's carved plaque as well as reliquaries that are believed to contain fragments of:

- The True Cross
- A nail from the crucifixion
- Thorns from Christ's crown
- The Good Thief's cross
- St. (Doubting) Thomas' index finger
- The scourging pillar

Helena also brought soil from the crucifixion mount and spread it at Santa Croce, making this one of the best places, outside Jerusalem, to meditate on the Passion of our Savior.

It is said that during the razing of Hadrian's pagan temples, Helena prayed for guidance from God. Then, one day, she urged workers to dig in a certain place, amidst the debris. There, the workmen unearthed a block of wood upon which a message had been written in Hebrew, Greek and Latin: Jesus of Nazareth, King of the Jews.

The startling discovery led to a feverish excavation in which more relics were soon discovered, including three crosses.

However, no one knew which was the cross of Christ until the bishop of Jerusalem, Macarius, suggested a test. In a nearby house, a woman was deathly sick. So, remains of the three crosses were brought to her bedside. When the first two crosses were pressed to her body, no response was seen. Then, upon touching the third, she immediately rose from her bed and began praising the Lord for her miraculous healing.

On display, is a full size replica of the enigmatic Shroud of Turin, precisely representing the wounds of Christ from:

- The scourging
- The crown of thorns
- The crucifixion
- The piercing lance

Accomplished investigators, using equipment of modern science, have attempted to prove this a forgery, but no one has succeeded. With carbon dating results now credibly challenged, the evidence supports the conclusion that the mysterious Shroud actually was Christ's burial cloth.

SAN GIOVANNI IN LATERANO

St. John Lateran
Daily: 7–7; Oct–March, closes at 6
Museum: 9–1 and 3–5, Mon–Fri
Cloister and museum require
small charge for admission.

St. John Lateran
is unique in status and history.
It is the oldest of the four 'Patriarchal Basilicas' and seven 'Pilgrim Churches.' It is also the Cathedral for the Bishop of Rome, a papal honor and responsibility. In the 4th century, Constantine ordered its construction and the Lateran Palace became the official papal residence until 1304. So, for a thousand years, the Lateran had the prestige of today's Vatican. Until 1870 all popes were crowned here and five ecumenical councils have been held on this site. This enduring church has survived the sacks of Alaric and Genseric (408 and 455 AD), the devastating earthquake of 896, and the fires of 1308 and 1360. Today's interior is primarily the work of Bernini's foe, Francesco Borromini.

The central bronze doors of the cathedral are normally shut. Originally, they enclosed the ancient Senate *Curia* in the Roman Forum. Imagine the historical figures who have walked through them. Above and right, they are pictured from outside and in. The small inset picture of a pilgrim demonstrates the massive scale of this enormous basilica and everything in it. Its mosaic floors were removed from declining Roman churches and inlaid in the 15th century.

The high altar's Gothic *baldacchino* seems somewhat undersized in such a massive cathedral, but it dates from 1369. At the top of it, are preserved the great treasures of this church: the unseen heads of Saints Peter and Paul. The altar is unique in the Catholic world, being made of wood, not stone, and not containing any relics. The altar is, itself, a relic. Though now encased in stone, it is the one upon which St. Peter celebrated Mass during his years in Rome. Only a pope may offer Mass at this altar.

In the *confessio*, before the papal altar, is the tomb of Pope Martin V (left) who ordered the Roman return of popes after seven decades in Avignon France. The *confessio* once displayed the wooden altar of St. Peter, under acrylic (below). It is believed popes celebrated Mass on this unpolished wooden table from St. Peter to St. Sylvester in the 4th century. For years, pilgrims tossed coins onto it out of respect. Now it is encased in the main altar.

In addition to St. John the Apostle, this basilica is dedicated to St. John the Baptist, as is indicated by his statue (left) in the *confessio*.

CHRISTIAN TRIVIA 4 PILGRIMS

The 4 Patriarchal Basilicas of Rome are:
1. St. John Lateran
2. St. Peter's Basilica
3. St. Mary Major
4. St. Paul Outside the Walls.

The list of Rome's 7 Pilgrim Churches includes the Patriarchal Basilicas plus:
1. St. Lawrence Outside the Walls
2. Holy Cross of Jerusalem
3. Sanctuary of the Madonna of Divine Love.

San Giovanni in Laterano

Every bishop has a chair, or *cathedra*, that represents the authority with which he speaks. As Bishop of Rome –one of the pope's many titles and responsibilities– the Pope's *cathedra* (left) stays in the apse of St. John Lateran, the Cathedral of Rome. The throne is decorated with precious marbles in detailed mosaics. However, above it are even more precious mosaics that have been painstakingly preserved through the centuries. Particularly important is the center of the upper apse that displays nine angels hovering around the figure of Christ. This historic remnant dates from the 4th or 5th century. One tradition even claims that it is identical to the Supernatural image that was manifested to worshippers on the occassion of the dedication of the church.

In the right transcept (below), we see one of the many ornately carved ceilings over large organ pipes and confessional boxes.

Walking through the nave of the cathedral, one's eyes are drawn to the colossal marble apostles, standing 15' tall (below). So, it is easy to miss the art above them, including exquisite high-relief sculptures, as well as beautiful frescoes.

In the cathedral's left transcept is an altar with an ornate tabernacle, placed under a gold-columned canopy (right). Mounted over it, we see a large, gold image of the Last Supper (above). There, visible behind that image, are fragments of the table from which Jesus ate his Last Supper and offered the first Mass. This relic is displayed publicly on Easter Sundays.

We see a pope's eye view of the nave of this church from behind the papal altar (left). From here, the pontiff regularly celebrates Maundy Thursday Mass in honor of the Last Supper.

The Holy Door of St. John Lateran is only opened every 25th year, or whenever a Holy Year is declared. Other years, pilgrims queue to pay homage to Christ by rubbing the patina from the bronze foot of Baby Jesus who is cradled in the arms of His Blessed Mother, in front of the Crucified Redeemer (right).

SCALA SANCTA AND CLOISTER
AKA SCALA SANTA OR HOLY STAIRCASE
DAILY, 6:30–11:45; 3:30–6:45

Across the street from St. John Lateran is a moving relic from the passion of Jesus Christ. At first glance, it appears to be just another flight of stairs (below). But these led to the *praetorium* of Pontius Pilate in Jerusalem. So, during His trial and passion, Jesus Christ trod them repeatedly. The 28 Tyrian marble steps have been covered with wood for preservation, but small glass sheets make visible the spots where Christ's blood is said to have fallen. Around 335, the mother of Emperor Constantine, St. Helena, arranged to transfer the *Scala Sancta* to Rome. Since then, they have been revered with deep devotion. Christian pilgrims honor the Passion of Christ by ascending them, on their knees, while saying a prayer on each step. Today, sadly, armed soldiers must sometimes guard the entrance, while pilgrims pray and children play (right).

ARE THESE THE STEPS ON WHICH THE PROTESTANT REFORMATION BEGAN?

An odd story survives from Martin Luther's famous visit to the *Scala Sancta* in 1511. Decades later, Luther's son claimed his father reached a theological turning point while following the tradition of ascending the staircase on his knees. Here, he was struck with the revelation: "The just shall live by faith alone." Luther suddenly understood, according to the story, that Christian works – such as this uncomfortable devotion – had no value before God. An unflattering version of the account claims Luther rose abruptly from his knees, blurted "Sod this for a game of gladiators!", then stormed away. Regardless of the accuracy of that quote, a key element of the Protestant Reformation became Luther's "faith alone" doctrine which, Catholics argue, contradicts Scripture:

"For as the body without the spirit is dead, so faith without works is dead also."
James 2:26

Through the wood covering, a glass medallion (left) allows pilgrims to see the marble steps below.

This statue is known as *Ecce Homo*, based on Pilate's dismissive Latin for, "Behold the man."

It is near the base of the Holy Staircase, and its feet are said to exude a miraculously fragrant scent, at times.

TIPS 4 PILGRIMS

Don't arrive at the last minute, if you plan to pray on these sacred steps. To allow time for unhurried prayers, the gate at the foot of the *Scala Sancta* is closed approximately 20 minutes before official closing.

The steps are crowded, at times, especially on days designated to honor the Passion. The ascent can be difficult on the knees and, consequently, not suited for children. Keep in mind that those who pray slowly do not yield to ascending speedsters!

At the top of the stairs is the *Sancta Sanctorum* (Holy of Holies, right) named so because of the great number of relics it houses. Once a prayer chapel exclusively for popes and few others, it is now seen only by special arrangement. This chapel has been known as the Sistine of the Middle Ages. In the silver frame, one can see a painting of Christ. It is called the Holy Face, and is said to have been started by St. Luke and finished by an angel. Many of these frescoes date to the 13th century.

Between the Scala Sancta and Baptistry is the tallest and possibly oldest of Rome's thirteen ancient obelisks. Amazingly, it dates from the 15th century B.C. and once was in the Egyptian Heliopolis at the Temple of the Sun. Now topped with a cross, the red granite monolith was originally placed at the Circus Maximus, where Christians were once butchered.

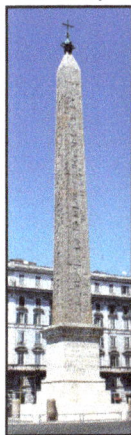

THE CLOISTER (below) is accessible from inside San Giovanni, but requires a modest charge. It once housed a community of monks who served the needs of the basilica. The structure was built by the Vassalletto family in the 13th century. Its Cosmati-style mosaics display elaborate, geometric inlays for a decorative effect. In fact, many of the bare columns pictured below were once covered with inlaid marble mosaics.

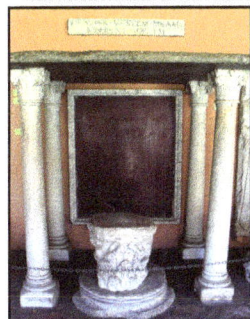

The Cloister preserves the red porphyry slab upon which Roman soldiers cast lots for Jesus Christ's seamless tunic. The columns that surround the slab are said to be the height of Jesus, which appears to be around 5' 10".

Also preserved here, is a 5th century papal throne (right), the oldest one known to have survived the centuries.

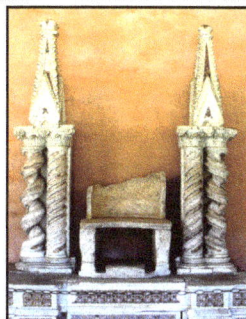

BATTISTERO LATERANENSE
The Lateran Baptistry
DAILY: 7:30 - 12:30 & 4 - 7:30

In the early centuries of Christianity, the unbaptized were not allowed into churches. So, Baptistries were located off site. The Baptistry is adjacent to the Cathedral of St. John Lateran in the historic building that became the prototype for future Christian Baptistries. Though restored through the centuries, it dates from the time of Constantine and is believed to be on the site of his Baptism. However, the ancient historian Eusebius claims Constantine received the Sacrament on his deathbed. Perhaps the emperor had lived by the philosophy of young Augustine, who once prayed, "Oh Lord, please make me holy... just not yet."

The Baptistry may have been circular, in the beginning, but it has maintained its octogonal shape since the 5th century. At its center was a circular pool in which Christian catechumens were baptized by triple immersion, while surrounded by eight solemn porphyry pillars.

Today, the immersion pool has been replaced by a large, green-basalt urn. For some time, it served well for immersing converts in the waters that welcomed them to the faith. Both the urn and its ornamented bronze cover date to the 17th century.

The Lateran Baptistry honors two similarly named saints, with a Chapel of St. John the Evangelist and a Chapel of St. John the Baptist. The proper name for the Baptistry is *San Giovanni in Fonte* (St. John at the Font). However, it is often remembered as the Baptistry of Constantine. The emperor's original frescoes have been painted over, through the centuries, with scenes in the life of St. John the Baptist. However, a mosaic in one of the smaller apses dates from the 5th century.

The serene Chapel of St. Venantius (left) is attached to the Baptistry. He was a missionary bishop, martyred in Dalmatian in 257. His remains, along with those of eight other martyrs rest beneath the altar. The chapel's beautiful ceiling (below) is carved from cedar.

SANTI QUATTRO CORONATI
FOUR CROWNED SAINTS
MON - SAT: 9:30 - 12 & 4 - 7:30 (MORNINGS ONLY: OCT - MAR)

During Emperor Diocletian's reign (284-305), four Roman soldiers were martyred here for refusing to sacrifice to Asclepius, a pagan god. Their names were Severus, Victorinus, Carpophorus and Severinus. Records suggest that a church on this site, in honor of the Four Crowned Saints, may have been established during the time of Pope Melichiades (311-314), making it one of the oldest Christian churches in Rome.

In 847, Pope Leo IV was elected here. Later, during a reconstruction project, he ordered that the relics of the Four Crowned Saints be removed from a cemetery and relocated to the church, along with the bodies of five martyred sculptors who had refused to sculpt a pagan god.

The bell tower (above) was added in the 9th century. Its truncated height suggests it may have been used for defensive purposes, rather than bells. However, the basilica suffered major damage during the Norman sack of Rome in 1084 After that, the church was rebuilt on a smaller scale. Its original apse (left), though oversized, remains with the newly narrower nave.

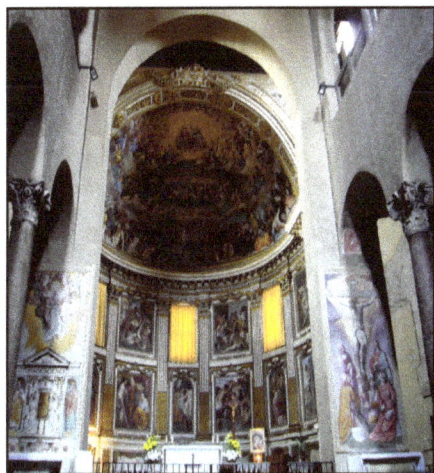

Over the entrance to this minor basilica (right), is a very old fresco of the four martyred soldiers in the clouds, with Augustinian nuns and orphan girls, praying for their intercession from below.

The apse (above) contains panels that depict the scourging deaths of the soldier martyrs. Along the nave, above the remains of 14th century frescoes, we see the *matronea,* or women's galleries. A cloister was established here in the early 13th century. In 1560, however, Pius IV gave the church and the adjoining convent to Augustinian nuns who cared for orphans. Today, Augustinian sisters continue to live here. The cloister has lovely gardens and a 12th century fountain. The Chapel of San Silvestro (1€ donation) has been preserved with the appearance of its 1254 origins, including ancient frescoes. Whenever seeking entrance, look for the bell to ring, and a nun will assist.

HISTORY 4 PILGRIMS

From birth, *baroque* masters Bernini and Borromini were different: Bernini, the prodigious, multi-talented son of a sculptor; Borromini, the rising stonemason, obsessed with only architecture and its accents. He became Bernini's star pupil. However, their relationship soured as their artistic style and personalities clashed. Charming Bernini attracted the best of commissions in his long life. Volatile Borromini shortened his own by suicide.

SAN CLEMENTE
ST. CLEMENT
DAILY: 9 - 12:30 & 3:30 - 6:30 (OCT - MAR: 6)

A church in honor of St. Clement, the third pope, has existed on this site since 384, and the early origin of the current structure is apparent from the front entrance (above) that rests well below modern street level. There, you may enter into the basilica's atrium (right) that dates from the to the 12th century. However, this entry point is often closed, leaving tourists to find their way to the less conspicuous, side entrance of the church. Here, entering into inspiring architectural beauty it is easy to forget that the church was nearly destroyed by Norman invaders in 1084. Today, however, from the nave's 12th century cosmatesque pavement to its ornately coffered, early 18th century *baroque* ceiling, this historic site proves the enduring tenacity of the Catholic faith.

The unusual apse mosaic (left) dates from the first half of the 12th century. Here, Christ's Cross is the Tree of Life where, from its base, waters of life flow, attracting all creatures that thirst for life. Also from the base of the Cross, lively acanthus leaves sprout, filling the golden apse. Representing the apostles are twelve white doves, perched on the Cross and, below it, twelve white sheep flank the Lamb of God.

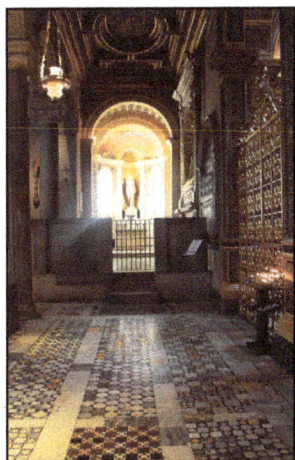

Viewing up the right aisle (left) pilgrims focus on the 16th century statue of St. John the Baptist, from an unknown artist. Nearby, another chapel (right) honors the 9th century saints, Methodius and also Cyril, who invented the Cyrillic alphabet and became the father of Slavonic literature. That chapel displays a lovely painting (below) of a young Virgin Mary, by Giovanni Battista Salvi.

Yet, as pilgrims soak up the antiquity of this church, they are surprised to find that this is only the beginning of a journey through time. That is because this house of worship was built upon an earlier 4th century basilica, and that was built upon the ruins of a 1st century pagan temple. All of this is available to explore by gaining admission at the vestibule of the sacristy, near the front, right of the church.

Stairs lead down to the narthex of the 4th century basilica where one finds ancient art. This fresco, pictured right, demonstrates that the earliest Christians venerated the Mother of God artistically, just as Catholics do, today.

San Clemente demonstrates that Rome was built, layer upon layer, in search of God. As pilgrims descend below the church, they find a 1st century Mithraic temple. (For more on Mithraism, see p. 115.) Pictured below, is the Mithraic banquet room, or *triclinium*. Tourists and pilgrims then continue on, through a series of 1st century rooms that, today, see no light of day.

HISTORY 4 PILGRIMS

Previous to Rome's Christian era, Vestal Virgins played an important role in the wellbeing of the state. Six physically perfect girls, between the ages of 6 and 10, were chosen by lottery from patrician families. They were given 10 years of training to serve Vesta, the daughter of Saturn. Enjoying the public role of deified beauty queens, still, each was required to keep the sacred fire burning in the temple of Vesta and to maintain her virginity. After 30 years of service, they were free to marry. However, beatings were in order if the sacred fire went out. Also, when any of them broke her vow of chastity, she was buried alive. Her lover was taken outside the city and clubbed to death.

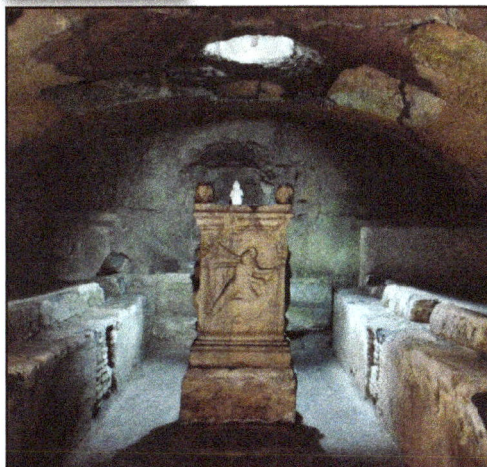

6

Palazzo Taverna

Palazzo Boncompagni Corcos

Palazzo Malvezzi Campeggi

Casa delle letterature

Palazzo Medici Clarelli

Palazzo Bennicelli

Oratorio dei Filippini

Odradek

Carrefour express

Palazzo Sacchetti

Palazzo Sforza Cesarini

Teatro dell'Orologio

5

Chiesa Nuova

Vicolo Sugarelli

Corso Vittorio Emanuele II

7

San Biagio della Pagnotta

monumento a Nicola Spedalieri

Palazzo dei Pupazzi

Palazzo degli Accetti

Chiesa Nuova

Vicolo Cellini

Il Goccetto

Via dei Cartari

Via Larga

Via Cers

Chiesa di Santa Lucia del Gonfalone

Trattoria Settimio

La Locanda del Pellegrino

Walking Tour 2
West of Piazza Navona

1. Piazza Navona
2. Sant'Agnese in Agone
3. Santa Maria dell'Anima
4. Santa Maria della Pace
5. Chiesa Nuova (aka Santa Maria in Vallicella)
6. Saint Giovanni of Fiorentini
7. Strolling lovely Via Giulia, you may wish to visit a variety of churches, including Chiesa dello Spirito Santo dei Napoletani and Santa Maria in Monserrato
8. Campo De' Fiori

Palazzo Incoronati de Planca

Piazza De' Ricci

Palazzo Ricci

Practical Tips
4 Pilgrims

1. This longer, but rewarding, tour can begin and end at Piazza Navona (far right). The terrain, here, is flat.
2. There are no Metro stops in this historic district but taxis and buses are plentiful near Basilica di Sant'Andrea della Valle (lower, right).

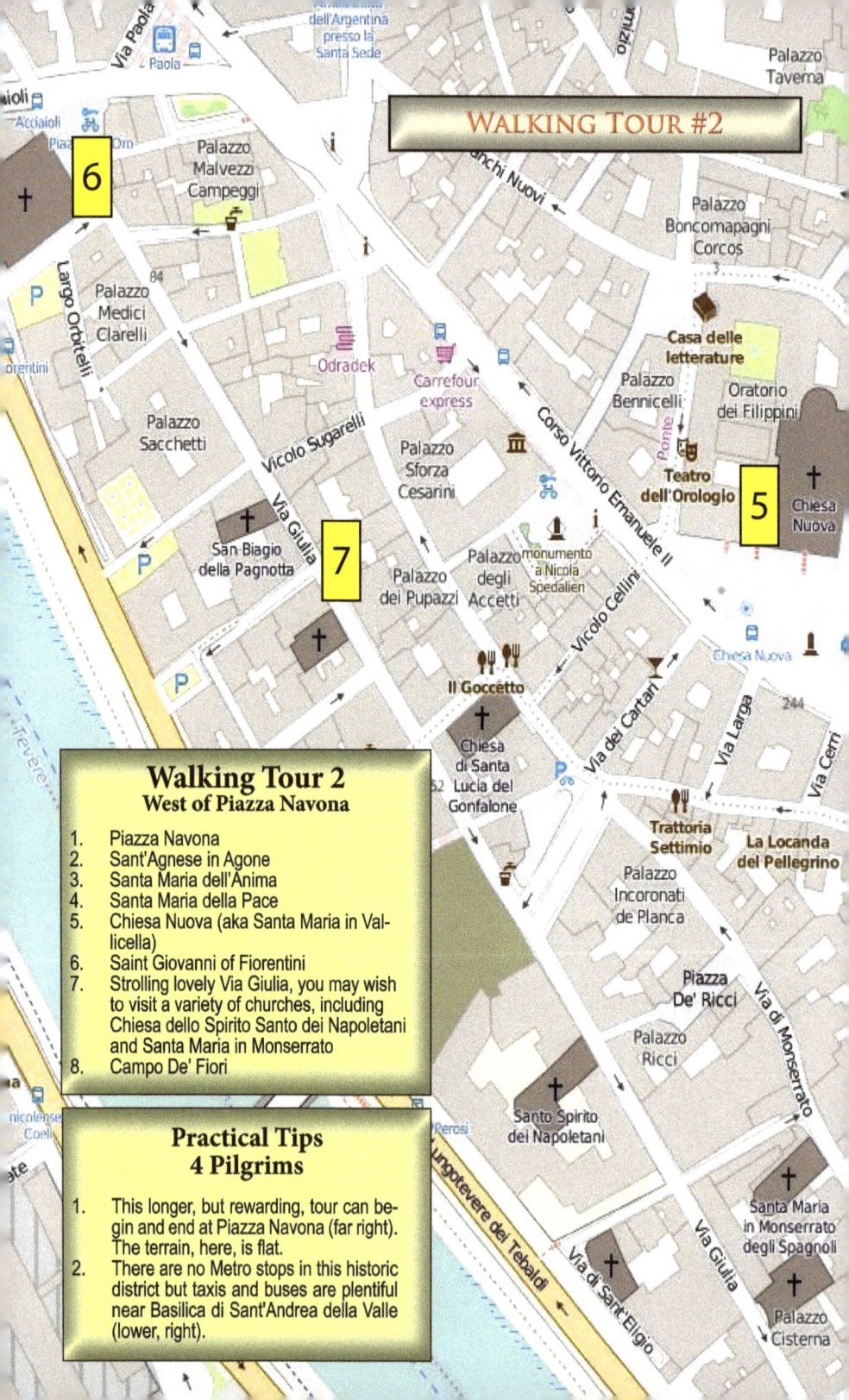

Santo Spirito dei Napoletani

Santa Maria in Monserrato degli Spagnoli

Via di Monserrato

Via Giulia

Via di Sant'Elgio

Lungotevere dei Tebaldi

Palazzo Cisterna

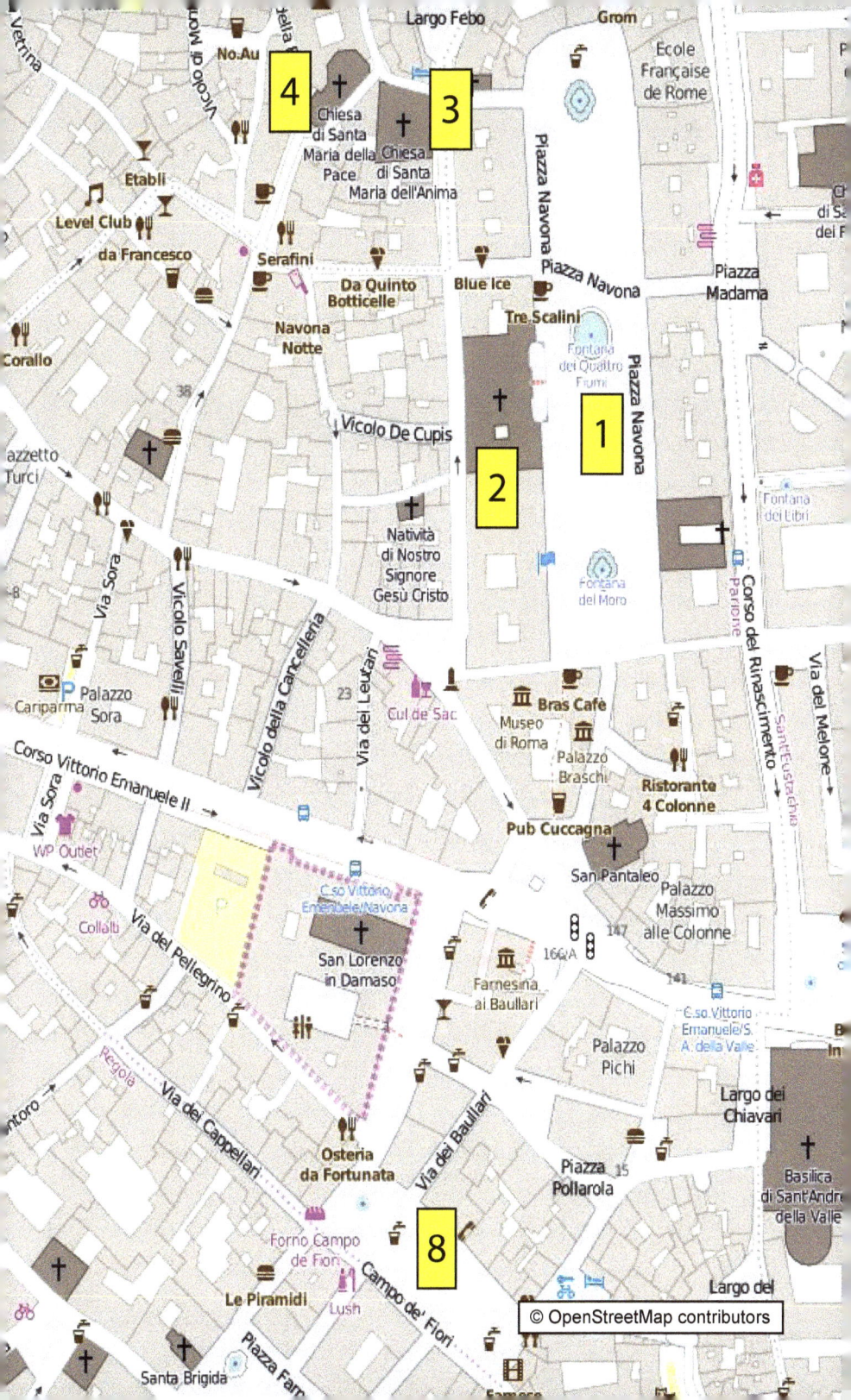

Largo Febo — **Grom**

Ecole Française de Rome

4

Chiesa di Santa Maria della Pace

3

Chiesa di Santa Maria dell'Anima

No.Au

Vicolo di Mo...

della...

Etabli

Level Club
da Francesco

Serafini

Piazza Madama

Piazza Navona

di S...
dei A...

Da Quinto Botticelle

Blue Ice

Navona Notte

Tre Scalini

Corallo

Fontana dei Quattro Fiumi

1

Piazza Navona

azzetto Turci

Vicolo De Cupis

2

Natività di Nostro Signore Gesù Cristo

Fontana dei Libri

38

Via Sora

Vicolo Savelli

Vicolo della Cancelleria

Via dei Leutari

Fontana del Moro

-8

Corso del Rinascimento

Via del Melone

23

Sant'Eustachio

Via del...

Caripama

Palazzo Sora

Cul de Sac

Bras Café

Museo di Roma

Corso Vittorio Emanuele II

Palazzo Braschi

Ristorante 4 Colonne

WP Outlet

Via Sora

Pub Cuccagna

Collalti

Via del Pellegrino

C.so Vittorio Emanuele/Navona

San Lorenzo in Damaso

San Pantaleo

Palazzo Massimo alle Colonne

147

166/A

141

Farnesina ai Baullari

C.so Vittorio Emanuele/S. A. della Valle

B...
In...

Regola

Via dei Cappellari

Palazzo Pichi

Largo dei Chiavari

Osteria da Fortunata

Via dei Baullari

Piazza Pollarola

15

Basilica di Sant'Andr... della Valle

8

Forno Campo de Fiori

Campo de' Fiori

Largo del

Le Piramidi

Lush

ntoro

Piazza Farn...

Santa Brigida

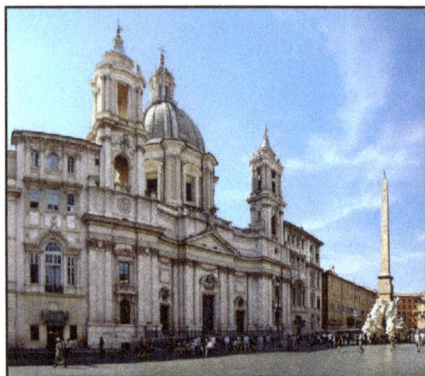

In the shadow of Francesco Borromini's church of *Sant'Agnese in Agone* (left) sits *Piazza Navona.* This historic and popular public square owes its unusual shape to Emperor Domitian's stadium (below) that once occupied the space.

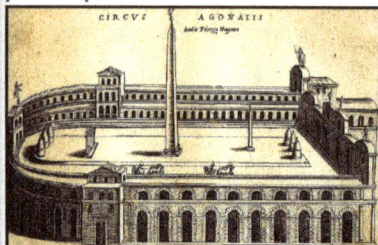

Domitian reigned from 81 to 96 AD. He ruled as a micromanaging monarch, ignoring the Senate and governing both political and moral law in the Roman empire. Some historians claim he was the first Emperor to proclaim himself *Dominus et Deus:* Master and God. So, when Christians and Jews naturally refused to worship him, they gained his suspicion and fell subject to his state-sponsored persecutions. Indeed, though he was an effiient bureaucratic adminstrator, ancient historians tend to portray Domition as a cruel tyrant, ruled by paranoia. However, some modern reviewers dispute these ancient accounts, suggesting Domitian's rule was not as brutal as portrayed by early historians.

Fountains are favorites, here. The Neptune Fountain (right) and the Moor Fountain at the other end of the *piazza,* were designed by Giacomo della Porta.

During frequent festivals (above), *Piazza Navona* can become uncomfortably crowded, causing it to lose much of its charm.

Today, the centerpiece of the *piazza* is Bernini's striking Fountain of the Four Rivers *(Quatro Fiumi, above),* at the base of an ancient Roman obelisk. (To get this commission, it is said that charming Bernini seduced the pope's neice.) Some of the fountain's sculpted characters (right and left) allegedly shield their horrified eyes from the disgusting church that Bernini's bitter rival, Borromini, designed. It's a great story, but the fountain was here first. The church—*Sant'Agnese in Agone*—is actually quite beautiful.

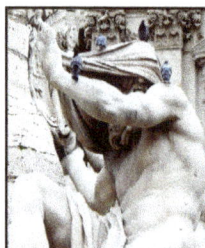

SANT'AGNESE IN AGONE
ST. AGNES IN AGONY
DAILY: 9:30 - 12:30 & 3:30 - 7; EXCEPT CLOSED MONDAYS

Saint Agnes was born in 291. Though her family had descended from Roman nobility, they were Christian and raised her in the faith.

By the age of 13, she was becoming a beautiful young lady and, because of her family's heritage and wealth, began attracting young suitors. However, Agnes had other plans, choosing a life of strict religious purity.

Whether from her open professions of faith, or the anger of rejected suitors, Agnes soon came to the attention of the authorities at a time when Emperor Diocletian was persecuting Christians. So, Prefect Sempronius condemned her to be stripped and dragged naked to a brothel, where she was subjected to terrible circumstances. (It was said that men who abused her were struck blind.) Still, she maintained her faith.

At trial, Agnes was sentenced to death, in Domitian's stadium, where tourists now stroll the *Piazza Navona*. There, executioners tied her to a stake and tried to light a fire at her feet, where either the wood would not ignite or the flames avoided her body. This angered the officer in charge who drew his sword and viciously beheaded the young saint. It is said that brave Christians rushed to her feet and soaked up her blood from the stadium floor.

A few days after the execution, Agnes' foster-sister, Saint Emerentiana, was found praying by her tomb. When confronted by angry Roman pagans, she refused to leave and, for that reason, was stoned to death.

Today, the skull of St. Agnes is preserved and on display (below) at Borromini's ornately detailed, *baroque* church. She is the patron saint of chastity, gardeners, girls, engaged couples, rape victims, and virgins.

Coincidentally, her name in Greek means "chaste."

Santa Maria dell'Anima
St. Mary of Soul
Daily: 9 - 12:45 & 3 - 7

Santa Maria dell'Anima was established in the 14th century as a hospice chapel for Germans. Today it is the national church of the German community in Rome.

Brilliant participants in the building of its current structure include Donato Bramante and Antonio da Sangallo. However, at the turn of the 19th century, Napoleon's troops ignored the church's beauty and sanctity, and converted its sacristy into a stable for their horses.

Today, pilgrims see not only a peacefully beautiful main altar area, but also 8 side chapels that display inspiring art and architectural accents. A serene courtyard is attached to the church, containing a number of ancient items.

Santa Maria della Pace
St. Mary of the Peace
Mon, Wed, Sat: 9 - 11:50

In 1480, an image of the Virgin Mary (right) was hit by a stone. (Another story says it was stabbed by a soldier's spear.) When viewers inspected the artwork for damage, they were shocked to find it exuding blood. The reigning pope was clearly moved by this miracle and called upon the Virgin to help prevent a war that had been brewing since the time of the murder of Giuliano de'Medici, two years earlier. When a peace agreement was reached, in 1482, Pope Sixtus IV dedicated this church to Our Lady of Peace.

This church includes notable art by Raphael Sanzio, including his *Sibille with Angels* (left), as well as architecture by Donato Bramante and Pietro da Cortona. The architecture of the adjacent cloister is highly praised and is also the work of Bramante.

CHIESA NUOVA (AKA SANTA MARIA IN VALLICELLA)
NEW CHURCH (AKA ST. MARY IN VALLICELLA)
DAILY: 8 - 12 & 4:30 - 7

Only in Rome will a 16th century church be known as "*Chiesa Nuova*" or "New Church." This was the home of St. Philip Neri, one of Rome's most beloved saints, a servant of the poor. Neri was an unconventional reformer. He attracted even young aristocrats to become servants of God and man. He humbled them by requesting that they parade in rags or work on this church as common laborers. Still, they followed the servant saint.

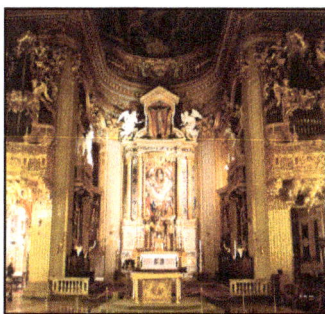

Perhaps responding to the persuasions of St. Philip Neri, Pietro da Cortona also humbled himself by spending two decades frescoing the beautiful nave, dome and apse (below).

Caravaggio's moving *Deposizione* (right) is located in the *Cappella della Pietà*. The relics of St. Philip Neri are entombed in another chapel (below).

SAN GIOVANNI DEI FIORENTINI
ST. JOHN OF THE FLORENTINES
DAILY: 7 - 11 & 5 - 7:30 (OCT - MAR: 4:30 - 7)

This basilica was dedicated to the Florentine community in Rome from 1518 until 1906, when it became a parish church. Its design and construction included many of Rome's most famous architects, including: Donato Bramante, Jacopo Sansovino, Antonio Sangallo the Younger, Michelangelo Buonarroti, Giacomo della Porta, Pietro da Cortona, Carlo Maderno, and Francesco Borromini. This impressive list is due largely to the fact that the church took 101 years to complete. However, Michelangelo's early design was rejected for being too expensive.

Inside are quality works of art and sculpture, as well as one of the most important organs of the 17th century. Pilgrims can hear this organ every Sunday at noon. This is the only Roman church where animals are welcomed and every Easter a lamb-blessing takes place here.

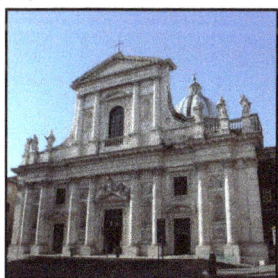

After Maderno was entombed here, Borromini designed the altar. The brilliant but volatile younger architect requested that he too be buried here, next to his famous uncle. Borromini further asked for an unmarked grave, and then committed suicide. Today, their tombstone under the cupola reveals only the elder's name. However, two nearby marble tablets commemorate both extraordinary architects.

VIA GIULIA

The route down Via Giulia to Campo de Fiori is a lovely stroll, more peaceful than in the hectic parts of Rome. Along the pleasant trail, you will pass a half dozen churches that are worth stepping into. However, the most unusual one is Santa Maria dell'Orazione e Morte (St. Mary of Prayer and Death, right).

Passing by, tourists are surprised by the macabre images on the facade of the church (below). However, the purpose was honorable, in a lawless age. The Confraternity of Prayer and Death was established to give burial to the numerous dead who were being found in the countryside or in the Tiber, without any identification. Without this public service, none would have received a dignified funeral. Beside the church, a cemetery was established. However, in 1886, it was almost destroyed by embankment construction on the Tiber. Inside, the oval church has an interesting crypt and a number of remarkable works that focus on the brevity and fragility of this life.

CAMPO DE' FIORI
FIELD OF FLOWERS
MON - SAT UNTIL 2PM

Campo de Fiori is a festive street market, offering tourists a wide variety of produce, flowers, spices, clothes and souvenirs. However, one ominous bronze statue there reminds us of a far less festive time, in a far more brutal age.

Giordano Bruno was a 16th century Italian. Though a Dominican priest, he began to espouse pantheism, along with denying the existence of the Trinity and the dogma of Transubstantiation. Over time, he established a reputation for rebellion, including even a charge of murder. Eventually, he published his thoughts and his writings were then condemned by the Inquisition as heretical. After 8 years of imprisonment in *Castel Sant'Angelo*, Bruno still refused to recant. So, he was sentenced to death and, on this site, burned at the stake.

UNUSUALLY GRAPHIC
TOMB AT
SANTA MARIA DEL POPOLO

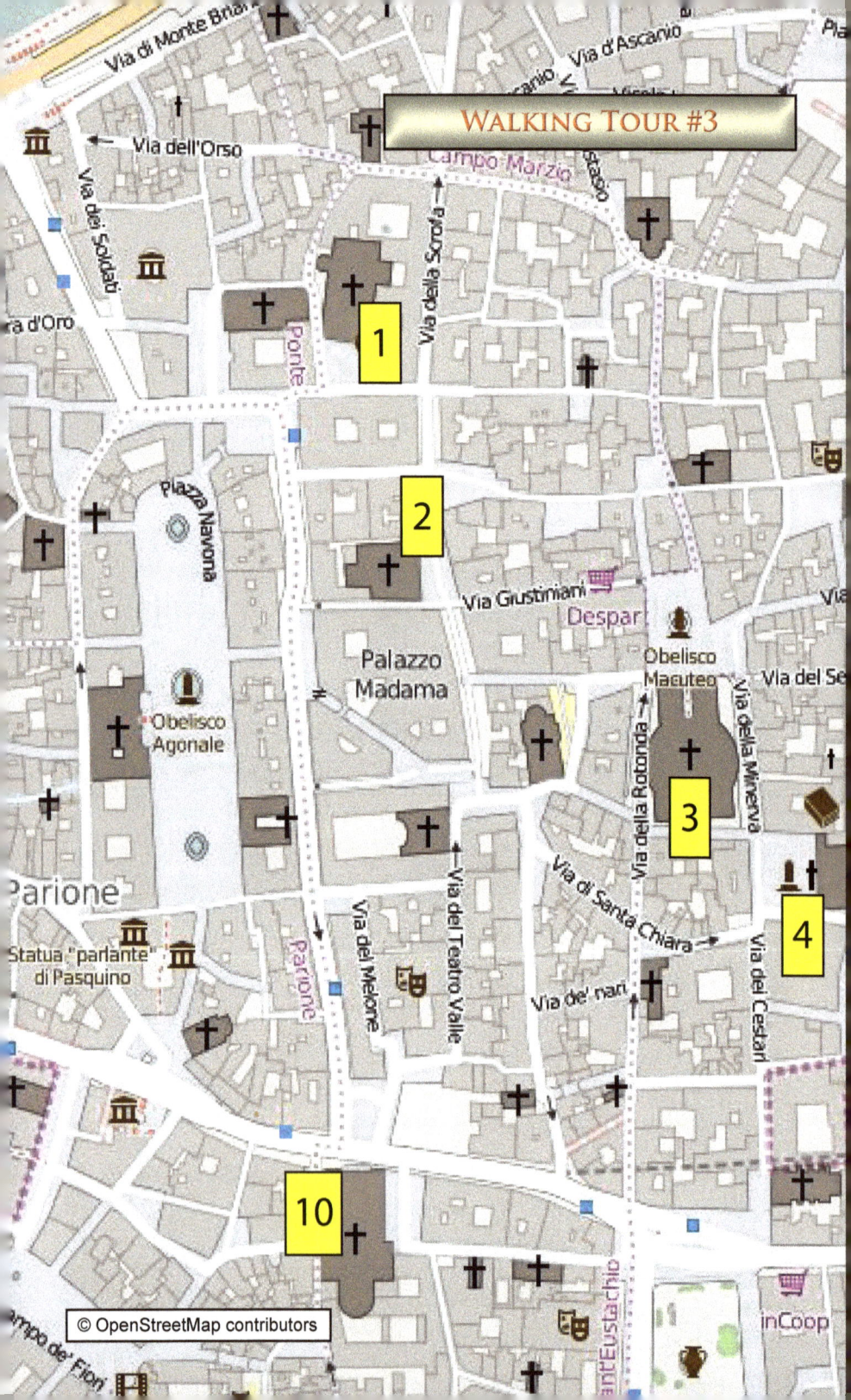

Via di Monte Brian
Via d'Ascanio
Via dell'Orso
Campo Marzio
Via della Scrofa
Via dei Soldati
a d'Oro

Ponte

1

Piazza Navona

2

Via Giustiniani
Despar

Palazzo Madama

Obelisco Macuteo

Obelisco Agonale

Via della Rotonda
Via della Minerva
Via del Se

3

Parione

Via di Santa Chiara

4

Via del Cestari

Via del Melone
Via del Teatro Valle

Via de' nari

Statua "parlante" di Pasquino

10

ntEustachio

inCoop

© OpenStreetMap contributors

Walking Tour 3
in the vicinity of The Pantheon

1. San Agostino
2. San Luigi dei Francesi
3. The Pantheon (aka Santa Maria dei Martiri)
4. Santa Maria Sopra Minerva
5. Sant'Ignazio
6. Santa Maria in Via Lata
7. San Marcello
8. Santi Apostoli
9. Chiesa del Gesu'
10. Sant'Andrea della Valle

Practical Tips
4 Pilgrims

1. This lvery worthwhile tour can begin and end at Piazza Navona (far left), where taxis and buses are plentiful, near #10.
2. There are no Metro stops in this historic district.
3. Though this is a longer tour, the walking is flat.
4. Always remember that street arrows on maps reflect only auto traffic patterns, not walking directions.

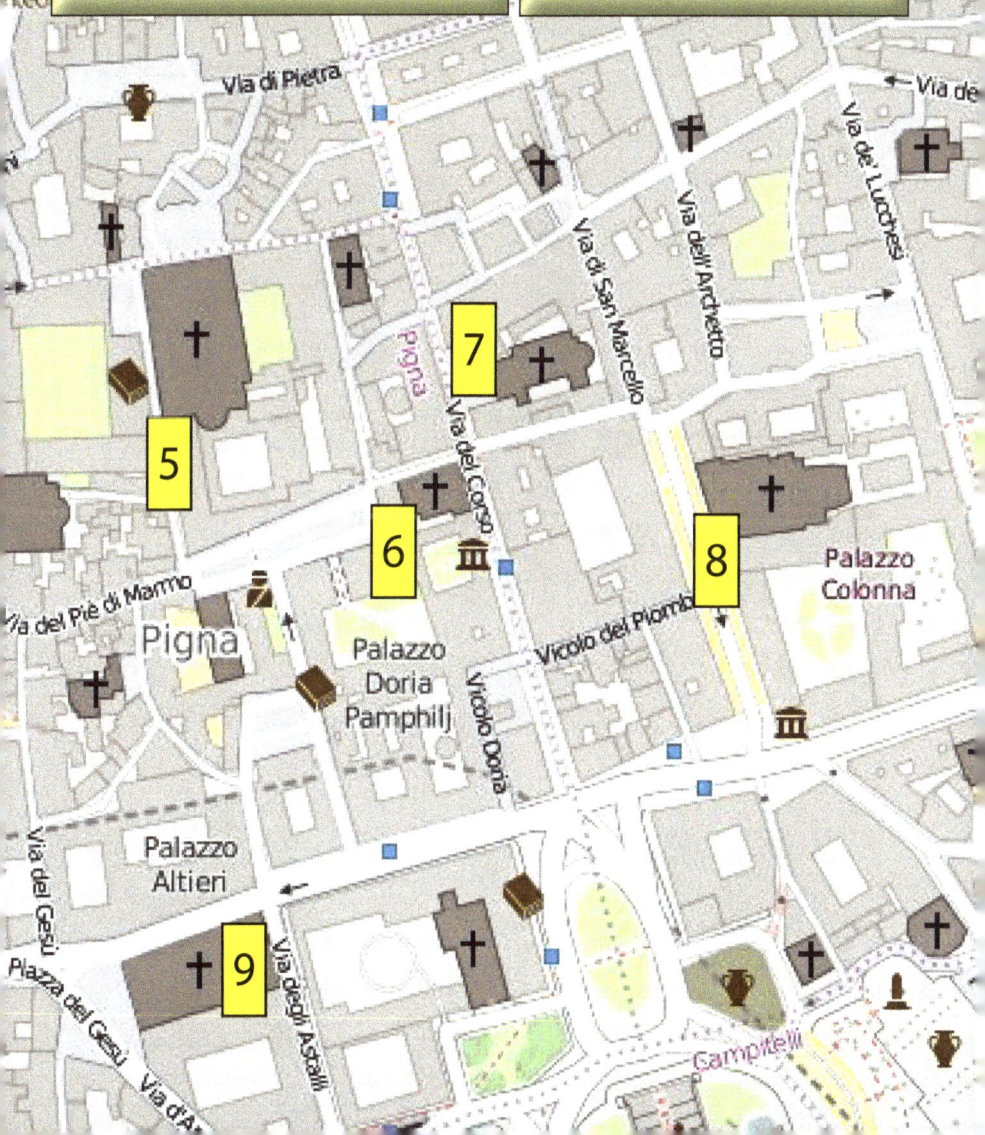

Via di Pietra

Via di Pol

Via de

Via

Via de' Lucchesi

Pigna

Via di San Marcello

Via dell'Archetto

7

5

Via del Corso

6

Via del Piè di Marmo

Pigna

Palazzo
Doria
Pamphilj

Vicolo del Piombo

8

Palazzo
Colonna

Vicolo Doria

Palazzo
Altieri

Via del Gesù

Piazza del Gesù

9

Via degli Astalli

Via d'A

Campitelli

SAN AGOSTINO
St. Augustine
Daily: 7:30 - 12:30 & 4 - 6:30

St. Augustine (354 - 430) was Bishop of Hippo in North Africa, and a prolific author who became a Doctor of the Church. The church that honors him was completed in 1483. However, this was also the site of *San Trifone*, a 9th century church. Around 1300, that structure was replaced by a new church that honored Augustine. Today, that church's nave is the current church's transept.

The 15 steps that lead up to the entrance of the church indicate that its design wisely predicted the occassional flood waters of the Tiber. An Augustinian monastery is next door, and St. Philip Neri (1515 - 1595) studied theology there. In this church is a carved wooden crucifix from the early 15th century that the saint often prayed before.

Even though St. Monica had been born a Christian, Augustine's mother was given in marriage to an abusive, adulterous pagan. In fact, Augustine, himself, squandered away his youth in sinful pursuits. But Monica never lost faith in the power of relentless prayer. Eventually, her prayers overcame all obstacles: Monica's husband converted on his death bed and Augustine not only changed his ways but became one of the Church's greatest of intellectual saints. Today, Monica is one of the most popular of patron saints, interceding for victims of alcoholism, difficult marriages, disappointing children, verbal abuse, and adultery. Her tomb (below) is on display in the St. Monica Chapel in this church but her remains have been moved to beneath the altar.

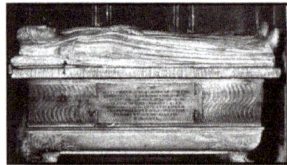

The main altar (left) was designed by Bernini with four columns of black marble and two of the master's angels. At its center is a Byzantine icon of the Virgin Mary from the famous church of Hagia Sofia in Constantinople. After the fall of that city, the icon was brought to Rome and given to this church in 1482.

The church's most important painting is *Madonna of the Pilgrims* (aka *Madonna di Loreto*, 1604, left). Two pilgrims, kneel while adoring the infant Christ. How do we know it is a Caravaggio? Check out those dirty feet!

In 1512, Raphael painted Isaiah (right) at the behest of a humanist from Luxembourg, Johann Goritz. When the dissatisfied sponsor complained to Michelangelo that Raphael had overcharged for the painting, Raphael's rival defended him by saying, "The knee alone is worth the price." The work is now displayed on the church's third column on the left.

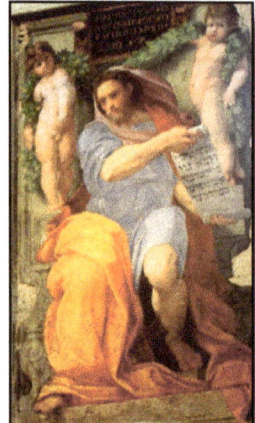

San Luigi dei Francesi
St. Louis of France
Daily: 8 - 12:30 & 3:30 - 7 except closed Thursday PM

This beautiful church is dedicated to St. Louis IX who was king of France until 1270. It is the national church of the French in Rome, and many well known Frenchmen are buried here. It was first commissioned for construction in 1518. However, various delays – including the infamous sack of Rome – prevented its completion until 1589. By that time, though, masters such as Giacomo della Porta and Domenico Fontana had contributed to its construction.

The coffered ceiling of the nave (below), by Antoine Derizet, is beautifully ornamented with white and gilded stucco work. The extravagant pattern is carried through to the apse and cupola.

Most extravagant of all, however, is the chapel of St. Louis (right), by artist Plautilla Bricci.

Other beautiful artworks include the impressive fresco at the center of the nave ceiling (left), by Charles-Joseph Natoire, showing the death of King Louis while on a crusade.

The 5th chapel on the left (right) is dedicated to St. Matthew and contains some of Caravagio's most famous masterpieces, his first great religious works. The artist's initial attempt at *St. Matthew and the Angel* (bottom, right) was rejected because of the shocking appearance of the inspired author: old, grey, and with dirty feet. In the dramatic *Calling of St. Matthew* (bottom, left), Christ's hand raises from the shadows, indicating that He chooses the astonished tax collector to follow Him while Matthew droops his head and ponders his coins. But the saint's memorial would not be complete without *Martyrdom of St. Matthew* (bottom, middle). Matthew has been dragged from an altar and is about to be slain, as others watch in horror.

PANTHEON (aka Santa Maria ad Martyres)

Greek: "All the Gods" (aka St. Mary of the Martyrs)
Mon - Sat: 9 - 4:30 (Jul - Aug: 6) Sun & Holidays: 9 - 1

This temple, first dedicated to all the Roman gods, was originally built in 27 BC, but burned down in 80 AD. Then, thirty years later, an apparent lightning strike caused the rebuilt Pantheon to be consumed by fire again. So, determined to establish an indestructible temple, Emperor Hadrian began reconstruction in 119 AD. It appears he accomplished his goal. However, by the 7th century, it had declined into a state of abandonment, leading its owner, the Byzantine Emperor Phocas, to give the Pantheon to the Catholic Church in 609. Pope Boniface IV promptly ordered 28 cartloads of martyrs bones delivered here and renamed the building *Santa Maria ad Martyres* (St. Mary of the Martyrs). The change in status immediately halted, here, the pilfering of ancient structures that had become common in Rome. Consequently, the Pantheon is considered the world's best preserved, great building from antiquity. Still, some significant filching was even authorized later by the Church.

SHHH!

Remember that the Pantheon is now consecrated to Christian worship. Maintain reverential quiet, no matter how disrespectful other tourists become.

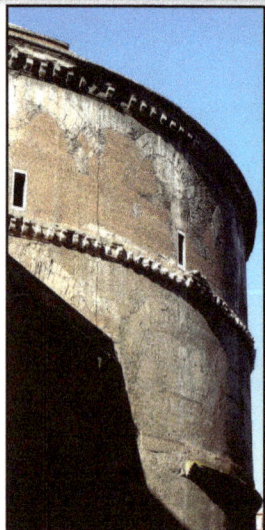

The outer walls (left and right) provide faint evidence of the beautiful facade that the temple once displayed. That marble veneer was all stolen in the neglectful early centuries. Pilgrims get a sense of the age of this building by noting that the rustic bronze doors are from the original temple. But a better indication can be found by walking to the side of the structure. There, you will discover (left) that street level was significantly lower at the time of the temple's construction.

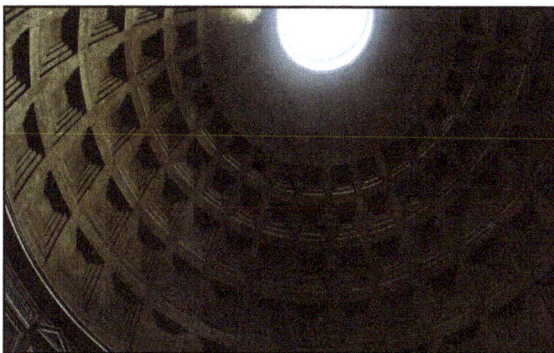

As you enter, past the portico's 16 granite columns that are 42' tall and 15' in circumference, note the *Chapel of St. Joseph in the Holy Land,* on your left. Soil from there was used to build it.

The precisely coffered dome (right) is the largest cast concrete structure ever constructed prior to the 20th century. It is 142' in diameter and proportioned like a section of a 142' sphere that could be resting on the ground. One of the walls that supports the massive dome is 23' thick.

The Pantheon's sole source of light is the dome's oculus. It appears much smaller than its 30' diameter. Rain freely falls through it, so the Pantheon's colorful marble floor has been designed to quickly drain away the many centuries of rainfall it has collected.

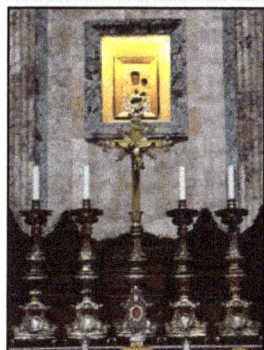

The perimeter of the interior (below) displays a Catholic altar (right) and the tomb of master artist Raphael (left). Also buried here is Victor Emmanuel II who became the first king of united Italy in 1870. The burial honor is somewhat surprising, considering that Pius IX excommunicated the king after his forces seized the Papal States, Years later, however, when the king lay dying in the Quirinal Palace – once a summer residence of popes – Pius reversed the excommunication and even sent his blessing.

Santa Maria Sopra Minerva
St. Mary above Minerva
Church Daily: 7 - 12 & 4 - 7; Cloister: 8 - 1 & 3:30 - 7:30

Over the ruins of Pompey the Great's Temple of Minerva (50 BC), Pope Zacharias (741-752) built this site's first church. In the 13th century, however, the monastery next door and, later, that church were given to the Domincan Friars. By 1370, the Dominicans – who continue to serve this church – completed this structure: the first Gothic church built in Rome. Today, Bernini's clever little pachyderm welcomes visitors, outside.

Near the main altar is *Christ the Redeemer* (right) that was begun by Michelangelo, but finished by one of his students. Its bronze drape was added later. In addition to medieval master artist Fra Angelico, two 16th century Medici popes are entombed here: Pope Leo X and one of the most unfortunate of all pontiffs: Clement VII, who reigned during the infamous sack of 1527. Most notably, however, this basilica holds the sarcophagus (below) of Dominican mystic St. Catherine of Siena who lived here. Her room has been preserved for viewing.

An Unforgettable Visit

This church was meant to be our last stop on what we (mistakenly) thought would be our final trip to Rome for research on this book. Just before noon, I was concluding my photo session as bright sunbeams pierced through the church's windows (right). I had previously photographed Corrado Mezzana's *Sacred Heart with Sts. Catherine of Siena and Margaret Mary Alacoque* (below, left). As I began to leave, however, I was stopped in my tracks when I noticed how the sunlight illuminated the Sacred Heart of Jesus (below, right). Just then, the noon bells began ringing and my wife approached to show me her last-minute purchases from outside.

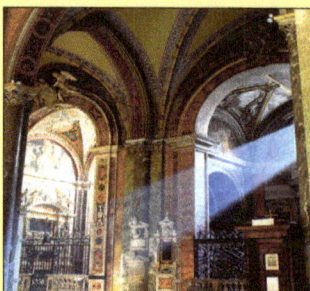

I shushed her and pointed at the shining Sacred Heart of Jesus. As the church bells finished tolling, we stood there in amazed silence.

Coincidence? Maybe... but we don't think so.

SANT'IGNAZIO DI LOYOLA

ST. IGNATIUS OF LOYOLA
DAILY: 8 - 12:30 & 4 - 7:15

This church, constructed in the 1620s, is dedicated to the Society of Jesus founder, St. Ignatius Loyola. It sits on property that was once a part of the Roman College, an institution operated by Jesuits.

The Chapel of St. Aloysius Gonzaga (right) displays a striking marble relief of the Annunciation, by Pierre le Gros. Gonzaga, a Jesuit, died while attending the Roman College. His relics are in a lapis lazuli urn, under the relief. Another chapel contains the relics (below) of Jesuit Cardinal St. Robert Bellarmine (d. 1621).

For the best view of the cupola, stand on the small yellow disk in the center of the nave, in line with the first pilaster. The success of Pozzo's cupola painting cleared the way for his masterful work on the apse and nave (below).

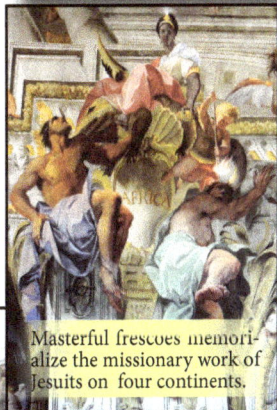

Masterful frescoes memorialize the missionary work of Jesuits on four continents.

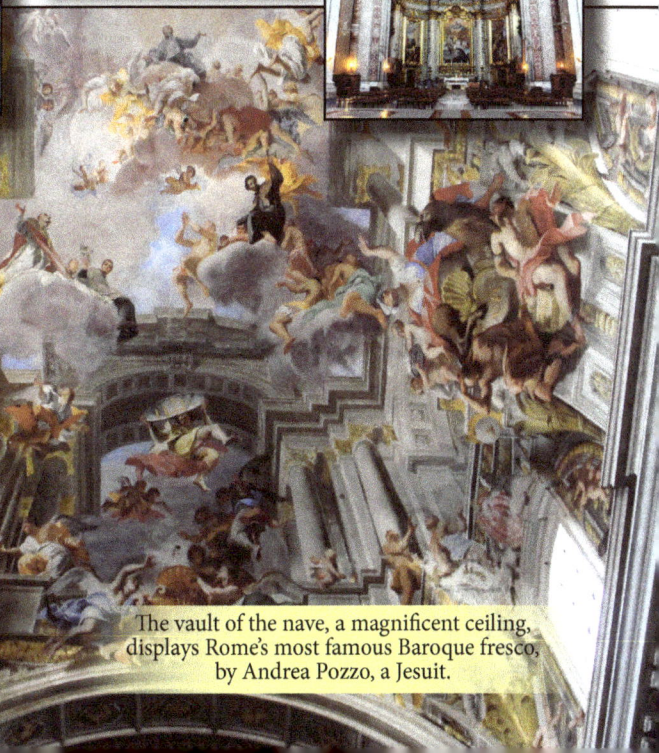

The vault of the nave, a magnificent ceiling, displays Rome's most famous Baroque fresco, by Andrea Pozzo, a Jesuit.

SANTA MARIA IN VIA LATA
ST. MARY IN THE BROAD WAY
CHURCH UPPER LEVEL: 5 - 7PM; CRYPT: 4 - 6PM

This church won't win any awards for cleanest facade but its history is important. St. Paul is believed to have been imprisoned here for two years. Below the church is a crypt that exhibits copies of medieval frescoes whose original works have been removed for conservation. However, more importantly, it holds a marble column to which St. Paul, it is believed, was bound. Pietro da Cortona and his students are responsible for many of the church's 17th century design elements. The upper church dates from the 9th century (below) with major renovations in the 15th. However, Tiber flooding forced new construction in the 1600s. Inside, over the relics of Agapito, a deacon and martyr of the 3rd century, is an icon of the Virgin Advocate, dating from the 13th century. Miracles have been attributed to the veneration of this icon.

CHURCH HISTORY
4 PILGRIMS

Each of Rome's four Patriarchal Basilicas has a Holy Door that is opened only for each Jubilee year. These Holy Years are based on Old Testament writings, but were established for Catholics by Pope Boniface VIII in 1300. The ceremonial use of the Holy Door, however, did not begin until the Holy Year of 1500. More recently, Jubilees have been declared every 25 or 50 years.

SAN MARCELLO AL CORSO
ST. MARCELLUS ON THE COURSE
DAILY: 7 - 12 & 4 - 7

Pope Marcellus I (d. 309) almost lived to see Rome's acceptance of Christianity. Instead, he was imprisoned on this site and then sent into exile, where he died just four years before the Edict of Milan, and one year into his papacy.

San Marcello al Corso, itself, has endured a similarly ill-fated history.

The Titulus Marcelli was established on this site, and Pope Boniface I was elected here in 418. Pope Adrian I built a church here in the 8th century, but in 1519 fire destroyed the structure. Soon, funds were raised for its reconstruction. However, the Sack of Rome, in 1527, created another problem: church coffers had to be emptied in order to bribe German mercenaries who were pillaging Rome's churches.

Jacopo Sansovino had been awarded the reconstruction contract, but he fled during the Sack, never to return. Then, after Antonio da Sangallo finished the project, a Tiber flood seriously damaged the church in 1530. The long-suffering construction project was not finished until 1597 with the completion of Carlo Fontana's facade.

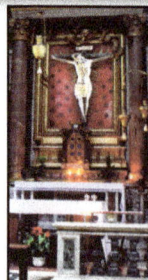

SANTI APOSTOLI
HOLY APOSTLES
DAILY: 6:30 - 12 & 4 - 7:15

After Rome's triumph over Totila and his invading Ostrogoth warriors, Pope Pelagius I wanted to commemorate the victory. So, in 560, he began construction on the first church to be located on this site. Later, but still in the 6th century, his successor, John III, placed the bones of the Apostle Saints Philip and James the Less (below, right). After the earthquake of 1348, however, the church remained empty for eight decades. Today, near the crypt, beneath the central nave, is an altar over "the well of martyrs." (lower, left). Into this well, Pope Stephen V (d. 891) is said to have placed many relics from early Christian cemeteries.

The painting over the main altar (right) is the largest altar piece in Rome. It is *Martyrdom of Saints Philip and James*, by Domenico Muratori, painted in 1715. In two distinct scenes, the artist depicts Philip being crucified in Hierapolis, and James being clubbed to death after having been hurled from the temple in Jerusalem. To the left of the church is the entrance (#51) to the monastery. With the porter's permission you may visit the two cloisters including a tomb where Michelangelo's body was kept for 17 days in 1564, before being secretly taken to Florence. This was the great artist's parish, but Florence, his home.

FRESCO FACTS 4 PILGRIMS

Artists who sought a more durable medium than paint on canvas or wood chose a technique called fresco. They mixed sand and lime and spread the mix over the wall. Then they applied their colors quickly, while the wall was still wet or fresh. When it dried, the colors fused chemically with the lime and became permanent. The fresco technique dates back at least to the ancient Egyptians. It is not an easy method to master.

For Michelangelo's frescoes, he painted watercolor sketches on canvas, called cartoons. But he had never before applied cartoons to walls or ceilings. So, because of his inexperience with frescoes, he invited capable artists from Florence to assist him, shortly after accepting his Sistine assignment. However, Michelangelo was not one for partnerships. He learned what they were able to teach in a week, or so, and then sent them on their way. After that, he locked himself in the chapel and proceeded with the frustratingly difficult project, unassisted.

CHIESA DEL GESU'
CHURCH OF THE MOST HOLY NAME OF JESUS (AKA CHURCH OF JESUS)
DAILY: 7 - 12:30 & 4 - 7:45 (EXCEPT SUN: 7:30 - 1)

This church can best be described as awe-inspiring, but it had a rough time just getting started. In 1537, St. Ignatius of Loyola–founder of the Society of Jesus (the Jesuits)– arrived in Rome and established his community. Eventually, they realized that their home church was proving too small. So, by the end of 1550, the cornerstone for the first Jesuit church was laid. However, construction was soon interrupted. Then, in 1554, Michelangelo received approval for a new design and another cornerstone was installed. Less than a month later construction, again, was halted. Finally, fourteen years later, a third foundation stone was laid and construction began in earnest. The Church of Jesus was consecrated in 1584. Today, it continues to be served by Jesuits.

Giacomo della Porta's facade (left) is not as eye-catching as the interior, but it represented a significant style transition from Renaissance to *baroque* and, consequently, was imitated throughout Europe.

The right transept holds an ornate chapel dedicated to St. Francis Xavier, one of Ignatius' first companions and venerated for the virtues that place him among the Church's greatest missionaries. A reliquary (right) displays the forearm and hand of the great saint. An equally ornate chapel occupies the left transept, where St. Ignatius is entombed.

The highly ornamented vault and cupola (left and below) are so beautifully executed that pilgrims are likely to get sore necks. With that in mind, church officials placed a large, angled mirror (right) in the central nave so that the ceiling can be viewed by comfortably looking down.

The fresco in the vault (left) is named *Triumph of the Name of Jesus*. It has been acclaimed as Baciccia's undisputed masterpiece and the most important art work of the Roman high *baroque*. The highly unusual overhead perspective creates the illusion of looking through the ceiling. Pilgrims watch as a bright light attracts the blessed saints, while the damned are repelled.

Again, Baciccia's hand ornamented the cupola (left and right). However, his fresco (*Vision of Heaven*) is somewhat deteriorated. In the drum are four windows lighting statues representing the four cardinal virtues: Prudence, Fortitude, Justice and Temperance.

SANT'ANDREA DELLA VALLE
ST. ANDREW OF THE VALLEY
DAILY: 7:30 - 12 & 4:30 - 7:30

An ancient church preceded this one here, named San Sebastiano, because this was the site on which the pierced body of Saint Sebastion was found. However, a newer church later replaced it, honoring the patron saint of Amalfi: St. Andrew. This is a titular church and minor basilica.

Around Rome, the size of this spectacular dome (below) is second only to St. Peter's Basilica. Completed in 1622, it is 16 meters in diameter by 80 meters high, and designed by Carlo Maderno. The lantern inside the dome was Borromini's first major work.

Behind the altar are paintings in the life of St. Andrew, including a huge image of his crucifixion on an X-shaped cross (bottom of page).

Carlo Maderno's supervision of this construction site was not without its difficulties. The extravagant dome fresco, *Glory of Paradise*, was executed by Giovanni Lanfranco. Its excellence earned him the church's highest commission. However, that did not go over well with Domenico Zampieri, known as Domenichino, who had been commissioned to paint the altar images of Saint Andrew's life and death (below). In the spirit of an Italian opera, Domenichino is said to have tried to kill his well-paid rival.

Like in Chiesa del Gesu', this ceiling is so magnificent, that a floor standing mirror (below) helps to prevent neck strain.

TRIVIA 4 PILGRIMS

This inspiring church is the scene of the first act in Pucini's popular opera, *Tosca*.

The son of a Duke, Joseph Mary Tomasi rejected the comforts of Sicilian nobility, eventually becoming a scholarly cardinal of saintly humility. His virtuous reputation was so revered that Clement XI initiated beatification just five months after his death. This church preserves the saint's largely incorupt relics (below).

The Trevi Fountain
(See page 109)

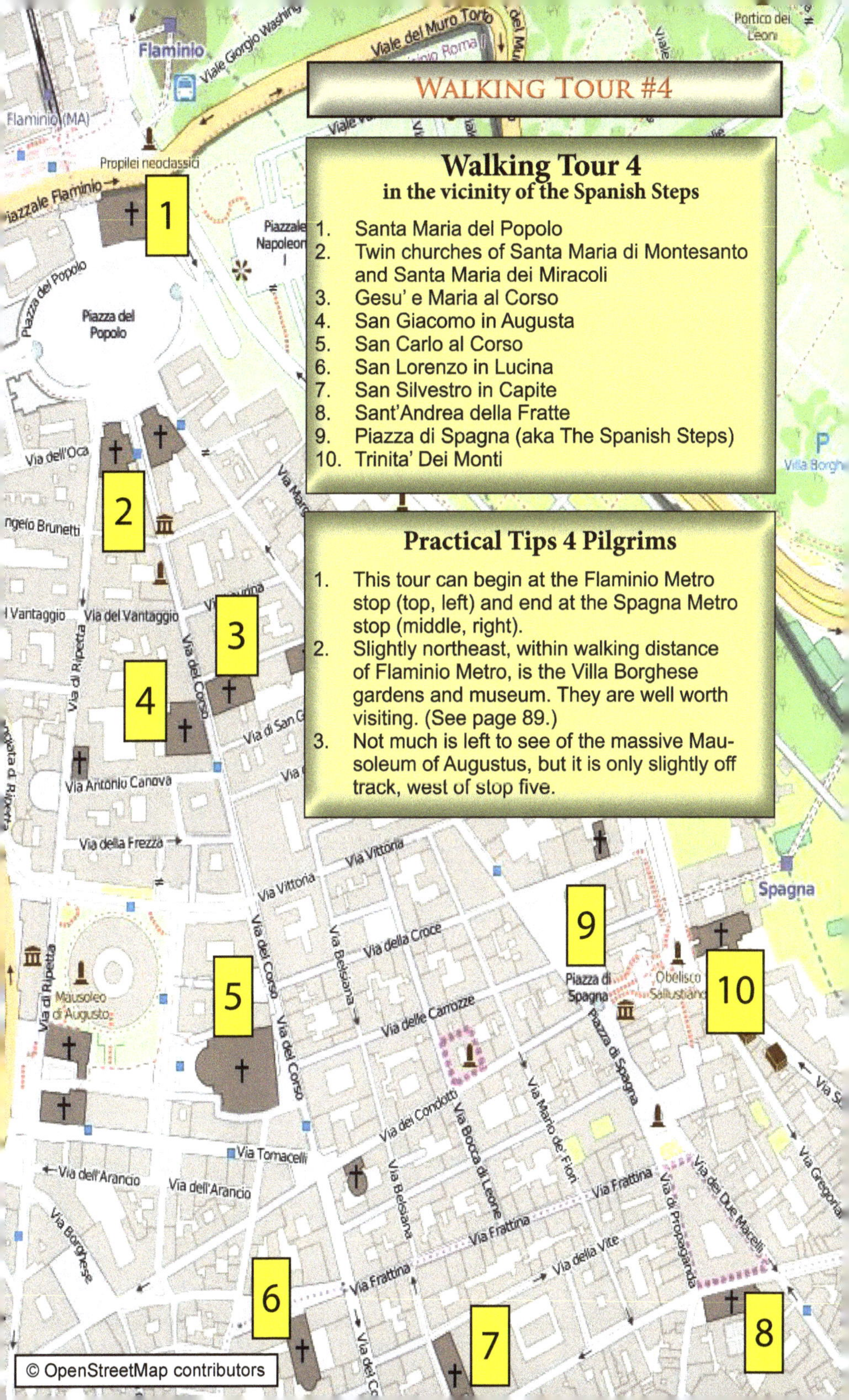

1

2

3

4

Walking Tour 4
in the vicinity of the Spanish Steps

1. Santa Maria del Popolo
2. Twin churches of Santa Maria di Montesanto and Santa Maria dei Miracoli
3. Gesu' e Maria al Corso
4. San Giacomo in Augusta
5. San Carlo al Corso
6. San Lorenzo in Lucina
7. San Silvestro in Capite
8. Sant'Andrea della Fratte
9. Piazza di Spagna (aka The Spanish Steps)
10. Trinita' Dei Monti

Practical Tips 4 Pilgrims

1. This tour can begin at the Flaminio Metro stop (top, left) and end at the Spagna Metro stop (middle, right).
2. Slightly northeast, within walking distance of Flaminio Metro, is the Villa Borghese gardens and museum. They are well worth visiting. (See page 89.)
3. Not much is left to see of the massive Mausoleum of Augustus, but it is only slightly off track, west of stop five.

9

Spagna

10

5

6

7

8

Santa Maria del Popolo
St. Mary of the People
Daily: 7 - 12 & 4 - 7 (Hol: 8 - 1:30 & 4:30 - 7:15)

This was the site of the grave of Nero, an emperor so evil that Romans feared his return from the grave. So, when 11th century Romans complained that an old tree, here, was attracting Nero's demon servants, in the form of crows, Pope Paschal II took action. He chopped down the oak, scattered Nero's ashes and built an oratory that was dedicated to the Virgin Mary. Though the oratory was enlarged 130 years later, the present structure dates from around 1475. Martin Luther slept in an adjacent Augustinian monastery during his influential visit in 1511. Sixteen years later, the monastery was destroyed during the Sack of Rome.

The main altar (left and right) dates from 1627, but the image of Madonna and Child, above it, was brought to this church from the Lateran in 1230. Above and below the image is the message: "You are the honor of our people."

This church holds many works from the hands of art masters. Caravaggio's famous *Conversion of St. Paul* (right) and *Crucifixion of St. Peter* (see p. 26) are in the chapel located left of the main altar. Bramante extended the apse, and Bernini added *baroque* decorations to the interior—including oak branches that entwine the organ pipes—as well as an altar in the right transept. The attractive Cybo Chapel was designed by Carlo Fontana and the Chigi Chapel contains not only works by Bernini (statues of Daniel and Habakkuk) but the overall design belongs to Raphael in addition to the ceiling mosaic design.

S. M. di Montesanto & S. M. dei Miracoli
aka The Twin Churches at Piazza del Popolo
Mon - Sat: 6:45 - 12:30 & 4:30 - 7:30; Sun & Hol: 8 - 1:45 & 4:30 - &:45

Santa Maria dei Miracoli (church pictured right of the obelisk) is one of the twin churches that face Piazza del Popolo. It is named for a miracle that occurred in 1325. After her baby fell into the Tiber, a panicked mother invoked the intercession of the Madonna and Child from an image on a nearby wall. After a miraculous rescue, the original image was preserved and is now displayed at San Giacomo in Augusta (bottom of next page). The altar image (left) is a copy.

The incorrupt remains of the virgin martyr Santa Candida (left) are preserved in Santa Maria dei Miracoli.

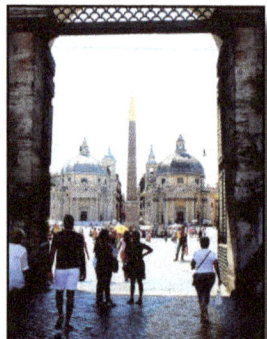

Gesu' e Maria al Corso

It seems everyone has difficulty with the name of this ornately *baroque* church. More formally known as The Church of the Holy Names of Jesus and Mary, this structure dates from 1633, when it was built for the Discalced Augustinian Order. In 1967, Pope Paul VI made it a cardinalate deaconry, but incorrectly labelled the church with the Italian equivalent of "The Most Holy Names of Jesus and Mary on Via Lata", even though that street is across town.

HISTORY 4 PILGRIMS

Rome has often attracted the world's greatest artists. But many pilgrims do not realize that some of the world's great literary lights also called Rome home. The English Romantics Keats, Shelley, Byron and Mary Shelley established a movement here in the early 19th century, especially associated with the area of the Spanish Steps. As one faces the steps, to the right, is the house where John Keats died in 1821. It is now a museum.

San Giacomo in Augusta

At the time of Jesus Christ's birth, no name was more revered than that of the recently deceased Caesar Augustus. Today, Rome's church of San Giacomo carries his name because it is located near the mausoleum of the great emperor. However, over the past two millennia, the name of Augustus has inspired no one to works of greatness, and his tomb has become an eroding monument to fleeting fame (right). In stark contrast, Roman churches such as this have overcome every obstacle placed before them, continuing to minister to mankind in the name of Jesus Christ.

In 1347, a chapel was established here to serve the Spiritual needs of the despairing patients of the Hospital of St. James of the Incurables. By the late 16th century, the hospital and church had to be expanded. Here, St. Camillo de Lellis offered the humble works of mercy that earned him the title of patron saint for patients, nurses and hospitals. However, during the 1849 Seige of Rome, this church was desecrated as a stable for Louis Napoleon Bonaparte's war horses.

The namesake of this church–St. James (below left)–was the apostle of Jesus and brother of John. He is usually portrayed with a walking stick because his extensive travels after the Ascension made him an appropriate patron saint of pilgrims. So, he is a particularly fitting saint to honor on pilgrimages to Rome.

The revered image of *Our Lady of Miracles* (right) is the one that inspired the construction of Santa Maria dei Miracoli, one of the twin churches, up the street, at Piazza del Popola.

This was one of the first churches to adopt an elliptical dome in its design. It became a prototype for many imitators.

SANTI AMBROGIO E CARLO AKA SAN CARLO AL CORSO

SAINTS AMBROSE AND CHARLES AKA ST. CHARLES ON THE COURSE
DAILY: 7:30 - 12:30 & 5 - 7

This basilica was the "national" church for Lombards in Rome. It is dedicated to two canonized bishops from Milan, the capital of Lombardy.

Bishop St. Ambrose died in 397, but when Charles Borromeo was canonized, in 1610, the church was renovated and renamed in his honor. Today, a large chapel for the saint is located in a room behind the altar. Under a painting of the Madonna and child, an elaborate monumental reliquary holds the heart of St. Charles (right).

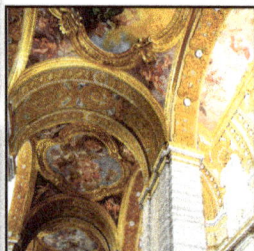

The magnificence of the *baroque* era comes alive in this church. The conclusion of construction was accomplished by Pietro da Cortona (1669), who also designed the dome. It is the fifth in Rome in terms of amplitude, after St. Peter's Basilica, the Basilica of St. John Bosco, the Basilica of Saints Peter and Paul, and the church of Sant'Andrea della Valle. and decoration in stucco of the time (1669).

CARAVAGGIO 4 PILGRIMS

Brilliant bad boy Michelangelo Merisi da Caravaggio wore out his welcome in Rome after 16 years of artistic genius. He was the master of light and shadow. But in 1606, the wayward painter killed a man for beating him at a game of tennis. So, Caravaggio fled Rome for Tuscany and died there, four years later. Yet, he left a treasure trove of masterpieces in Rome. They can be found at the Capitoline Museums, the Borghese Gallery, the Doria Pamphilj Gallery, Palazzo Barberini, the Vatican Museums, and the churches of San Luigi Francesi, Santa Maria del Popolo, and Sant'Agostino.

SAN LORENZO IN LUCINA

This basilica was originally built in the 4th century, and Damasus I (366-384) was elected pope in it. The church was built on the site of the home of a Roman matron, named Lucina, who had protected Pope St. Marcellus I (308-309) when he was being hunted by Emperor Maxentius. Since then, it has undergone various renovations and transformations in the 8th, 12th, 17th, 19th and 20th centuries.

Though the design of this church originally included three naves, the current floorplan has just one, with chapels along each side. As pilgrims follow through these chapels, they may contemplate important Spiritual journeys of the past. For example, in the first chapel on the left – the baptistry – the Baptism of Jesus is displayed. Then, moving around the church, notice other chronological scenes in the life of Christ.

Particularly striking, over the altar, is *Christ on the Cross* by Guido Reni (right). Upon entering, it is the focal point of the church. The series of Christ's images concludes with His Ascension. Taking other paths through San Lorenzo, one also discovers chronological stories being told through images from the lives of the Blessed Mother (left). Finally, a third path can be taken to witness the Spiritual journey of St. Lawrence, the martyred patron of this basilica. The gridiron upon which Lawrence was martyred is below the altar.

The Fonseca Chapel was designed by Bernini and contains a marble bust of the chapel's namesake that was sculpted by Bernini himself.

San Sylvestro in Capite
St. Sylvester at the Head
Daily: 7 - 7; Sundays 9 - 1 & 3:30 - 6:30

"'Whatever you ask, I will give you,
up to half my kingdom.''
She went out and said to her mother,
'What shall I ask for?'
'The head of John the Baptist,' she answered."

Mark 6:23-24

This church was dedicated to Pope St. Silvester and first constructed in the 8th century for the purpose of housing the remains of numerous saints and martyrs, particularly from the catacombs. It is called *in Capite* because a revered relic, said to be the head of St. John the Baptist, is kept here.

The bell tower (left) dates from 1198. Today, San Silvestro is designated for Rome's English speaking Catholics.

The relics of Pope St. Sylvester, Pope St. Stephen I and Pope St. Dionysius were exhumed and re-enshrined beneath the high altar (far right) when the new church was consecrated in 1601. It is thought that this altar, which is older than the present church, was designed, or at least influenced, by Michelangelo. At the entrance, two 8th century marble tablets display lists of some of the saints whose relics were brought here. At the crypt, a huge block of masonry is believed to have been owned by the two brothers who originally built this church in the 8th century.

Recent excavations have revealed that this church is situated over the ruins of the colossal sun temple, built by Emperor Aurelian (d. 275 AD). The golden organ (below) is from the 1600s.

Jesus Christ said of him:
"I tell you,
among those born of women
there is no one
greater than John."

Luke 7:28

In a chapel to the left of the entrance is the crowned head of St. John the Baptist (left). It rests on a tabernacle altar by Michelangelo, in a reliquary made of parts dating to the 13th and 14th centuries. Though Pope Benedict XVI seemed to vouch for the relic's authenticity in August of 2012,, this church is not the only site that claims to hold the head of this great saint.

SANT'ANDREA DELLA FRATTE
ST. ANDREW OF THE THICKETS
DAILY: 6:30 - 12:45 & 4 - 9

The Basilica of Sant'Andrea della Fratte was once on the outskirts of Rome but now in the heart of town, near the Spanish Steps. The unusual bell tower (left) was designed by Francesco Borromini. The second chapel on the left may also be the work of Borromini. This church contains two monumental statues that were originally designed for *Via Crucis* series on the *Ponte Sant'Angelo*. The two angels hold instruments of Christ's torture and were the work of Gian Lorenzo Bernini. However, upon completion, they were considered too excellent to be exposed to weather. So they were donated back to the

artist. In 1729, Bernini's heirs, who lived nearby, donated the angels (one, right) to this church, pitting two baroque geniuses – Bernini and Borromini – against each other, just as they had been in life. Below this church is Rome's only *putridarium*, in which cadavers are kept until the meat decomposes and only the bones are left, for storage in ossuaries.

TRINITA' DEI MONTI
TRINITY OF THE MOUNTAINS
DAILY: 8:30 - 12 & 4 - 6

This church is well known because of its unusual twin bell towers that dominate the view of the popular Spanish Steps. The obelisk in front of the church is of Roman origin, imitating Egyptian style with hieroglyphics that were copied from an authentic Egyptian obelisk in Piazza del Popolo. During the Napoleonic occupation, this church, like many others in Rome, was despoiled of its art and decorations. In 1816, however, after the Bourbon restoration, the church was restored at the expense of King Louis XVIII.

This church holds an unusual work of art. One of Michelangelo's last friends and students was Daniele da Volterra. In fact, he gave one of the only descriptions of the last days of the great master. However, Volterra tried a different style in his *Assumption of the Virgin* (right). No doubt, it is beautifully executed. But, to some, it has an almost blacklight, psychedelic look, perhaps more reminiscent of the 1960s than the 1550s.

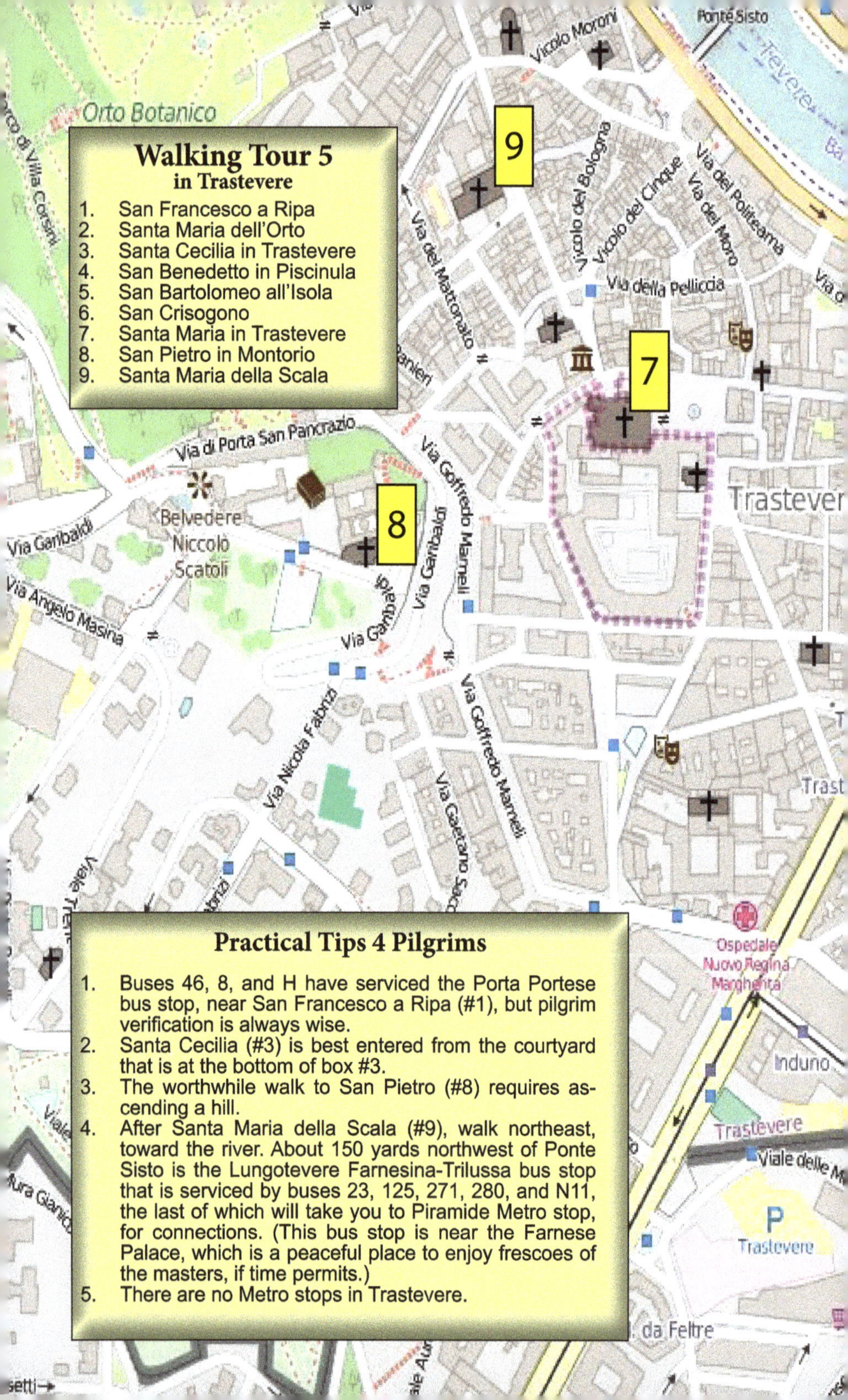

9

Walking Tour 5
in Trastevere

1. San Francesco a Ripa
2. Santa Maria dell'Orto
3. Santa Cecilia in Trastevere
4. San Benedetto in Piscinula
5. San Bartolomeo all'Isola
6. San Crisogono
7. Santa Maria in Trastevere
8. San Pietro in Montorio
9. Santa Maria della Scala

7

8

Practical Tips 4 Pilgrims

1. Buses 46, 8, and H have serviced the Porta Portese bus stop, near San Francesco a Ripa (#1), but pilgrim verification is always wise.
2. Santa Cecilia (#3) is best entered from the courtyard that is at the bottom of box #3.
3. The worthwhile walk to San Pietro (#8) requires ascending a hill.
4. After Santa Maria della Scala (#9), walk northeast, toward the river. About 150 yards northwest of Ponte Sisto is the Lungotevere Farnesina-Trilussa bus stop that is serviced by buses 23, 125, 271, 280, and N11, the last of which will take you to Piramide Metro stop, for connections. (This bus stop is near the Farnese Palace, which is a peaceful place to enjoy frescoes of the masters, if time permits.)
5. There are no Metro stops in Trastevere.

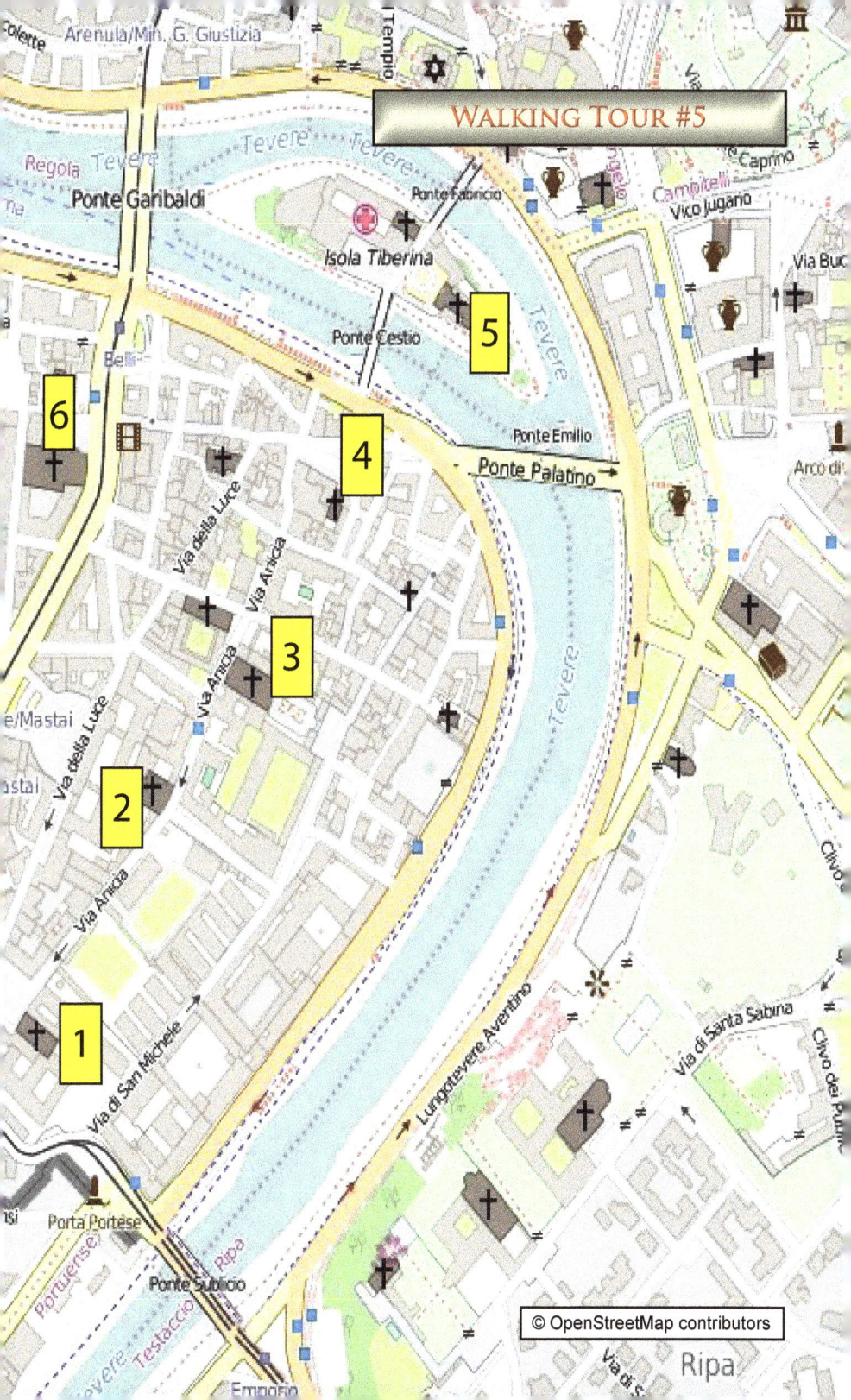

Arenula/Min. G. Giustizia

Tempio

Caprino

Tevere

Tevere

Tevere

Regola

Campitelli

Tevere

Ponte Garibaldi

Vico Jugario

Ponte Fabricio

Via Buc

Isola Tiberina

5

Tevere

Belli

Ponte Cestio

6

Arco di

Ponte Emilio

Via della Luce

4

Ponte Palatino

Via Anicia

e/Mastai

3

Via della Luce

Via Anicia

2

Tevere

Clivo

Via Anicia

Via di Santa Sabina

Clivo dei Pubb

Lungotevere Aventino

1

Via di San Michele

Porta Portese

Ripa

Ponte Sublicio

Portuense

Testaccio

Emporio

Ripa

SAN FRANCESCO A RIPA

When visiting Rome in 1219, St. Francis of Assisi lived on this property. He is the first saint documented to have shared the *stigmata*, the wounds of the Crucified Christ. In his cell, the black stone pillow and crucifix of Francis are preserved. Ask the sacristan to see the cell, as well as an altar that is said to contain 1,000 relics. Though the current church building only dates from the 17th century, it has an important collection of art and sculpure, as well as relics and remains of saints. In the friary's garden, nearby, an orange tree is said to have been planted by the saint. This is an excellent place to ponder some of the mystical mysteries of our faith.

In the 4th chapel on the left of the nave is Bernini's moving masterpiece *The Ecstasy of Beata Ludovica Albertoni* (right). Completed in 1675, this is the last work completely sculpted by the great artist.

In the Chapel of the Holy Family, amidst paintings from the life of Christ, is the glass-encased body (below) of Saint Leontia, a martyr from the 5th century and daughter of a bishop.

The chapel of St. Michael the Archangel (left and right) contains a striking painting of the angel's domionion over Lucifer. The work's origin is disputed, but believed to be by Guido Reni. This chapel was once called the Pietà because of the painting by that name, by Annibale Carracci, that was once displayed as the altarpiece. In 1797, however, it was taken on orders of Napoleon and now resides in the Louvre Museum.

Under St. Michael is the body of a 17th century saint, Charles of Sezze. He has been described as a humble friar minor, an apostle of Trastevere, and a writer of ascetic works. He was also a mystic who was stigmatized by the Holy Eucharist when he received a wound in the heart while attending Holy Mass.

Santa Maria del'Orto

In 1488, this area was covered by vegetable garden fields. Nearby, an image of the Madonna and Child graced the face of an old tombstone. One day, a man suffering from an incurable illness passed by and stopped to pray before the image. He vowed that if he would be healed he would light a lamp, in honor of the Blessed Mother and Son, and insure that it would remain perpetually lit. Of course, he recovered and kept his promise. But even more, with the help of the arts and crafts "university," he built a chapel. As the healing shrine gained prominence, Pope Alexander VI approved the plans for a larger church. Construction began in 1494. But a variety of setbacks, including a lack of funds, caused construction to languish for 9 decades until its completion in 1585.

Today, parishioners remain true to the promise, maintaining the perpetual lighting in the church. On the 3rd Sunday, every October, the church is adorned with fruit and vegetables. At the end of Mass, apples are consecrated and distributed to congregants. According to tradition, each member of the church's Brotherhood – members of crafts, trades and professions involved in food production – then divides his apple and shares a piece with each member of his family.

THE LEGEND OF ROME'S FOUNDING

Eight centuries before Christ, King Numitor of Alba Longa was overthrown and exiled by his younger brother Amulius. Fearing revenge in the future, Amulius murdered Numitor's sons. He also forced Numitor's daughter, Rhea Silvia, to become a vestal virgin, obligating her to guard her virginity or suffer penalty of death. However Mars, the god of war, became enchanted by her beauty and had his way with Rhea Silvia while she slept. As a result of this she bore twins, Romulus and Remus.

Upon learning of the births, an enraged Amulius had Rhea Silvia thrown into the Tiber, and the twins were set adrift on the river in a reed basket. They were found by a she-wolf who suckled them on Palatine Hill, preserving their lives until a shepherd found them. (A more credible version of the story suggests the shepherd's wife was a former prostitute who had recently lost a stillborn child. She, more likely, nursed the boys. Adding credibility to this version is the fact that "lupa" in Latin means both "she-wolf" and "prostitute.")

The boys were raised knowing their family history and, when they grew to adulthood, devised an attack on Alba Longa. Amulius was slain and Numitor, restored to his throne. The heroic twins, however, decided to found a new city close to where they had been washed ashore. But they disputed which hill their city should be built on, Romulus favored the Palatine; Remus, the Aventine. However, the brothers clashed and, eventually, Remus was either killed by his brother or one of Romulus' chief followers. Had it happened the other way around, the Eternal City might have been named "Reme."

SANTA CECILIA IN TRASTEVERE

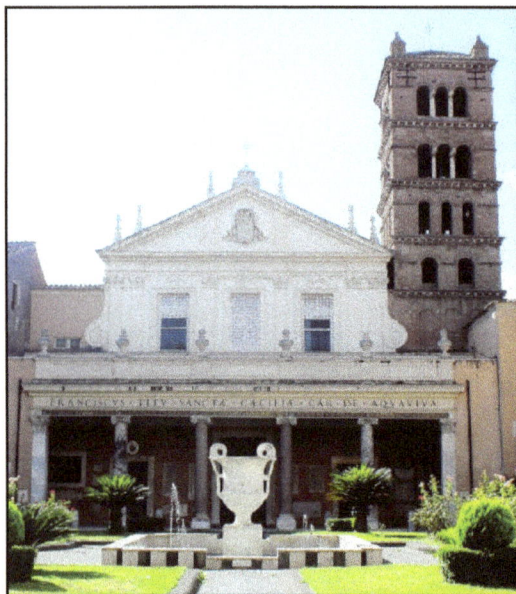

St. Cecilia lived here and, around 230 AD, died here. Today, the basilica church that was built above the ruins of her ancient house is a popular destination for pilgrims from around the world. Spotting the church can be a bit tricky, however. Pilgrims must pass through an outer facade (below) before entering the church's courtyard (left).

Once inside (right), Arnolfo di Cambio's beautifully detailed, black and white marble canopy draws every eye to Stefano Maderno's unforgettable statue of the slain saint, at its base. The canopy dates from 1293 and the statue was sculpted in 1600. However, the apse mosaic is from the time of Pope Paschal I, in the early 9th century.

Available for viewing during limited hours (see above hours) is Pietro Cavallini's highly praised fresco known as the *Last Judgment*. This masterpiece that dates from 1293 is located in the nun's choir upstairs and well worth the small admission charge.

TIPS 4 PILGRIMS

Rome's *centro storico* (historic center) is bounded by these rough landmarks: Villa Borghese to the north, *Stazione Termini* to the east, the Roman Forum to the south, and the Tiber River to the west. Because of the rich history of Rome buried below this area, Metro access is mostly lacking here. But the tight area puts an incredible number of important sites within walking distance, and buses are plentiful.

Young Cecilia was the daughter of a Roman senator who offered her in marriage to Valerianus, a pagan nobleman. However, on their wedding night, the devout Christian bride explained to her husband that she was protected by an angel who guarded her virginity. When he asked to see the angel, she sent him to the 3rd milestone on the Via Appia, where he would be baptized by Pope Urbanus. He obeyed and, upon returning, he and his bride were graced with a visitation from the angel who crowned them with roses and lilies. Now, zealous for the faith, they soon converted his brother, Tiburtius. Together, they began to contribute alms to Christian causes and, when they refused to sacrifice to pagan gods, Prefect Turcius Almachius condemned them to death. Nearing execution, the brothers converted their executioner and, consequently, all three were killed.

Before Cecilia could be captured, she bravely witnessed her faith and arranged for her house (pictured below, right, and accessible from today's church with permission from the sacristan) to be preserved as a place of worship. She was condemned to be suffocated in the bath of her own house, where she was led down a hall (pictured, left) to the *calidarium* that is now a chapel, where conduits are still visible. Inside the overheated steam room, however, she remained unharmed. So, the prefect ordered that she be decapitated there. The inept executioner botched three horrifying attempts, and finally fled from the bloody virgin.

The highly ornamented crypt (below), is adjacent to the ancient house and contains Cecilia's remains along with those of Saints Valerian, Tiburtius, Maximus and two popes.

Cecilia lingered three more days, managing to dispose of her property to the poor and the Church. She was entombed in the Catacombs of Callistus, but when her body was exhumed, in 1599, it was seen as incorrupt for a time. Sculptor Stefano Maderno, at just 23 year of age, witnessed the miracle and sculpted Cecilia, exactly as he remembered her. Today, we see that the slain saint still gives witness to the three Persons in one God as she extends three fingers on two hands.

SAN BENEDETTO IN PISCINULA
ST. BENEDICT BY THE LITTLE BATH
DAILY: 8 - 12 & 4:30 - 7:30

This little church is easy to miss but has an interesting past. The great St. Benedict of Nursia lived on this site in the 5th century, before commiting to a hermit's lifestyle. His cell and an image of the Virgin Mary, that he prayed to, are preserved here, along with its original cosmatesque pavement.

The current church structure was built on the former site of the neighborhood's public toilets. It maintains bragging rights for Rome's smallest bell tower, housing a diminutive ringer that dates from 1069.

SAINT TRIVIA 4 PILGRIMS

The relics of St. Bartholomew were stolen in 1981 and not found and returned until four years later.

SAN BARTOLOMEO ALL'ISOLA
ST. BARTHOLOMEW ON THE ISLAND
MON - SAT: 9 - 1 & 3:30 - 5:30: SUN: 9 - 1 & 6:30 - 8

A lovely walk through Trastevere and over a pedestrian bridge brings pilgrims to a peaceful island that is surrounded by the rippling waters of the Tiber. Here is one of the great tributes to twenty centuries of Christian martyrs: San Bartolomeo (below). This 1,000 year old minor basilica was built on the ruins of the Temple of Aesculapius, dating from 293 BC.

Connecting the east side of the island to the Campus Martius is Rome's oldest Tiber bridge, still in use. The Ponte Fabricio (left) was built in 62 BC. Today, the charming pedestrian overpass welcomes toursists and street artists.

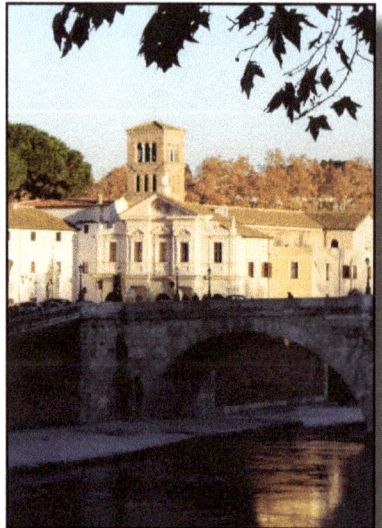

Bartholomew is believed to be the same person named Nathanael, in John's Gospel. Upon first hearing of Jesus, Bartholomew wondered aloud how anything good could come from Nazareth. Still, the Lord appreciated his honesty and made him an apostle. After witnessing the Ascenscion, Bartholomew travelled widely, professing the Gospel. In Armenia, he converted King Polymius. However, the king's brother deeply resented the change and ordered Bartholomew's execution. The saint was flayed alive and crucified, head down.

St. Bartholomew's remains are entombed in the church's altar (below), making this house of worship one of the most moving for remembering the heroic virtue of Christian martyrs around the world.

Flanking the nave, are six small chapels, such as the one below. Each honors the *Nuovi Martiri,* or New Martyrs, from certain parts of the world and during various persecutions. The chapels honor martyrs from Asia, Oceana and the Middle East; from the Americas; from the communist persecutions; from the Nazi persecutions; from Europe; and from Africa and Madagascar.

ROME TRIVIA 4 PILGRIMS

- Population (city): 2.7 million.
- Population (metropolitan): 3.8 million.
- Number of tourists per year : 12 million.
- Number of water fountains: 300+.
- Number of public toilets: 40 (estimate) Way too few!

SAN CRISOGONO
ST. CHRYSOGONUS
MON - SAT: 7 - 11:30 & 4 - 7; SUN: 8 - 1

San Crisogono (or Grisogono) is a minor basilica and one of Rome's oldest churches. This site served as an early titulus until its first church was built during the reign of Pope Sylvester I, sometime between 314 and 335. The church was rebuilt in the 12th century, but this structure dates from 1626. The name and coat of arms for Cardinal Scipione Borghese are displayed prominently. He was a major promoter of this church's construction.

This church is dedicated to St. Chrysogonus, a Roman military officer who was martyred circa 304 in northern Italy, during the persecution of Diocletian. A church has existed on this site since the 5th century. This church retains the structure of one built in the 12th century, but the interior decor (left) is from the 17th. A pair of gigantic porphyry columns support the triumphal arch. Because of their size, they are very rare. Twenty-two ancient Egyptian granite columns flank the nave. They are from earlier Roman buildings, possibly the Baths of Septimius Severus (d. 211). Detailed designs are included in the gilded coffered ceiling (1620) as well as the cosmatesque pavement, which dates from the 13th century. At the end of the right aisle is a lovely chapel, designed by Bernini. At the end of the left aisle is a dramatic chapel (below, right) that features a statue of Christ over an oval reliquary that contains a relic of St. John of Matha. Under the main altar, are the relics of the apostle, St. James the Less, as well as the church's namesake. Along the left aisle, the peaceful remains of Blessed Anna Maria Taigi (below; see p. 199) are displayed. In the 19th century, she lived in a building nearby.

Through the sacristy, a 5th century subterranean church is found. The walls still retain their early frescoes.

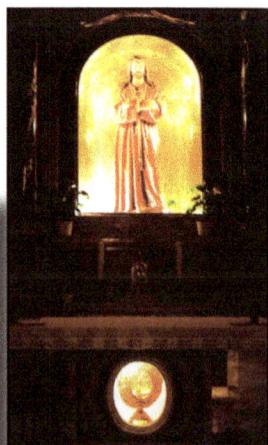

SANTA MARIA IN TRASTEVERE
ST. MARY IN TRASTEVERE
DAILY: 7:30 - 1 & 4 - 8

This minor basilica is one of the oldest churches in Rome and possibly the first in which Mass was openly offered. A Christian house-church was established here about 220 and its first sanctuary was completed by 227. In 340, Pope Julius I rebuilt the structure, enlarging it.

In the portico, pilgrims will see fragments (left) displayed from earlier churches, here, dating back to the 4th century. Though the portico was not added until the 19th century, the faded mosaics on the church's facade are from the 12th or 13th.

Resting on a balustrade above the portico (right), statues of four saints are displayed. They are Callistus, Cornelius, Julius, and Calepodius. Their relics are entombed beneath the main altar.

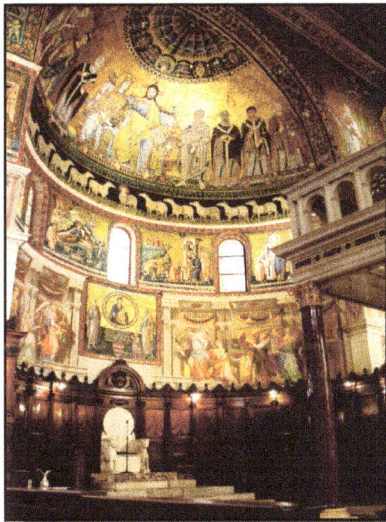

The heart of Trastevere is the church's piazza. This area is very pedestrian friendly and great for a stroll or dinner. The piazza's 17th century fountain (below) is by Carlo Fontana.

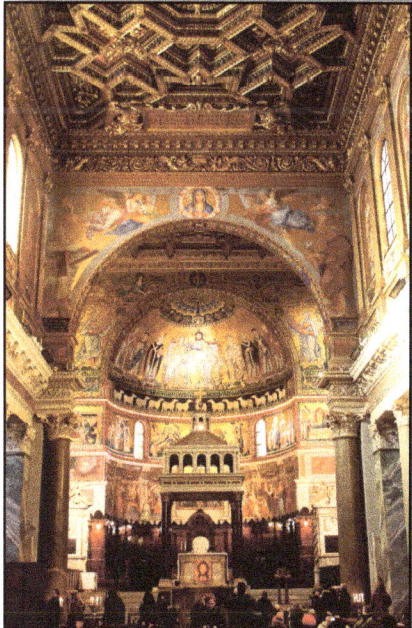

The 22 granite columns that flank the nave (right) were removed from the ruins of the Baths of Carcalla in the 12th century. Their unmatched capitals give an indication that their age likely pre-dates the Christian era. Some of the church's interior mosaics date to the 13th century. However, the exceptional mosaics on the apse vault and triumphal arch were restored around 1140. A lovely cosmatesque candle stick holder, at the right of the altar, is marked with the words "Fons Olei," indicating the location of a legendary miracle. On the pavement, nearby, this message is engraved: "Here oil flowed when Christ was born of the Virgin."

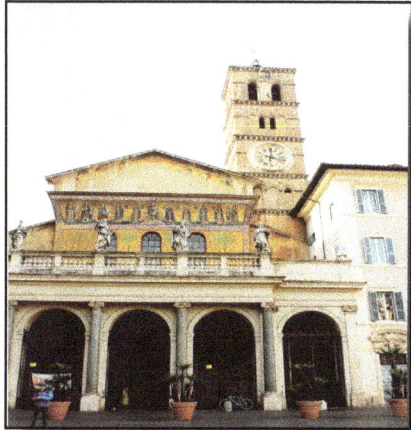

SAN PIETRO IN MONTORIO

ST. PETER IN MONTORIO
DAILY: 9 - 12 & 4 - 6:30

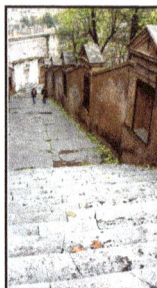

A church and monastery have existed on this site since at least the 8th century because it was once believed that Peter was crucified here. Modern scholarship, however, has shown that the true place of Peter's execution was in Nero's Circus, on today's grounds of St. Peter's Basilica. Pilgrims should prepare themselves for stairs (right) when they make this trek because the church sits atop Janiculum Hill.

Though the facade (left) appears ordinary, this church contains some very interesting art and architecture.

On the spot where Peter was believed to have been crucified, for example, Ferdinand and Isabella of Spain commissioned Donato Bramante, in 1502, to build the *Tempietto*, or Little Temple (right). Its diminutive size does not detract from its careful proportions and architectural excellence. The second large chapel on the left of the main church's nave displays paintings of Christ's life including David van Haen's moving *Way to Calvary* (left). Also, among the many other visually engaging art and decorative accents (left and below) pilgrims will find the small chapel, that is located first on the left, was designed by Bernini and, among other tributes to St. Francis, exhibits a striking marble relief (right) of *St. Francis in Ecstasy* by Francesco Baratta.

View from San Pietro in Montorio on the Janiculum.

GEOGRAPHY 4 PILGRIMS

Rome was founded upon seven famous hills. Originally, they were more pronounced. Through the centuries, though, Rome's development filled the valleys and shaved the peaks. The seven hills include:

1. Capitolino
2. Palatino
3. Aventino
4. Esquilino
5. Viminale
6. Quirinale
7. Celio

Other hills in the region include Vaticano (never one of the seven hills upon which Rome was founded), Pincio and the Gianicolo. Also, a long ridge along Trastevere is called the Janiculum.

HISTORY 4 PILGRIMS

In world history, Rome has played a dominant role during many of its definable eras:

1. Etruscan era
2. Foundation of Rome
3. Rise of empire
4. Decline and fall of empire
5. Rise of Christianity
6. Counter-Reformation
7. Napoleonic Occupation
8. Italian Unification
9. Fascism and WWII
10. Modern era

SANTA MARIA DELLA SCALA
ST. MARY OF THE STAIRS
MON - SAT: 6:30 - 12 & 4 - 7 (6:15: OCT - MAR) SUN & HOLIDAYS: 6:45 - 12:15

This church was completed in 1610 to be a place of honor for a miraculous icon (below, left). In a nearby house, the image had been placed on a staircase landing, and when a mother prayed before it, her deformed daughter was cured. This church is also well known for the adjacent monastery that served as a respected pharmacy for the papal court. In 1849, as the Roman resistance fought French troops, the church was converted into a hospital. It also holds, as a revered relic: a foot of St. Teresa of Avila. But its most scandalous story involves Caraggio, who had displayed here his *Death of the Virgin*. It was eventually removed because not only was the Virgin Mary's body bloated but, for the model, Caravaggio had used a local prostitute.

St. John Paul II
by Oliviero Rainaldi

In May of 2011, when this 16' high bronze statue was first erected on the grounds of Termini Station, it was widely criticized for resembling Benito Mussolini more than the beloved pope. After an 11-month remodeling project, however, we love it!

Walking Tour 6
in the vicinity of
Piazza Repubblica

1. Sacro Cuore di Gesu'
2. Statue of John Paul II
3. Baths of Diocletian
4. Santa Maria degli Angeli
5. San Bernardo alle Terme
6. Santa Susanna
7. Santa Maria della Vittoria
8. Moses Fountain (aka Fontana del'Acqua Felice)

Practical Tips 4 Pilgrims

1. This short tour can begin at the Termini Metro stop. and end by retracing your steps back to either the Repubblica or Termini Metro stop. Or, if time permits, head west on Via Barberini to begin Tour #8 (page 107), another of the shorter tours.
2. Because of a long fence, the best way to cross to and from Sacro Cuore (#1) is by walking through the Termini building to the door on the northeast side.
3. If staying near Termini Station, Sacro Coure (#1) is convenient for daily Mass, which is offered every weekday at 6:30, 7:00, 7:30, 8:00 and 9:00, as well as at 6:00 pm. Morning Masses are offered on Sundays at 7:00, 8:00, 9:00, 10:00 and 11:30.
4. Also, if staying near Termini Station, this can be a practical first tour since it is relatively short and convenient for dealing with first-day orientation and jet lag.

© OpenStreetMap contributors

Roma Termini
Stazione Termini

Ministero della Difesa

Repubblica

Piazza dell'Indipendenza

Sacro Cuore di Gesu'

Sacred Heart of Jesus
Daily: 6 - 12 & 4 - 7:30

Within view of Termini Station is a shimmering golden image of Christ, elevated high into the Roman sky. Its comforting presence seems to be blessing the tourists as they scurry in and out of the station. The memorable statue is perched atop the belltower of Sacro Cuore di Gesu – Sacred Heart of Jesus – a minor basilica and parish church that was visited by Pope John Paul II in 1987.

Built on the site of the ancient barracks of the Praetorian Guard, still, this is a relatively new church, by Roman standards. It was constructed 1887. Though it lacks the rich history of many Roman churches, its interior is beautifully adorned with elaborate architectural details. It is well worth a visit. Today, the church is served by Salesians, and a boarding school for arts and industries is attached to the church.

Tips 4 Pilgrims

Dealing with beggars in Rome is a difficult issue, especially for Christians. That is why someone sits at each church entrance, with a hand out. However, for tourists, revealing where money is kept can be a mistake.

I am reminded of a time when I brought my family to Paris. We decided to go to Mass at *Sacre Coeur* one morning. At a crowded Metro station a group of cute children approached, pleading for money while bumping and hugging us. I had encountered playfully aggressive little pickpockets in Russia, so I ignored my manners and shouted "Get away!" while protecting my wallet pocket.

Soon, we boarded the Metro car, but there was no place for me to sit. As I gripped the rail, standing, I noticed a very well dressed man – he could have been a model for GQ – moving past me very slowly. So, I lowered my hand to my wallet. I was shocked to realize, however, that his fingers were already there: deep in my pocket. (I couldn't believe it. I had felt nothing.) Immediately, he snatched his hand out and responded to my angry stare with a look of complete shock, as if from a false accusation.

I realized he had been watching the little ones – probably *his* kids – as they tricked me into revealing which pocket held a jackpot. With my wife and children beside me, however, I was not about to make a scene ... especially on Christmas morning.

So, ever since, I prefer to privately drop coins into the coffers of each church I visit and let them sort out the charity issues. After all, the Catholic Church is the most charitable institution in human history.

However, on the other hand, if you prefer a more direct approach, just make sure you always have easy access to change ... lots of it.

Statue of St. John Paul II

He was a beloved, groundbreaking pontiff. The first pope:
- from Poland;
- from a communist country;
- to ski;
- to climb mountains;
- to claim the two names of his predecessor;
- to be shot in public.

When Cardinal Karol Wojtyla arrived at the Conclave of 1978, he carried with him the rough equivalent of just $10 because Polish communist officials had forbidden him from taking more out of the country.

He had personally witnessed the evils of Nazi and communist totalitarianism. Eventually, he would be credited with playing a major role in the fall of Soviet communism and its domination of Poland and the rest of Eastern Europe.

He became the second longest-serving pope in history and the most travelled, visiting 129 countries during his pontificate. Adding to his global popularity was the fact that he was a brilliant linguist, learning a dozen languages and using 9 of them regularly.

Along with Pope John XXIII, Pope John Paul II was canonized on April 27, 2014, a date of extreme significance for him: Divine Mercy Sunday.

Statue located near the bus lot
at Termini Station

Terme di Diocleziano
Baths of Diocletian
Tues - Sun: 9 - 7:45

Dedicated in 306, these were the grandest of imperial baths, covering an area of almost 1.3 million square feet, or roughly 26 football fields. A tour of these baths might provide an interesting historical perspective on ancient Roman life. However, the last time we checked, European Union citizens were granted free admission, while others were required to pay a hefty entrance fee. So, some tourists decided to pass.

For more of what remains of the baths today, visit Santa Maria degli Angeli (see p. 90) and San Bernardo alle Terme (see p. 91), both of which survive as modern-day churches, where admission is free.

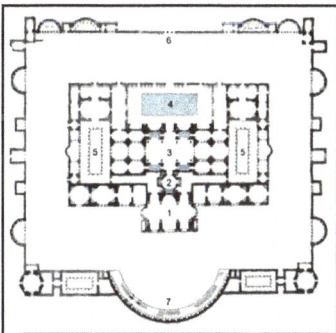

Floorplan: 1: Caldarium (hot water); 2: Tepidarium (warm water); 3: Frigidarium (cold water); 4: Natatio (swimming pool); 5: Palaestra (gymnasium); 6: Main entrance; 7: Exit.

Villa Borghese Tips 4 Pilgrims

The Villa Borghese is one of Rome's great art museums. It is located within walking distance of Flaminio Metro stop, through the lovely Borghese park. Tickets must be reserved in advance (11€; www.tosc.it). The gallery is open Tuesdays through Sundays, 8:30 to 7:30. So, the Baths (above) and the Borghese Gallery can fill the mid-day down time when many sites are closed for siesta.

SANTA MARIA DEGLI ANGELI E DEI MARTIRI
ST. MARY OF THE ANGELS AND MARTYRS
DAILY 8 - 12:30 & 4 - 6

St. Mary of the Angels may hold the honor of Rome's oddest church facade. It was carved from the spectacular complex known as the Baths of Diocletion (emperor 284-305). Some historians claim that, during the zenith of Imperial Rome's Christian persecutions, tens of thousands of the faithful were forced into slave labor to construct it. Today, this large basilica occupies only a small part of what may have been the largest bath complex in the world.

It housed spacious cold, warm, and hot rooms, as well as a swimming pool that covered almost 26,000 square feet. But baths were only a part of this pleasure center. It also contained libraries, gymnasia, conference rooms and gardens.

In 1561, Pope Pius IV became convinced to initiate the project after a Sicilian priest persisted in telling the pope of his mystical vision in which a bright light rose from the ruins of these baths. So, the pontiff commissioned Michelangelo who, by now, was eighty-six years old. Construction began in 1563, but the great master only lived another year. The project was completed by his students. Today, the Baths of Diocletion still contain water: holy water.

HISTORY 4 PILGRIMS

The initials S.P.Q.R. are often seen around the city. They represent an expression that dates back to the ancient Roman Republic, standing for "*Senatus Populus Que Romanus*" or "The Senate and People of Rome."

A recent addition is the jarring sculpture of *St. John the Baptist* (right), by Polish artist Igor Mitoraj. He also created the church's bronze doors.

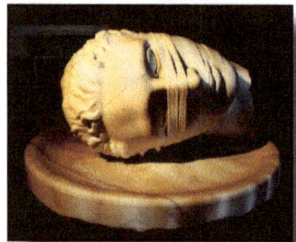

Pilgrims will notice that in this basilica's unusually long right transept a diagonal line is embedded into the pavement (below, right and left). For preservation, it is protected from pedestrian traffic.

In the 16th century, Pope Gregory XIII revised the Julian calendar by shortening it approximately 11 minutes per year. That does not amount to much over the life of a man, but over the life of the Church, it was significant. The Gregorian Calendar became a global standard. Then in 1701, Pope Clement XI desired further verification of the calendar's accuracy. So, he commissioned the world's most accurate meridian line for this church. Since then, every clear day at solar noon (approximately 11 am), a shaft of sunlight falls precisely on this line. Every year, from summer solstice to winter solstice, the sun tracks the line from one end to the other, until it reverses course and begins again.

PART THREE: SITES AROUND ROME

SAN BERNARDO ALLE TERME
ST. BERNARD AT THE BATHS
DAILY 6 - 6:30

Upon entering, pilgrims will be surprised at this church's dome. In many ways, it resembles the Pantheon's, only smaller. San Bernardo owes its unusual shape to the fact that it was once incorporated into the Baths of Diocletian. Approximately 750 feet away, another round tower has survived, only to be incorporated into a hotel.

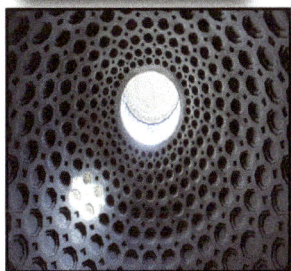

Eight large statues of saints are displayed in wall niches around the circular perimeter. They are the work of Camillo Mariani (ca. 1600). The Chapel of St. Francis was more recently added to the ancient rotunda. It displays a sculpture of the revered saint (right) by Giacomo Antonio Fancelli.

SANTA SUSANNA
ST. SUSANNA
MON - SAT: 9 - 12 & 4 - 7; SUN 10 - 12

On this site, St. Susanna was martyred, and a titular church has existed here since 280 AD. In 1603, the present Renaissance-style structure was completed, under the direction of Carlo Maderno, who also was responsible for the facade of St. Peter's Basilica. Paulist Fathers serve this house of worship and, since 1921, it has been designated as the Catholic Church for the Americas, as indicated by an American flag near the altar.

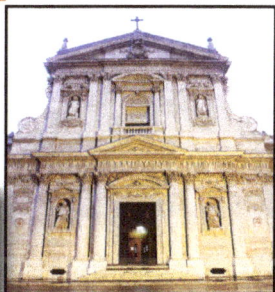

The church organ pipes (below) are surrounded by fading frescoes, a marble sculpture in high relief and a colorfully ornate, coffered ceiling.

Frescoes around the church depict the life of Roman St. Susanna who was martyred here by beheading. The church's crypt houses her remains, as well as those of her father, St. Gabinus, who was starved to death. Also, a 2nd century noblewoman, St. Felicity, is buried here. After refusing to renounce her Christian faith, she was subjected to something worse than torture: having to witness the martyrdom of her seven children.

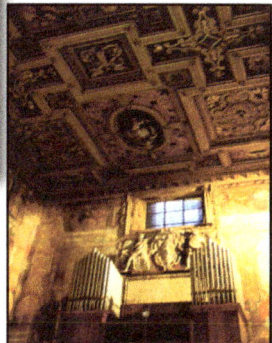

Santa Maria della Vittoria
St. Mary of the Victory
Daily: 7 - 12 & 3:30 - 6

This is a titular church and minor basilica that replaced a small but ancient chapel to St. Paul. However, the current structure is relatively new, by Roman standards, being built by Discalced Carmelites between 1608 and 1620, under the direction of the famous architect Carlo Maderno. The church owes its present name to the victory of the Catholic army at the Battle of White Mountain near Prague (November 8, 1620). There, Ven. Dominic of Jesus and Mary, a Carmelite priest and chaplain general, wore an image of *Mary Adoring the Child* around his neck. As certain defeat loomed, however, vivid rays flashed from the eyes of Jesus, dazzling their opponents and causing them to stampede to defeat. On May 8, 1622, the miraculous image was solemnly enthroned in this church, which has since been called St. Mary of the Victory.

A saintly relic (above) is said to consist of the wax-encased bones of St. Victoria, a 3rd century martyr.

The dazzling ornamentation over the altar (above), harkens back to the miracle of the Christ Child's image blinding and confusing enemy troops.

This ceiling (above) and organ loft (above, right) are excellent examples of the power of religious art to draw us into prayerful meditation and a closer relationship with God. This is the magnificence of the *baroque* style of architecture that became popular in Rome in the late 16th century.

Gian Lorenzo Bernini's masterpiece of *baroque* art, *The Ecstasy of St. Teresa*, is displayed in the Cornaro Chapel on the left. Sculpted in 1646, it depicts St. Teresa of Avila in an ecstasy of joy after being pierced in the heart by an angel.

FONTANA DEL'ACQUA FELICE
FOUNTAIN OF HAPPY WATER
AKA THE FOUNTAIN OF MOSES

SIXTVS V PONT MAX PICENVS
AQVAM EX AGRO COLVMNAE
VIA PRAENEST SINISTRORSVM
MVLTAR COLLECTIONE VENARVM
DVCTV SINVOSO A RECEPTACVLO
MIL XX A CAPITE XXII ADDVXIT
FELICEMQ DE NOMINE ANTE PONT DIXIT

COEPIT PONT AN I ABSOLVIT III MDLXXXXVII

Only in Rome, can a fountain as grand as this become the subject of ridicule. In 1585, Pope Sixtus V initiated a project to bring fresh drinking water to this part of the city for the first time. A year later, the water it yielded was declared the best in Rome. However, the structure that Domenico Fontana competently designed still required statuary. So, the imposing figure of Moses was commissioned for the center niche, hopefully, one that would rival Michelangelo's masterpiece. But on the big day a chubby Moses was unveiled, looking as if he had indulged in too much pasta. It is said that, here, Moses will forever frown at the incompetence of his sculptor, though no single artist has ever claimed credit or blame.

The Tiber River

Amidst Rome's bustling urban energy and opulent spectacles, we rarely note the enduring significance of the Tiber River. Silently, it has sustained the Eternal City through eras of turmoil, Renaissance, tragedy and triumph. Rome, however, could not have become *Caput Mundi* without its Tiber lifeblood.

4

5

3

2

1

7

6

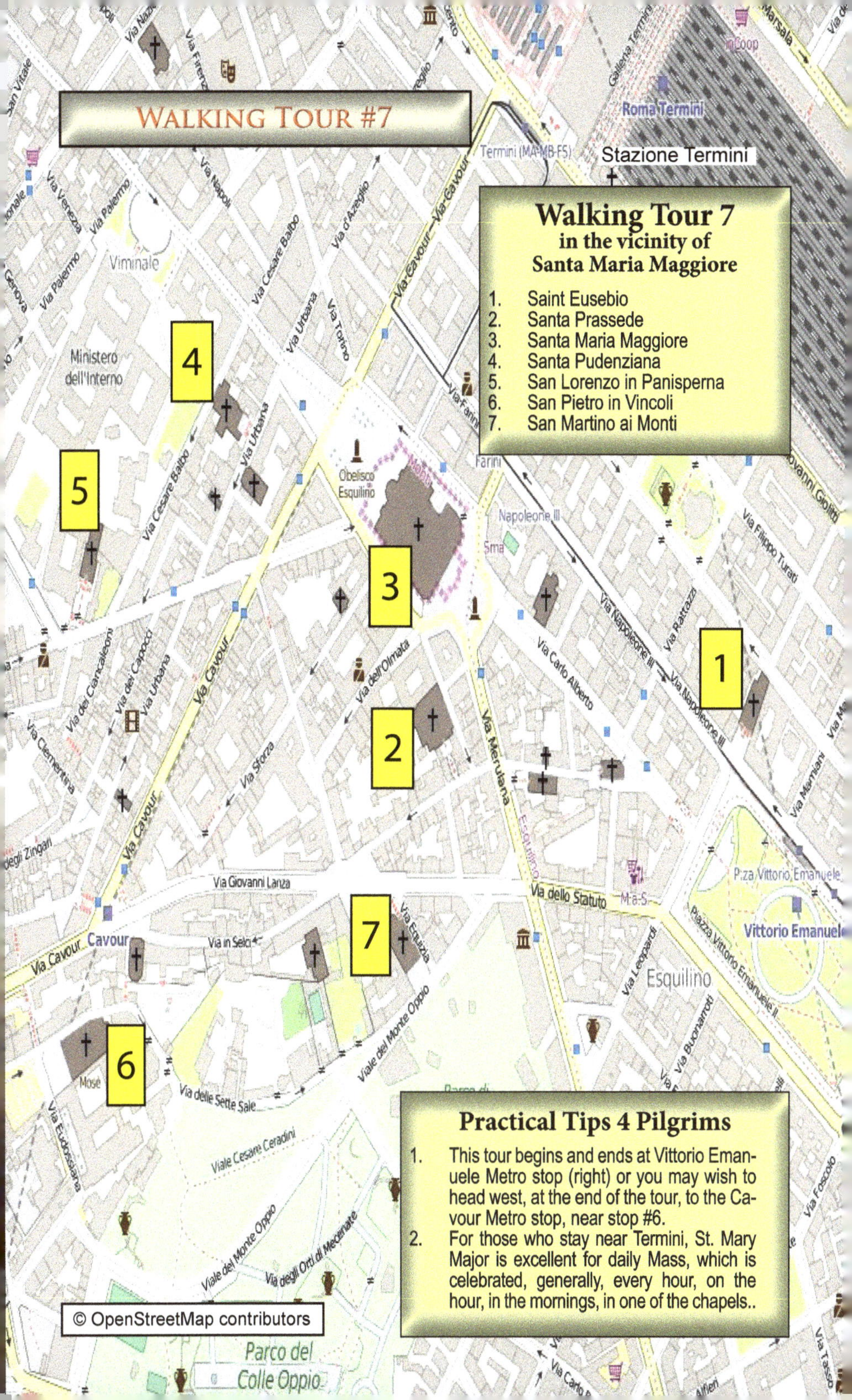

Walking Tour 7
in the vicinity of
Santa Maria Maggiore

1. Saint Eusebio
2. Santa Prassede
3. Santa Maria Maggiore
4. Santa Pudenziana
5. San Lorenzo in Panisperna
6. San Pietro in Vincoli
7. San Martino ai Monti

Practical Tips 4 Pilgrims

1. This tour begins and ends at Vittorio Emanuele Metro stop (right) or you may wish to head west, at the end of the tour, to the Cavour Metro stop, near stop #6.
2. For those who stay near Termini, St. Mary Major is excellent for daily Mass, which is celebrated, generally, every hour, on the hour, in the mornings, in one of the chapels..

SANT'EUSEBIO
ST. EUSEBIUS
WEEKDAYS: 8:30 - 9:30 & 6:15 - 7:15

Sant'Eusebio is a minor basilica and titulus, devoted to Saint Eusebius of Rome, a 4th-century martyr. The church's construction is believed to have been funded by the saint and placed on the site of his home. Recorded evidence of this church was found in the catacombs. So, we know it dates from at least the year 474. The present interior preserves the Romanesque style that dates from 1238, however, restorations have occurred in the 17th, 18th and 20th centuries. The floorplan dates from 1600 when Onorio Longhi redesigned it. The ceiling fresco is considered a neoclassical masterpiece by Anton Raphael Mengs (1757). The relics of St. Eusebius are preserved under the main altar, along with those of Saints Orosius and Paulinus.

Chiesa di S. Eusebio
by Giuseppe Vasi (1710-1782)

HISTORY 4 PILGRIMS
*"Thou art Peter,
and upon this rock I will build my church;
and the gates of hell shall not prevail against it."*
Matthew 16:18

Except for the Catholic Church, no institution on earth can claim an uninterrupted line of leadership over twenty centuries. Yet many have attempted to destroy it. Here is a partial list of attacks and sacks that have significantly harmed the Church and its leadership in Rome:
- In 410 AD, Alaric the Visigoth sacked Rome.
- In 455 AD, Vandals and African allies under the command of Gaiseric and Huneric invaded Rome, even more brutally.
- In 536, Belisarios stormed Rome.
- Goth leader Witigis besieged Rome from spring 537 to spring 538.
- Totilia and his Ostrogoth warriors invaded Rome in 545, and took it in December 546.
- In 547, Belisarios retook the city.
- Totila besieged Rome again in 549.
- A coalition of Arabs (Saracen pirates) sacked various parts of Rome in 846.
- Soon after, Pope Leo IV ordered construction of Vatican walls – 44' tall, with 44 towers – giving rise to the Vatican's nickname: The Leonine City.
- In 1084 Normans sacked the city, led by Robert Guiscard.
- In 1527, Spanish Emperor Charles V facilitated Rome's invasion by mostly Germanic mercenaries. This vicious sack focused on the Church's valuable or sacred objects, as well as clergy.
- Beginning in 1796, Napoleon Bonaparte's troops took control of the Papal States in Italy. Eventually, he was excommunicated by Pius VI. So Napoleon's men captured the pope and imprisoned him under house arrest until his death. Then, while weighing his options, Napoleon delayed the pope's burial for five months. The papal successor, Pius VII, continued having stormy relations with Napoleon and eventually was imprisoned for six years while Napoleon raided the Vatican treasury and art collections.

SANTA PRASSEDE
AKA ST. PRAXEDES
DAILY: 7:30 - 12 & 4 - 6

Most pilgrims never see the front entrance to *Santa Prassede* (left) but, instead, enter through the inconspicuous alley door (right) that is close to *Santa Maria Maggiore*. This minor basilica was built in 780 on the site of the titulus home of sister saints Prassede and Pudentiana who are buried near the main altar. They were the daughters of St. Pudens, reputedly Peter's first convert in Rome. In the Middle Ages, this was a favorite stop for Christian pilgrims.

The crypt (left) below the main altar provides a sense of the historic antiquity of this church. The sister saints offered their home and property to the faithful, even for the burial of martyrs, and for that offense they were murdered. About 2,000 saints are interred here, to this day. A large disc in the floor of the nave covers an ancient well in which Prassede is said to have poured the blood of martyrs.

The apse, triumphal arches (above), and the Chapel of St Zeno (below) display dazzling 9th century mosaics. The chapel was meant to be the mausoleum of Pope Paschal I's mother. However, today, it houses a marble fragment that is believed from the flagellation column of Jesus Christ (left).

This scourging pillar was first brought to Constantinople by St. Helena and, finally delivered to this church in 1223. The chapel is a masterpiece of Byzantine art and a fitting place to meditate on the sacrifices and sufferings of Jesus Christ and His saintly martyrs.

Santa Maria Maggiore

St. Mary Major
Daily 7 am – 6:45 pm

- On the lists of Rome's four 'Patriarchal Basilicas' and seven "Pilgrim Churches.'
- Among the oldest of Christian churches, approved by Constantine in the 4th century.
- The 250' bell tower was added in 1377 and is the tallest in Rome.
- The 1929 Lateran Treaty established that the basilica, which is located in Italian territory, is owned by the Holy See and enjoys extraterritorial status similar to that of foreign embassies.
- This church was once known as "Our Lady of the Crib" but is now popularly called "Our Lady of the Snows," for the reason described below.
- Of the five front doors, the one on the left is the Holy Door, only open during a Holy Year.

Tradition: In 350 AD, a wealthy Roman named Ioannes Patricius prayed to the Virgin Mary to give his life meaning. On August 5th, she appeared to him in a dream, asking for a church to be built in her honor where he would find snow. The next morning, when he spoke to his friend, Pope Liberius, the pontiff revealed that he had experienced the same dream. A papal aide then burst into the meeting with the news that the summit of Esquiline Hill had been blanketed by summer snow. The two friends rushed to the site, where the pontiff dragged his crosier through the icy terrain to outline the future basilica.

The colonnaded triple nave (above) is 280' long and part of the original design, with thirty-six Ionic columns, hewn from single blocks of Athenian marble. Old Testament mosaics span above the columns, most dating to the 5th century. The porphyry high altar is original, donated by Ioannes Patricius and his wife in the 4th century.

Below: In front of the altar, twin staircases descend into the deep well of the *confessio* that offers serene, intimate moments with Christ and Christian history.

A large, gold and silver reliquary (above) holds the remains of what is said to have been the cradle of Jesus Christ. It rests upon the crypt of the martyred St. Matthias, the apostle chosen to replace Judas.

Right: An oversized sculpture of Pope Pius IX, by Ignazio Iacometti, offers ecstatic prayers before the holy relic and martyr.

Also entombed here: six popes, Pauline Bonaparte and the creative genius whose understated tombstone simply reads: "Gian Lorenzo Bernini, who brought honor to art and to the city, here humbly lies."

Since its origin in 350, the church's interior (above) has seen many modifications, notably:

- The richly ornamented ceiling is from Giulio Sangallo, one of the architects of St. Peter's Basilica.
- The ceiling is gilded with the first gold from the Americas, a gift from Ferdinand and Isabella of Spain.
- The high altar's porphyry *baldacchino* was added in the 1700s.
- These Cosmati-style inlaid marble floors have welcomed the shoes of pilgrims for nine centuries.

The vaulted ceiling over the Baptistry (below) was completed in 1610, by Passignano. The Assumption of Mary into heaven is at its center.

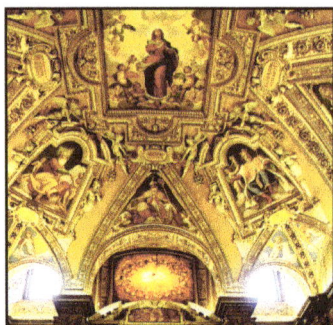

The rear facade of the basilica (right) was requested by Clement X in the 17th century. At that time, the octagonal apse was transformed into a semicircular one. The rear entrance of the basilica is punctuated with an obelisk, topped with a cross. The front entrance displays a colossal fluted column, topped with the Madonna and Child.

Spanning over the canopy of the main altar (left), we see the ancient mosaics of the Triumphal Arch (ca. 430 AD). They provide evidence that the life and role of the Mother of God was highly revered by the earliest Christians. Depicted scenes include: The Annunciation, Christ's Nativity and Infancy, the Presentation of Jesus at the Temple, the Magi with Herod, and the Slaughter of the Innocents. At the center peak is a jewel encrusted throne of God.

Perched atop the canopy is the Papal Insignia, indicating that this is a papal altar. The crossed keys are typically gold and silver, symbolizing the Keys of the Kingdom that were given to Simon Peter and the power to bind and loose sins. The triple crown (or tiara) represents the pope's three functions as "supreme pastor", "supreme teacher" and "supreme priest." Of course, the tiara is topped with the Cross, indicating the sovereignty of Christ.

The main altar (right) has red porphyry columns supporting an ornate, 15th century canopy. Gilded bronze palm branches encircle the columns, spiraling toward heaven. The perimeter of the canopy is skirted with gilded heads of seraphs – angels of the first rank in the Christian hierarchy. An ornately gilded dome is at the center of the canopy.

This excellent apse mosaic (left) is relatively "new" by the standards of this ancient church. But the "Coronation of the Virgin," still dates from the 13th century.

SANTA PUDENZIANA

St. Peter is said to have lodged on this site in the home of a dedicated Roman senator named Pudens. Later, in the late 4th century or early 5th, this basilica was built above a 2nd century Roman titulus that had provided a place for Christian worship during the dangerous early period of Roman persecution. The church is named after one of two saintly daughters of the senator. He is said to have been Peter's first convert in Rome.

The church's frescoed altar dome (left) is easy to miss. Its Romanesque belltower (above left) is from the early 13th century. The 4th century apse mosaic (above) is one of the oldest in existence. It has been restored through the centuries, but not always with the greatest of skill, leaving two disciples without legs. It features Jesus Christ enthroned at the center, with followers at his feet and two women (probably St. Pudenziana and her sister St. Prassede) crowning Peter and Paul.

The age of this ancient church is demonstrated by the blending of old and very old. In the walls (right) we see layers of age that are revealed by bricks that are similar to the ones found in the 3rd century Aurelian walls of Rome or in the 9th century Leonine walls of the Vatican. Even the often repaired floor (lower right) displays pavement that predates the more decorative Cosmatesque floors of more recent churches. However, true antiquity has been found in the underground excavations below the church. They extend to approximately 9 meters below the basilica floor.

Pilgrims descend through the centuries as they tred the steps (left) that lead to the church's front entrance. It is well below modern street level. In fact, as pilgrims approach the current front door (right), they might ask themselves: "Am I walking in the footsteps of St. Peter?"

SAN LORENZO IN PANISPERNA

ST. LAWRENCE AT PANISPERNA
DAILY: BEFORE 7:45 MASS

St. Lawrence of Rome was a friend and associate of Pope Sixtus II, who had elevated him to archdeacon and entrusted with control of the treasury of the Church. In 258, however, Emperor Valerian ordered the execution of all Catholic leaders along with the confiscation of all Church property. So, Lawrence stalled for three days, claiming it would take that amount of time to produce the treasures of the Church. When allowed that delay, the saint diligently set out to distribute all church valuables to the poor of Rome. Then, when he was forced to appear before Valerian's prefect, he explained that he was honoring his commitment to present to him the true treasures of the Church: the poor, the lame, the sick and the blind.

One tradition claims that Lawrence was promptly beheaded. However, a more prominent tradition says that Lawrence was ordered roasted to death. To demonstrate his resolve, it is said that he told his executioners, "Turn me over. I'm done on that side." The gridiron believed to have been used for his torturous death is displayed at San Lorenzo le Fuori Mura, but the location of his cruel execution is this site.

Perhaps in no other city does the eye roam so effortlessly through the eras of mankind, from ancient arches, to modern streets, to bygone temples. The Arch of Janus was built in the early 4th century. The Temple of Hercules Victor (commonly called Temple of Vesta) is the oldest marble structure to have survived Roman antiquity, dating from the 2nd century BC.

SAN PIETRO IN VINCOLI
ST. PETER IN CHAINS
DAILY: 8 – 12:30 & 3:30 – 6:30

Perched on the scenic northern slope of the Esquiline Hill is an important church with an unadorned entry. This church was first built on Roman ruins dating from the 3rd century BC. The present building dates from 438 AD, when the the wife of Emperor Valentinian III ordered the church's construction. She did so for the purpose of finding a suitable place to preserve and revere the chains (*vincoli*) of St. Peter that had restrained him during his last periods of arrest.

The elegant *baldacchin* (left) is relatively new (19th century), however, Iacopo Coppi's fresco in the half dome dates from 1577.

According to tradition, the displayed chains (below) include one strand from St. Peter's imprisonment in Jerusalem and another from his Mamertine incarceration in Rome. When they were initially placed next to each other in Rome, it is said that the two chains miraculously fused together. They are housed in a glass casket, under the golden baldacchin of the high altar (below).

Nearby, stairs lead to a crypt in which a 4th century compartmented sarcophagus is said to contain the remains of the seven Maccabee brothers – Jewish warrior martyrs from the Old Testament. It is likely that these relics have rested here since the church's founding.

Copy of Domenichino's *Liberaton of St. Peter from Prison* by an unknown artist, over second altar on right.

WERE THESE CHAINS MENTIONED IN THE BIBLE?

The night before Herod was to bring him to trial, Peter was sleeping between two soldiers, bound with two chains, and sentries stood guard at the entrance. Suddenly an angel of the Lord appeared and a light shone in the cell. He struck Peter on the side and woke him up. "Quick, get up!" he said, and the chains fell off Peter's wrists.

Acts 12:6-7

A popular attraction for pilgrims and tourists, alike, is the church's collection of fine statuary that includes Michelangelo's famous Moses. The great sculptor's hard-driving patron was Pope Julius II, a proud pontiff who carried the nicknames, "The Fearsome Pope" and "The Warrior Pope." Among the many projects that Julius placed under the direction of Michelangelo was the sculpting of 40 individual statues that were to be placed at the pontiff's grand tomb in the new St. Peter's Basilica. The testy partnership between the two geniuses proved one of the most unhappy, but artistically fruitful, in history. The ambitious pontiff pushed the devout artist to the limits of his endurance, driving him to produce numerous masterpieces, including the Sistine's ceiling. Today, however, only a simple marble stone marks the tomb of the former pontiff, in the floor of the basilica that he made possible: St. Peter's.

Upon completion of Moses, Michelangelo is said to have been so taken by the perfection of the sculpture that he struck his hammer against its knee and commanded, "Speak!"

The marred knee, however, is not the sculpture's only source for folklore. The protrusions from the statue's forehead are obvious. However, they are not intended to be horns, but beams of light. Still, considering that Michelangelo knew this statue was intended for the tomb of the pope who had driven him to exhaustion, could it be that the artist preferred a horned individual to watch over his stern patron throughout eternity?

Below: The nave is bordered by twenty fluted white marble columns with Doric capitals. Because of this design – unknown in classical Rome – they may have once adorned an ancient Grecian temple.

TIPS 4 OLDER PILGRIMS

Many find this church from the Cavour Metro station. If you do, however, be ready for a lengthy series of steps along the way.

San Martino ai Monti

On this site, the Trajan Baths and Nero's Domus Aurea stood. This *Monti* district was once a defensive outpost for Rome's protection. But because it was mostly populated by the poor, it became a welcoming area for early Christians. The church was ordered by Pope Simmaco in the 5th century over the titulus Sylvestri, from the 3rd century. Many of the early church's excellent mosaics have been concealed by later renovations. The crypt (below, right) preserves two rooms of the ancient titulus, as well as strips of 9th century frescoes.

Today's basilica has a Carmelite monastery next door (above, left). The church has been served by Carmelite friars since it was granted to them in 1299 by Pope Boniface VIII. This is the resting place of the recently beatified Blessed Angelo Paoli, O.Carm. (1642– 1720). He was revered throughout Rome for his service to the poor.

The Papacy 4 Pilgrims

Through the centuries, central Italy was ripped apart by feuding families, at times. So, naturally, some viewed the papacy as the crown jewel. Consequently, not every pope ruled with honorable restraint. Among the 266 pontiffs who have reigned, over two millennia, a few have been complete scoundrels.

The Carmelite Order is believed to have been founded in the 12th century on Mt. Carmel, at the cave of Prophet Elijah. Carmelites claim that Jewish hermits occupied the site in an uninterrupted succession since the time of the prophets, until the era of the Carmelite's uninterrupted residence. The oldest scapular is associated with the order. St. Simon Stock – a Carmelite – received the brown scapular from the Virgin Mary, who is sometimes referred to as Our Lady of Mt. Carmel. Today, they are organized into three orders: friars, nuns, and lay people. Each is dedicated to contemplative prayer, especially in association with the Blessed Virgin Mary.

The Crypt of San Martino ai Monti, by François Marius Granet (1806).

Christian Facts 4 Pilgrims

The mother tongue of Jesus and his apostles was Aramaic, which has a 22 letter alphabet and is read from right to left. The language that most closely resembles it today is Middle Syriac. The only group known to continue using this language is a small Syrian settlement of about 1000 Syriac Christians in the hills outside Damascus. Tragically, at the time of this writing, terrorists are attempting to overtake the community.

Walking Tour 8
in the vicinity of
Fontana di Trevi

1. Santa Maria della Concezione (Capuchin Crypt)
2. Fontana di Trevi
3. Saint Carlino alle Quattro Fontane
4. Sant'Andrea al Quirinale
5. Santi Vitale e Compagni Martiri in Fovea

Practical Tips 4 Pilgrims

1. Begin this short but hilly tour at Barberini Metro stop and, at the end, try a window shopping stroll up Via Nazionale to Repubblica Metro stop (east of this map).
2. If time permits, some may wish to tour the Quirinale Palace (directly above) where popes, royals and presidents have resided. Tickets are mandatory and can be reserved in advance at http://www.coopculture.it/en/
3. Map street arrows indicate directions for auto traffic, not pedestrians.

© OpenStreetMap contributors

Santa Maria della Concezione
St. Mary of the Immaculate Conception aka The Capuchin Crypt
Church: 7 - 12 & 3:45 - 7:30: Crypt 9 - 12 & 3 - 6

This church is restrained in its minimally *baroque* decor, but still a strong draw for pilgrims. Among other well known artworks, the altar piece for the first chapel on the right is the original of Guido Reni's famous *St. Michael* from 1635 (below, right).

Visiting here, one cannot miss the theme that this life is fleeting; only the next one lasts. Directly in front of the presbytery, for example, is the tomb of the church's founder, Cardinal Barberini. In the pavement is his simple tombstone, without name or date. It merely states in Latin, "Here lie dust, ashes and nothing."

Most pilgrims come to see the cemetery that is located below the church's chapels on the right side. Here, neatly arranged, are five rooms filled with the bones of over 4,000 Capuchins. Some are still clothed in Capuchin robes (below). Two of these rooms contain soil from the Holy Land. The somber display is not meant to be garish or morose, but simply to reflect the sentiments of a sign in the last alcove: "You are what we once were; you will be what we now are."

Michelangelo 4 Pilgrims

Michelangelo Buonarroti left famous works in Florence. But, in Rome, his abilities to produce masterpieces in many forms of art proved him worthy of the title "Renaissance Man." His architecture, for example, was designed as sculpture, capable of being appreciated from all directions. In St. Peter's Basilica, near his dome that proved to be an engineering miracle, he left the moving *Pietà*. Not far away, in *San Pietro in Vincoli,* is the *Moses* that had been planned for the tomb of his hard-driving patron. Perhaps that is why Moses – with the face of Julius II – has horns, even though the artist insisted that they were meant to be beams of light protruding from Moses' head.

Michelangelo resisted frescoes, until he was forced to prove that his talents equalled that of the greatest masters of the art. Brilliant frescoes in the Sistine Chapel portray Biblical history from the Creation to the Last Judgment. But, as always, critics abounded. So, fig leaves were added by others later, covering the human form that he believed was God's greatest creation. For those naysayers, however, he was capable of inflicting lasting revenge. For example, one severe critic – Cardinal Baigio da Cesena – is surrounded by demons in *The Last Judgment*. The cardinal is naked, except for the coiled serpent that tortures him, and his long pair of donkey ears.

Unlike most artists of his day, Michelangelo's goal was not money or pleasure. He lived a spartan existence, driving himself to the point of exhaustion "for God and St. Peter." In Rome, his wide-ranging talents can also be appreciated at Piazza del Campidoglio, Palazzo Farnese, Palazzo dei Conservatori and the Arco Farnese on Via Giulia. When he died, more than 100 of the day's greatest artists attended his funeral in Rome. But he was secretly spirited away, and buried in Florence.

Fontana di Trevi
Trevi Fountain

The Trevi Fountain is popular for every tourist in Rome. At 86' high by 116' wide, it is Rome's largest *baroque* fountain and one of the most famous in the world. Its construction began under Bernini and Pietro da Cortona. However, the project then languished for over a century before Nicola Salvi completed it in 1751.

The Trevi has been made famous by such films as *Three Coins in the Fountain* and *La Dolce Vita*. Still, this iconic monument once served a practical purpose: providing Romans with fresh water from the *Acqua Vergine*, a 14 mile aqueduct that had been constructed during the reign of Caesar Augustus.

Today, thanks to a generous supply of modern chemicals, the fountain stays clean and its coins, shiny. The treated water is attractively clear, but don't try to drink it.

Every week, the Roman Catholic charity, *Caritas*, retrieves coins from the Trevi to pay for AIDS shelters and food for the poor. In recent years, however, fountain pilferers have been nabbed repeatedly. Some even became famous. But when a television show used a hidden camera to record men sweeping coins from the fountain with a broom, a crackdown finally occurred and, since then, the value of retrieved coins has increased as much as 30%.

Legend has it that tourists inevitably return to the Eternal City after tossing a coin into the Trevi. However, the correct procedure must be followed carefully:

1. Stand with your back to the fountain;
2. Hold a coin in your right hand;
3. Toss it backwards, over your left shoulder.

Sadly, as the above picture demonstrates, some tourists just can't follow directions!

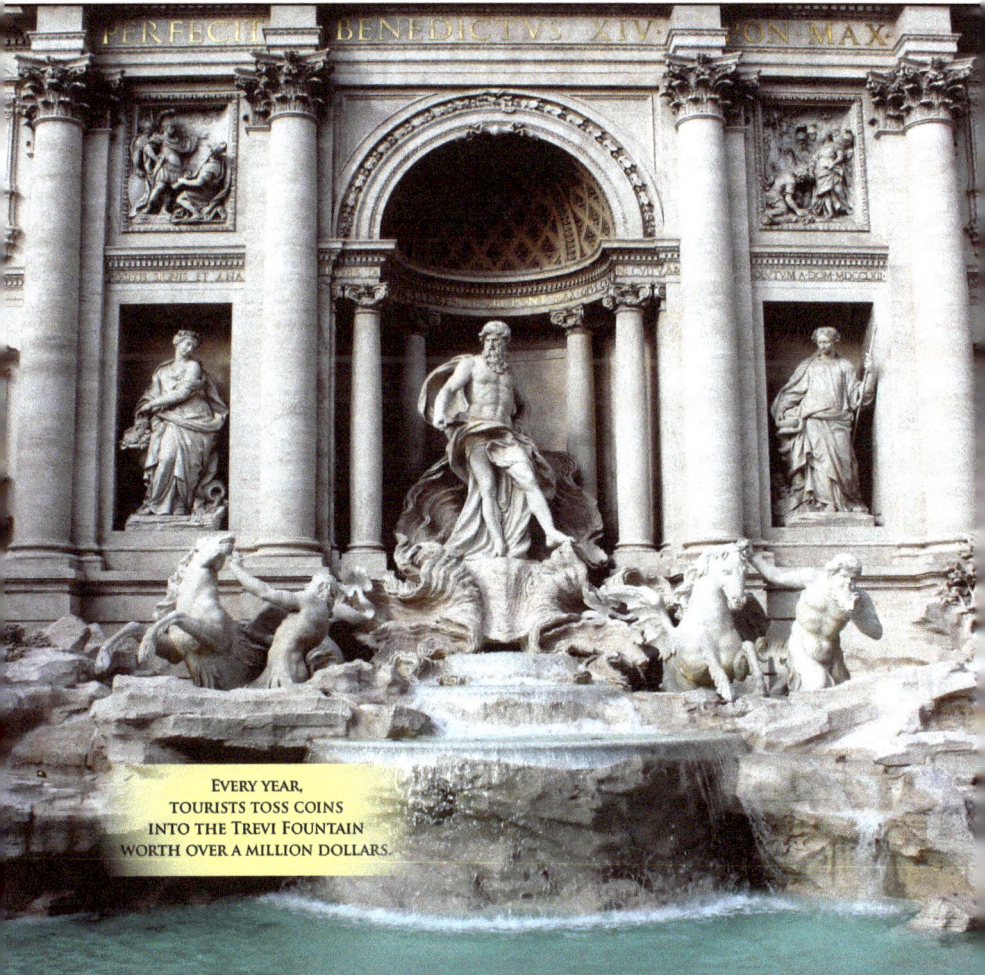

EVERY YEAR, TOURISTS TOSS COINS INTO THE TREVI FOUNTAIN WORTH OVER A MILLION DOLLARS.

SAN CARLINO ALLE QUATTRO FONTANE
ST. CHARLES AT THE FOUR FOUNTAINS
MON - FRI: 9 - 12 & 4 - 6; SAT: 9 - 12 ONLY

Nestled in the busy intersection of the Four Fountains (Via delle Quattro Fontane and Via del Quirinale), this diminutive but worthwhile church is easy to miss. It was Borromini's first independent commission.

The church's unusual serpentine facade (left) as well as its beautifully coffered oval ceiling (facing page) – presenting the *baroque* style in geometric patterns – prove Borromini's innovative brilliance. Tragically, however, he never lived to see its completion. (See page 30.)

The church is dedicated to St. Charles Borromeo the Milanese cardinal who died at just 46 years of age in 1584. Though the correct name is San Carlo, this church is commonly called San Carlino because of its small size.

The historic cloister and crypt (right) are also viewable by the public.

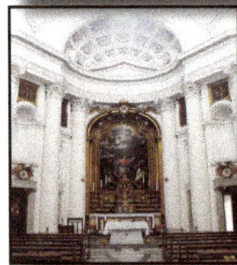

SANT'ANDREA AL QUIRINALE
ST. ANDREW ON QUIRINAL HILL
TUES - SUN: 9 - 12 & 3 - 6; CLOSED MONDAYS

Designed by Gian Lorenzo Bernini and completed in 1670, this church was built for a Jesuit seminary, here, in honor of the martyred apostle. It was the third Jesuit church built in Rome, after the churches in honor of the *Gesù* and *Sant'Ignazio*.

The High Altar (right) is flanked by fluted, roseate marble columns with Corinthian capitals and a white marble canopy. Over the altar, a dramatic oil painting displays the "Martyrdom of Saint Andrew" (1668) by French painter Guillaume Courtois. Above the canopy, St. Andrew rises through the clouds (below), to be greeted by lounging apostles and playful cherubim in heaven.

The genius of Bernini is displayed throughout Rome. He may have been most proud, however, of this church. His son, Domenico, recalled that in his later years, Bernini would sit inside for hours at a time, appreciating what he had accomplished for the glory of God: a visually integrated story of St. Andrew's life, martyrdom and ascencion into heaven. As the eye raises to the dome (facing page), one feels a sense of looking up from the depths of a pond where, on the banks, apostles and angels enjoy the comforts of heaven under a golden, vaulted sky. Bernini was a devout Catholic who took no compensation for this work, except a daily donation of bread from the novitiate's oven.

Stanislaus Kostka was raised in a wealthy Polish family. On his 17th birthday, in 1567, he left Vienna on foot, determined to come here and become a Jesuit priest. The arduous journey was so taxing on the frail but pious young man that he lived just 10 more months, but long enough to prove his heroic virtue to his Jesuit community. The saint's remains are entombed here (above) and his living quarters are preserved, just the way they looked when he lived here.

SAN CARLINO
ALLE QUATTRO FONTANE

DUELING DOMES ON QUIRINAL HILL

They were exceptional enemies: Borromini and Bernini; dueling for patronage, fame and enduringly tran-
scendent art. Architecture, however, was the one field in which Borromini believed he surpassed the artistic
talents of his popular and versatile competitor. Borromini's beautiful oval dome (above) is inventive and
complex; brilliant, but colorless. That is a description that might describe the architect himself. Yet, just a
block away, Bernini's dome (below) is more traditional, in some ways, but accentuated with evidence of
why he became Rome's greatest Baroque sculptor. This dome reveals a story that is active and dramatic,
the very essence of Bernini's genius.

SANT ANDREA
AL QUIRINALE

San Vitale is a titular basilica that was completed in 400 and dedicated by Pope Innocent I shortly after. Its more extensive name (above) refers to Vitale and other saints who were martyred with him, including Valeris, Gervase and Protase.

The portico (left) dates from the 5th century, a couple meters below the level of the bustling street of Via Nazionale.

In keeping with its age, the church offers a simple floorplan with just a single nave. The walls are frescoed with scenes of martyrdom, including that of St. Ignatius of Antioch, a Church Father who was fed to the lions in 107. The bold, coffered ceiling (right) is made from carved wood. The apse (right) is of 5th century construction but displays a fresco, *The Ascent to Calvary*, from the 16th century artist, Andrea Commodi.

Exiting the church (below), pilgrims realize the age of this ancient church that initiated construction in the 4th century. However, the steps down from the street were not needed until 1859.

This church offers one of Rome's rare examples of *trompe l'oeil* art. Here (right), we see what looks like colorful columns beside the altar. In fact, they are two dimensional paintings, providing the illusion of three dimensional columns.

Roman Arches

The triumphal arch is one of the most iconic examples of ancient Roman architecture. Though Romans did not invent these monumental structures, they popularized the use of them (along with sculpted columns) for the purpose of memorializing military conquests. Today, Imperial Roman arches, dating from as early as the 1st century BC, survive in at least 14 countries. Prior to that time, Republican Rome also built arches, but none have survived. At least ten famous arches have been destroyed in Italy since the 12th century.

The largest Roman arch, and one of the most famous, is the Arch of Constantine (right), located just a stone's throw from the Colosseum. It commemorates the victory of Constantine I in his decisive Battle of the Milvian Bridge. (*Ponte Milvio* is still in use in northwest Rome.) Though he was no saint, Constantine credited a Christian miracle for his victory and went on to declare an historic edict of Christian toleration. Yet, even with all its historical grandeur, this arch has been criticized for shamelessly snatching reliefs from earlier monuments. Critical Romans have derisively called it "Aesop's Crow."

Today, churches throughout Rome incorporate the arch in their entrances and, especially, before their altars, as a symbol of spiritual triumph. (See above.)

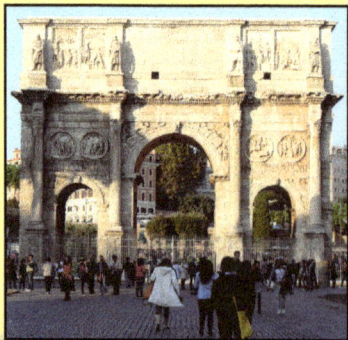

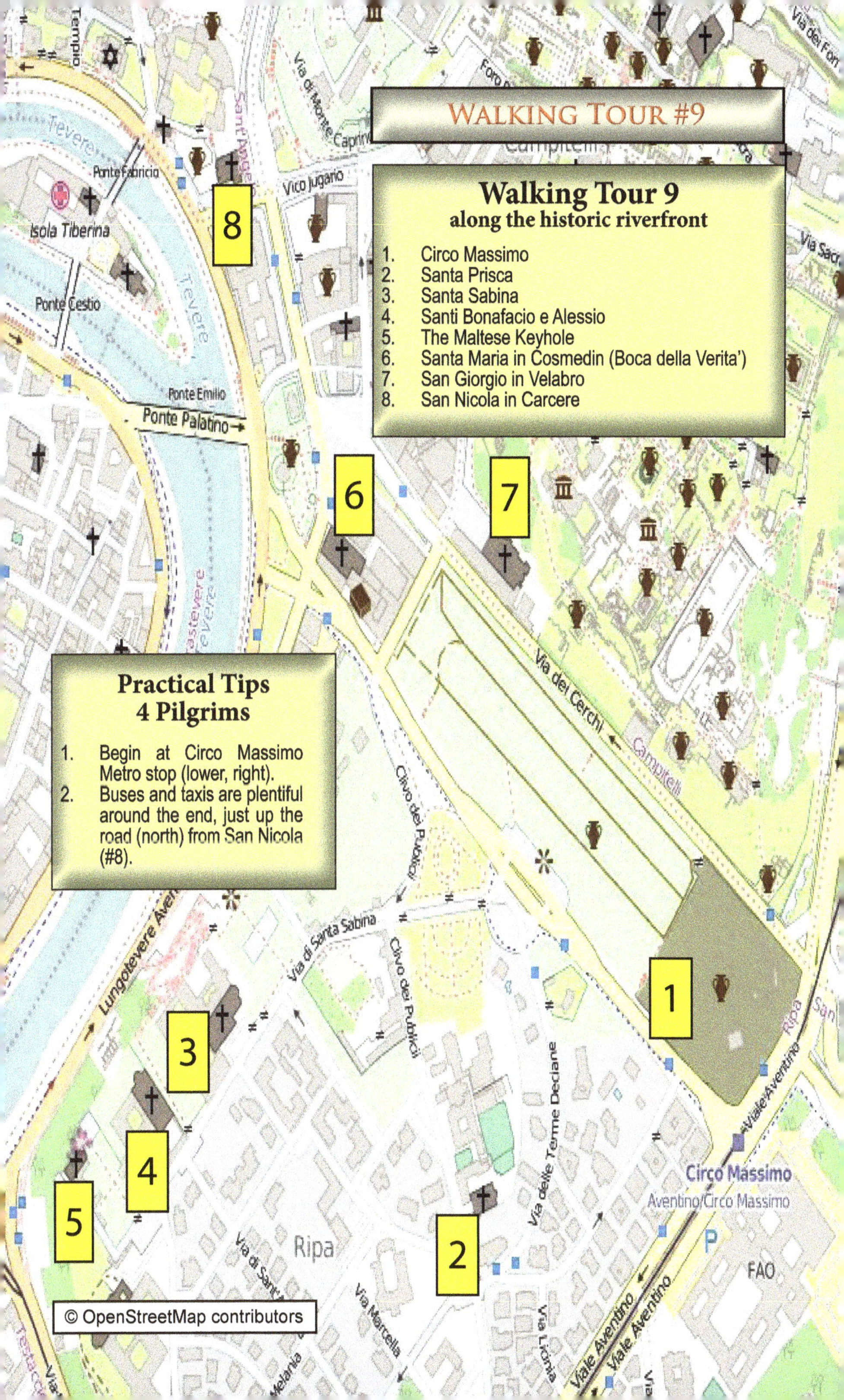

WALKING TOUR #9
Walking Tour 9
along the historic riverfront
1. Circo Massimo
2. Santa Prisca
3. Santa Sabina
4. Santi Bonafacio e Alessio
5. The Maltese Keyhole
6. Santa Maria in Cosmedin (Boca della Verita')
7. San Giorgio in Velabro
8. San Nicola in Carcere
Practical Tips
4 Pilgrims
1. Begin at Circo Massimo Metro stop (lower, right).
2. Buses and taxis are plentiful around the end, just up the road (north) from San Nicola (#8).
1
2
3
4
5
6
7
8
Tevere
Ponte Fabricio
Isola Tiberina
Ponte Cestio
Ponte Emilio
Ponte Palatino
Vico Jugario
Via di Monte Caprino
Via dei Cerchi
Campitelli
Clivo dei Publicii
Via di Santa Sabina
Lungotevere Aventino
Via delle Terme Deciane
Circo Massimo
Aventino/Circo Massimo
Viale Aventino
Ripa
Via Marcella
Via Licinia
FAO
© OpenStreetMap contributors

Constructed in 326 BC, covering an area that could fit almost 14 football fields, the Circus Maximus (above) was the first and largest stadium in the Roman empire. Few modern tourists realize that this "entertainment" venue (below) could accomodate three to five times as many spectators as the well preserved Colosseum. Emperors and their pampered guests watched horse and chariot races, religious processions, beast hunts and gladiator games from their exceptional "box seats" in the Palatine Palace (right).

In the summer of 64 AD, however, a fire broke out near the Circus Maximus. Nine days later, the raging flames had been brought under control, but two-thirds of Rome was smoldering, including Nero's palace. Romans soon began to suspect that their wicked emperor had started the conflagration, allegedly hoping it would allow him to rebuild Rome according to his own plan. So, Nero responded to the rumors by conveniently skapegoating an obscure new sect: Christians. Then he initiated the first great persecution of them. At one of his palaces, he had believers dipped in tar before impaling them on poles and setting them afire. As they lit his gardens, the sadistic emperor is said to have shouted at them, "Now, you truly are the light of the world!"

The Circus Maximus was the main venue where Christians were killed for entertainment, not the Colosseum. Here, Nero would have Christians wrapped in animal skins and then confronted by hungry dogs or lions that would tear them apart. At other times he would have them crucified and, when the crowd grew bored, set them on fire. In this modern era, we are shocked by such brutality, committed simply because Christians refused to worship Rome's pagan gods or, at times, their emperors. But we easily ignore that Christians continue to be persecuted or martyred in many countries today.

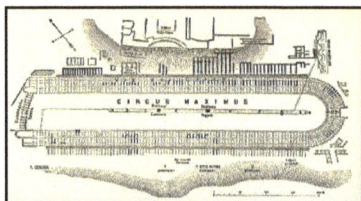

From its infancy, Christianity has been continually confronted by evil that wishes to exterminate it. With that in mind, perhaps, a memorial plaque has been mounted, overlooking this field where Christians were once slaughtered. It quotes George Santayana: "Those who cannot remember the past are condemned to repeat it." The memorial indicates a date that Americans, in particular, will always remember: "11 Settembre 2001."

SANTA PRISCA
ST. PRISCA
DAILY: 8:30 – 12 & 4:30 - 6:30

Aventine Hill is rich in Christian and pagan history, There, inconspicuously tucked between a convent and a sacristy is the small but historic parish church known as Santa Prisca. In the earliest Christian centuries, a home here was known as the Titulus of Aquila and Prisca. That house of Christian worship is believed to be the oldest on Aventine Hill, once offering hospitality to Saints Peter and Paul. It is also said that Trajan lived on this site before becoming emperor.

Before all that, however, a Mithraic temple (right) was here. It is preserved in the crypt below the church, and is considered the most complete of any known to exist. It includes three ceremonial rooms that were adjacent to the temple. At the time of this writing, special tours of the Mithraic temple may be arranged by emailing pierreci@pierreci.it.

HISTORY 4 PILGRIMS

Mithraism was a secretive Roman cult that based its religion on the Persian god Mithras. Their mysterious rituals were conducted, primarily, in caves and included communal meals. Initiation required a progression through seven stages, guided by astrology. As many as 35 Mithraic temples have been discovered around Rome.

Perhaps the most revered relic of this church is its 1st century baptismal (below). It is said that St. Peter baptized St. Prisca at this very font. Its small design provides evidence that the earliest Christians were not solely baptized by full immersion, as some modern Christians claim.

Though this church has a lovely little chapel that is dedicated to the Holy Family (below), the architecture and interior details of the rest of the church are modest, by Roman standards (above and below). Still, Santa Prisca's history alone would make it special anywhere else in the world.

According to the *Acta Sanctorum*, Prisca was 13 years old when Emperor Claudius imprisoned her for refusing to worship Apollo's statue. When she continued to profess her Christian faith, she was whipped and then thrown to the lions at the nearby Circus Maximus. However, the animals only laid at her feet. So, she was imprisoned again, then whipped and tied to a stake for burning. But the flames caused her no harm. Finally, the faithful little saint was taken away and beheaded.

PAPAL RESIDENCES
PAST AND PRESENT
"Ubi est papa, ibi est Roma"
"The seat in Rome is
wherever the pope is."

1. Lateran Palace
2. Quiranale Palace
3. Avignon's Palace of Popes
4. Vatican Papal Palace
5. Castel Gandolfo
6. Castel Sant'Angelo (involuntarily)

SANTA SABINA
ST. SABINA
DAILY: 7 - 12 & 4 - 7

This minor basilica was constructed prior to 432 and is one of Rome's best preserved to continue looking much like what 5th century visitors saw, though restorations were conducted during the 9th, 16th and 20th centuries. This structure was probably built over the house and tomb of the Roman matron Sabina, which recent excavations appear to have uncovered under the nave. In 1219, Pope Honorius III gave this church to St. Dominic and the Dominicans continue to serve it.

After 1870, during Victor Emmanuel's suppression of monasteries, this church became a military hospital. Today, Santa Sabina is the first Station Church of Lent (see p. 200). Here, popes have traditionally celebrated Mass on Ash Wednesday .

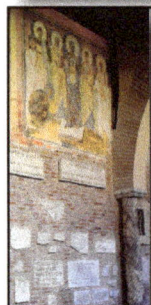

Santa Sabina's 24 white Corinthian columns (above and right) previously supported the ceiling of the nearby temple of Juno Regina. That dates these columns to at least 396 BC. The 5th century carved cypress door is the oldest of its kind, exhibiting the first known image of Christ crucified between the two thieves. In addition to having no facade, this church displays other indications of its ancient origins (above), including ceiling designs that are modest in comparison to later standards, and its rear-wall mosaic of gold Latin words on a dark blue background that is from the 5th century. On an outside wall (left), is an ancient fresco, along with fragments from antiquity. In a side chapel (below, right), the excavations can be accessed with the assistance of the sacristan. However, a pilgrim's time might best be spent by taking a few moments with one of the prayerful priests (left) who patiently await your Confession.

The main entrance is through a lobby that opens to the rear of the nave where you will find this lovely statue of Blessed Mother and her Divine Child (left).

SANTI BONAFACIO E ALESSIO
STS. BONIFACE AND ALEX
DAILY: 8:30 - 12 & 3:30 - 6:30 (OCT - MAR: 6)

The stories of Saints Boniface and Alex are so old that they are somewhat obscure. However, this minor basilica is associated with an even more mysterious saint.

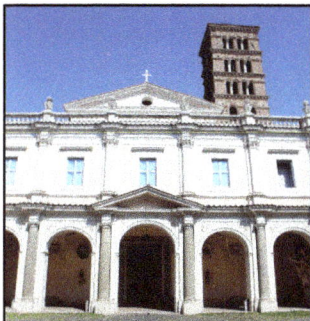

The crypt below this church is said to contain the remains of St. Thomas Becket, Archbishop of Canterbury. In 1170, he clashed with King Henry II over rights and privileges of the Catholic Church in England. When four knights interpreted the king's condemnation of Becket to be an order, they tracked the bishop down and murdered him in Canterbury

An arched passageway leads to the courtyard at the front of the church

Cathedral. An eyewitness said the saint's final words were, "For the name of Jesus and the protection of the Church, I am ready to embrace death."

In 1220, Becket's remains were moved from his first tomb to a shrine that brought many pilgrims to Canterbury. However, during King Henry VIII's dissolution of the monasteries in 1538, the king also ordered confiscation or destruction of everything owned by the Church. This is said to have included the annihilation of Becket's shrine and remains, as well as the obliteration of all mention of the saint's name.

After that, the public record of Becket's bones remains shrouded in mystery. While the king's men stripped away Catholic gold, silver and jewels; while statues, images and sacred books were burned or trashed; could it be that the humble monks who were tasked to oversee the shrine managed to preserve an inconspicuous but precious relic?

The Romanesque crypt is from the 10th century, the only one like it in Rome. It is only open during Christmas time when a popular crib is displayed. The relics of St Thomas Becket are under the crypt's altar, near a 12th century fresco of the Agnus Dei.

THE KEYHOLE OF MALTA

Next door to St. Boniface is an unusual sight. First noticing it, one wonders why tourists are standing in line at a green door. They don't seem to want to go in, but each one just leans against the door and then walks away with a smile.

Give it a try! You will be looking through the only keyhole in the world that has a view of three countries.

Just inside the door is a hedged passageway that is officially part of the tiny country of Malta. Farther away are the Italian rooftops of Rome. Finally, you will see St. Peter's unmistakable dome in Vatican City.

Santa Maria in Cosmedin (Boca della Verita')

This basilica stands on the site of an ancient Roman temple that was dedicated to Hercules Invictus. In the 300s, this site became the Roman market inspector's office, but by 600 it was being used as a Christian welfare center for the poor. By the late 8th century, however, this multi-layered complex had evolved into a large church.

The word 'Cosmedin" comes from the Greek word for "decoration" and probably refers to the rich ornamentation that originally graced its interior. By the mid 800s, this site included an oratory, a triclinium and a papal residence. But in 1084 it was one of the many churches that were sacked in the Norman invasion. Soon after, the church was renovated and a Romanesque tower was added. This church has the tallest medieval bell tower in Rome.

The age of this ancient church is made obvious (right) by its simply beamed ceiling, fading frescoes, and deteriorating stone columns.

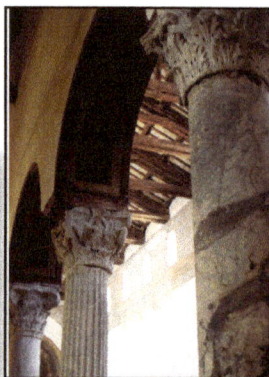

The skull of Saint Valentine (above), along with a few bones, are displayed in a golden reliquary. Unfortunately, his life was not as romantic as his holiday. Valentine was a devoted priest in Rome who assisted martyrs during the persecutions of Claudius II. When the authorities arrested him, he refused to renounce his faith. So, he was condemned to be beaten with clubs and then beheaded. His martyrdom occurred on February 14, 270 – the first Valentine's day. More of his relics are placed in the church of St. Praxedes.

The entrance to the crypt (right) can be found at the left side of the altar. It was built by Pope Adrian, twelve centuries ago, to store the relics of martyrs.

Tourists queue (above) in the portico of the church to have fun with the *Boca della Verita* – the "Mouth of Truth." Those who dare to accept the risk, slide their hands into the mouth of this strange character. A medieval legend has it that only a truth teller will remove the hand, unharmed. The popular disc is believed to be an ancient Roman fountain or drain cover. Through the centuries, however, contracts were actually sealed by this practice. The *Boca* has tested tourists and tasted hands at this location since 1632.

Tips 4 Little Pilgrims

Warning: Small Bocas can be dangerous too!

(This one was found on the Appian Way.)

BOCCA DELLA VERITA

SAN GIORGIO IN VELABRO
ST. GEORGE IN VELABRO
TUES, FRI, & SAT: 10 - 12:30 & 4 - 6:30

This church was highlighted in international news reports in 1993 when, along with St. John Lateran, it was bombed by the Mafia. From May to August, five car bomb attacks occurred in Rome, Florence and Milan leaving 10 people dead and dozens wounded. Fortunately no one was killed during the Roman church attacks, which were said to have been ordered in retaliation for Pope John Paul II's opposition to the Mafia. In a visit to Sicily, shortly before the bombings, the pontiff had urged the Catholics of Sicily to rise up against Mafia domination.

At this church, the explosion left the 12th century portico almost totally collapsed and blew a large opening into the wall of the main church. Next door, the residence of the Generalate of the Crosiers (Canons Regular of the Order of the Holy Cross) was severely damaged. In the other related bombings, art museums and a news reporter also were targeted.

Today, the church has returned to normal operations, even though renovations through the centuries reveal its antiquity. The well-worn, unmatched columns (left) indicate they probably originated in pagan temples from before this church's 7th century construction. From those columns we notice also that various renovations have used different floor heights.

SAN NICOLA IN CARCERE
ST. NICHOLAS IN PRISON
MON - SAT: 7:30 - 12 & 4 - 7; SUN: 10 - 1; CLOSED AUG UNTIL MID-SEPT.

This titulus is also a Lenten Station Church (see page 200). Since the 6th century, Christian churches have occupied this historic site. Yet, here, stood places of worship that pre-date the Christian era. The *Temple of Juno the Savior*, which dates from the second century BC, was directly under the present structure. Also, immediately to the right and left of this church stood Temples dedicated to the *Goddess Hope* and the *Two-Faced God, Janus*. Those temples, along with an adjacent vegetable market, date from the third century BC.

Evidence of such antiquity is observable in and around the church. Some believe that the earlier temples, beneath, had been transformed into a prison, leading to the current church name. However, others claim that the prison dates from many centuries later, during the Byzantine era. The bell tower is adapted from a medieval fortress tower. The remains of St. Nicolas are entombed under the altar and, below that, stairs lead to the ancient crypt. Next door are the impressive ruins of the ancient Theatre of Marcellus (see page 120).

The Theatre of Marcellus

Construction of this center for Roman entertainment was initiated by Julius Caesar. It was not completed, however, until the reign of Augustus Caesar, who dedicated it in 12 BC. This ancient theatre held up to 20,000 spectators.

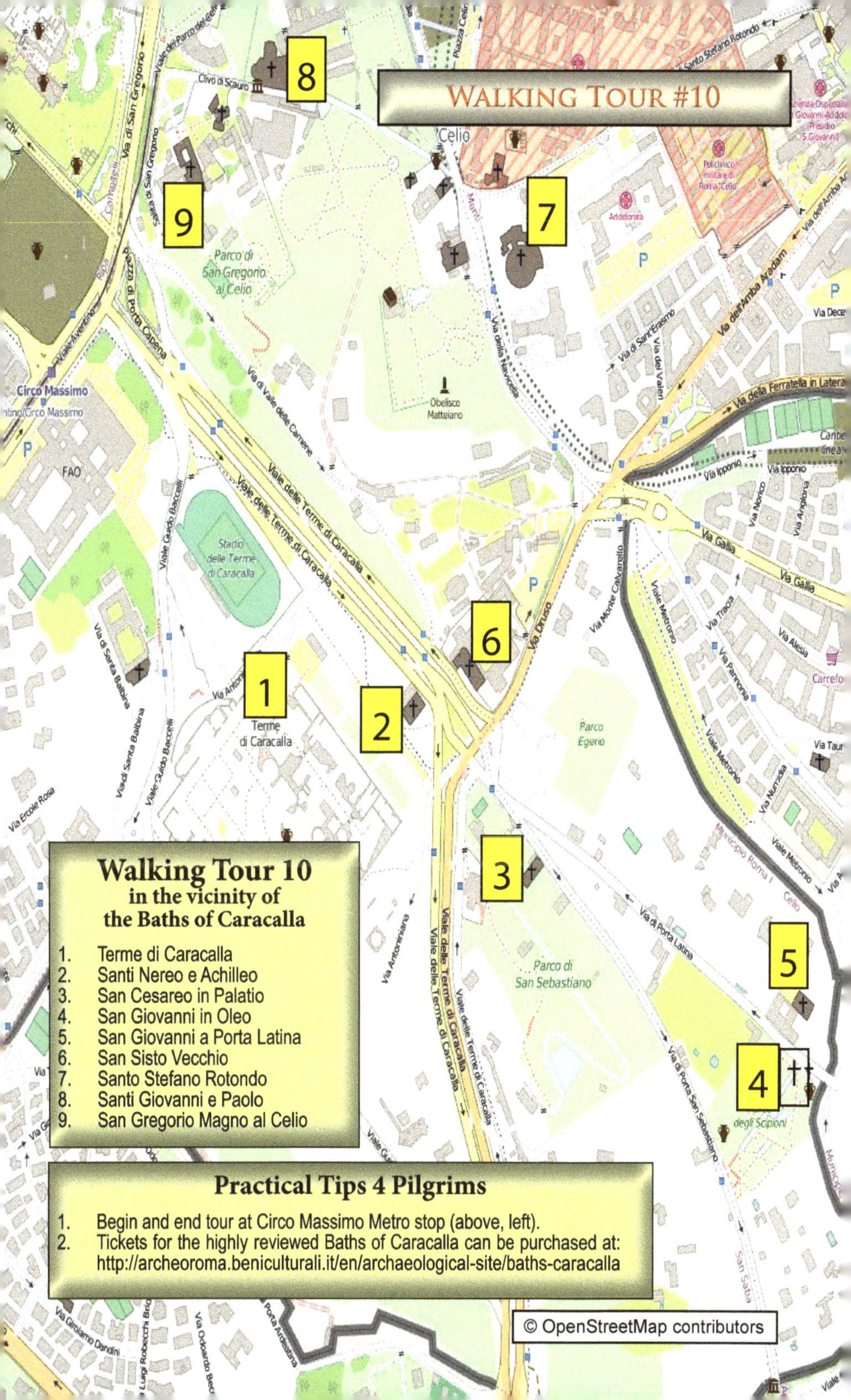

8

Celio

9

7

Parco di
San Gregorio
al Celio

Circo Massimo
ento/Circo Massimo

FAO

Obelisco
Matteiano

Stadio
delle Terme
di Caracalla

6

Parco
Egerio

1

2

Terme
di Caracalla

3

Parco di
San Sebastiano

Walking Tour 10
in the vicinity of
the Baths of Caracalla

1. Terme di Caracalla
2. Santi Nereo e Achilleo
3. San Cesareo in Palatio
4. San Giovanni in Oleo
5. San Giovanni a Porta Latina
6. San Sisto Vecchio
7. Santo Stefano Rotondo
8. Santi Giovanni e Paolo
9. San Gregorio Magno al Celio

5

4

degli Scipioni

Practical Tips 4 Pilgrims

1. Begin and end tour at Circo Massimo Metro stop (above, left).
2. Tickets for the highly reviewed Baths of Caracalla can be purchased at:
http://archeoroma.beniculturali.it/en/archaeological-site/baths-caracalla

TERME DI CARACALLA
THE BATHS OF CARACALLA
TUES - SAT: 9 - 7 (CLOSES AT 4, OCT - MAR)

The Baths of Caracalla were Roman public baths, built between 212 and 216. The complex covered approximately 33 acres. The bath building was 750 feet long, 380 feet wide, with an estimated height of 125 feet. It could hold an estimated 1,600 bathers.

In the 12th century, 22 well-preserved columns were relocated from these ruins to the church of Santa Maria in Trastevere. Today, the central part of the bath complex is the summer home of the Rome Opera company. It was a memorable backdrop for the first Three Tenors concert in 1990.

SANTI NEREO E ACHILLEO
STS. NERO AND ACHILLES
SAT - THURS: 10 - 12 & 4 - 6

Before the year 330, a church arose on this site dedicated to St. Peter in honor of a memorable event that is said to have happened here. Peter, who had been imprisoned in the Mamertine, escaped. Because of his shackles, Peter's feet were wounded and bandaged. On this site it is said that Peter lost a foot bandage as he fled Rome. However, not far from here, where to-day's church called *Domine quo vadis?* stands, Peter saw the Lord and decided to return to Rome, regardless of the consequences. (See p. 179.)

During the reign of Pope St. Gregory the Great (590-604), the church was dedicated to mar-tyred Saints Nero and Achilles. This ancient church is a titulus and minor basilica.

SAN CESAREO IN PALATIO
ST. CAESARIUS ON PALATINE HILL
SUNDAY ONLY: 9:30 - 12, OR BY APPT. (CLOSED AUG)

San Cesareo in Palatio is a titular church near the beginning of the Appian Way. It is dedicated to Saint Caesarius of Africa, a 2nd-century deacon and martyr.

In the 4th century, Emperor Valentinian attributed his own miraculous cure to the intercession of San Cesareo when the emperor visited a shrine at the site of the saint's martyrdom. Subsequently, the emperor decided to move the saint's relics to Rome, where they would be placed in a new church on the Palatine Hill.

On February 15, 1145, this was the site of the election of Cistercian Abbot Peter Bernard of Paganelli, who took the name of Pope Eugenius III .

SAN GIOVANNI IN OLEO
ST. JOHN IN OIL
OUTSIDE VISIT ONLY

On this site, it is said that St. John the Apostle was miraculously protected from harm after being submerged in boiling oil (thus, "*oleo*") when emperor Domitian grew angry with his evangelizing. The failure of the emperor's assassins, it is said, necessitated John's forced exile on Patmos. So, instead of silencing the great evangelist, Domitian unwittingly provided John with the Spiritual retreat and prayerful solitude that allowed him to write his book of Revelation.

In 1657 a cardinal named Paolucci endeavored to renovate a church he had been assigned: the nearby San Giovanni a Porta Latina. So, he also took on this project. To design this little *tempieto*, he commissioned Francesco Borromini, who had recently completed renovations for the Lateran Baptistry – another octagonal structure. Though small, this memorial achieves its purpose: to be memorable. Inside, 17th century frescoes depict stories of St. John the Evangelist, along with stuccoes that depict chain motifs. This tiny oratory is not a church and, consequently, rarely open.

TIPS 4 PILGRIMS

Use extra caution when walking narrow Roman roads that have no sidewalks, such as the one that leads to the Latin Gate (right and above).

SAN GIOVANNI A PORTA LATINA

ST. JOHN'S AT THE LATIN GATE
DAILY: 8 - 12:30 & 3:30 - 6

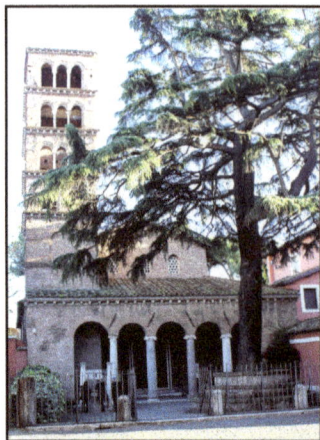

This minor basilica dates from the late fourth century, but the church underwent restoration as early as the fifth century. Then in the eighth, ninth, eleventh and thirteenth centuries further renovations were accomplished.

Indications of its antiquity are visible inside and out. As pilgrims approach, the Romanesque bell tower does not appear particularly old, by Rome's standards. But entering the portico, one notices unmatched columns and an ancient well. Inside, we see again the unmatched columns that are said to have been relocated from Rome's Temple of Diana, constructed in the 6th century BC.

Its fading frescoes, beamed ceiling and simplicity of interior design further enhance an ambiance of antiquity.

SAN SISTO VECCHIO

OLD ST. SIXTUS
DAILY: 9 - 11 (CLOSED AUG)

This titulus and minor basilica is said to have been approved for construction by Pope Anastasius I (399-401). The church houses the relics of Pope Sixtus II, that were transferred here from the catacombs of San Callisto in the sixth century.

San Sisto Vecchio was rebuilt in the early 13th century, by Pope Innocent III. The current church is the result of the restorations of Pope Benedict XIII (18th century), which left only the bell tower and the apse from the medieval church. A 13th-century fresco depicting scenes from the New Testament and the Apocrypha is conserved here.

Dominican nuns still occupy the convent and cloister at San Sisto Vecchio, just as they have done since the 16th century.

TEMPL · S · SYXTI ·

SANTO STEFANO ROTONDO
ST. STEPHEN'S IN THE ROUND
MON - FRI: 9 - 12

There may be no more moving tribute to name-less martyrs who sacrificed everything for Christ, through the centuries, than Santo Stefano Rotondo. It is dedicated to the protomartyr Stephen whose remains are believed to have been moved here after his stoning in Jerusalem. This ancient church is from the 460s and is now a virtual gallery of martyrdom. Encircling the round inner sanctum is a sometimes shocking col-lection of oil paintings characterizing the elaborately sadistic tortures that Christian martyrs endured.

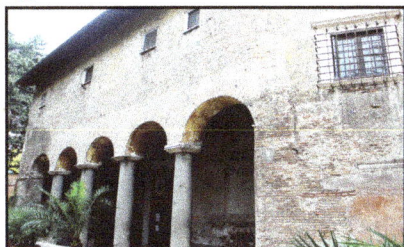

The domed structure at its center, surrounded by many of the church's 58 granite columns, dates from the time of Nero, and the vicious emperor is recorded to have feasted here, at his meat market.

Pope St. Gregory the Great (590-604) often preached here and his wooden throne is preserved near the en-trance.

The church's modest exterior (above) and its off-the-beaten-path location make it one pil-grims might consider skipping. But by doing so, they will miss a truly unforgettable experience. The images here, however, are too intense for small children.

... yelling at the top of their voices, they all rushed at him, dragged him out of the city and began to stone him. Meanwhile, the wit-nesses laid their coats at the feet of a young man named Saul.

While they were stoning him, Stephen prayed, "Lord Jesus, receive my spirit." Then he fell on his knees and cried out, "Lord, do not hold this sin against them." When he had said this, he fell asleep.

Acts 7:57-60

Santi Giovanni e Paolo al Celio

Sts. John and Paul in Celio
Daily: 9 - 11 & 4 - 5:30

Santi Giovanni e Paolo al Celio is an ancient basilica, titulus and Lenten church. It was constructed in 398 over the home of two Roman soldiers, John and Paul. They were martyred in 362 under Julian.

This church was damaged during the sack by Alaric I in 410 and, in 442, by an earthquake. It was restored by Pope Paschal I in 824. However, Rome was sacked again by the Normans in 1084. Again, the church was restored, with the addition of a monastery and a bell tower.

This is the mother church of the Passionists and houses the tomb of St. Paul of the Cross. The dimly lit interior is peaceful, quiet and well furnished. The interior is popular for its use of chandeliers, making it a good choice for Roman weddings.

San Gregorio Magno al Celio

St. Gregory the Great on Caelian Hill
Daily: 9 - 12:30 & 3:30 - 6:30

He was the first of the popes to come from a monastic background. Pope Gregory I was widely respected, even by Protestant reformers such as John Calvin. Today, he is a Doctor of the Church, one of the Latin Fathers, and considered a saint in the Roman Catholic, Eastern Orthodox, Anglican, and some Lutheran churches.

Gregory is the only pope who lived from the 5th through 11th centuries whose writings have survived intact as a comprehensive body of work. He standardized the form of Western ceremonial song. So, Gregorian Chant gained its name from him, although that label only was first used centuries after his death. Many attribute the roots of Medieval Spirituality to Gregory.

One historian criticized him, however, for being "excessively devoted to saints, miracles and relics." Perhaps that spoke more to the historian's flaws than the saint's.

In the 1970s, Blessed Teresa of Calcutta, M.C. was allowed to set up a homeless shelter and food kitchen for the poor in a building attached to the monastery here. Her religious congregation, the Missionaries of Charity, still continue the work.

The marble *cathedra* – official chair of the bishop of Rome – that is associated with Gregory the Great is preserved in the stanza di S. Gregorio in the church (left).

Angel Bearing Holy Water
Santa Maria degli Angeli
Page 90

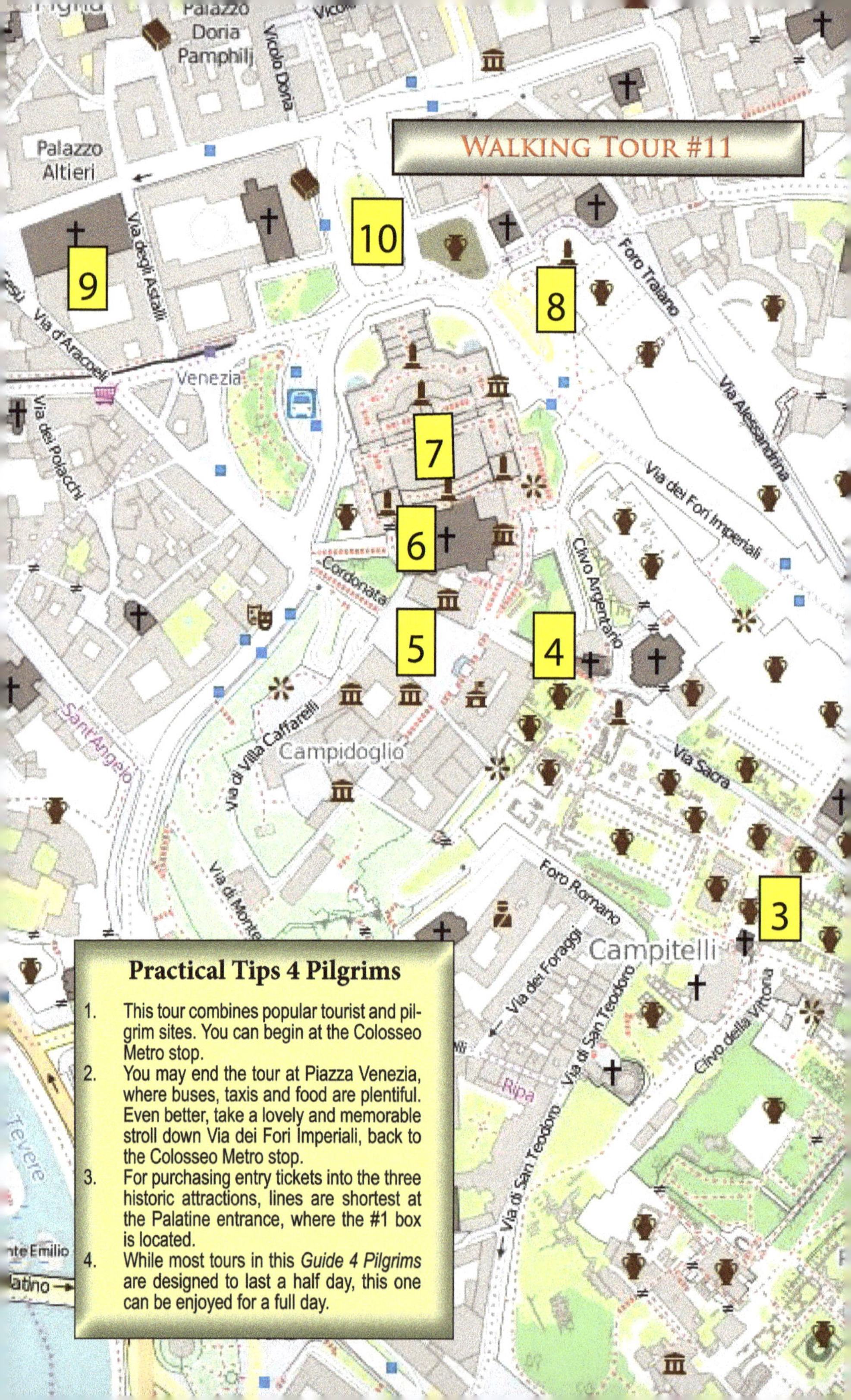

Palazzo
Doria
Pamphilj

Palazzo
Altieri

Via degli Astalli

Via d'Aracoeli

9

10

8

Venezia

Foro Traiano

Via Alessandrina

7

Via dei Fori Imperiali

Via dei Polacchi

6

Cordonata

Clivo Argentario

5

4

Sant'Angelo

Via di Villa Caffarelli

Campidoglio

Via Sacra

Foro Romano

Via di Monte

3

Campitelli

Via dei Foraggi

Clivo della Vittoria

Ripa

Via di San Teodoro

nte Emilio

Tevere

alatino

Practical Tips 4 Pilgrims

1. This tour combines popular tourist and pilgrim sites. You can begin at the Colosseo Metro stop.

2. You may end the tour at Piazza Venezia, where buses, taxis and food are plentiful. Even better, take a lovely and memorable stroll down Via dei Fori Imperiali, back to the Colosseo Metro stop.

3. For purchasing entry tickets into the three historic attractions, lines are shortest at the Palatine entrance, where the #1 box is located.

4. While most tours in this *Guide 4 Pilgrims* are designed to last a half day, this one can be enjoyed for a full day.

Walking Tour 11
in the Vicinity of
Foro Romano

1. The Palatine
2. The Colosseum
3. The Forum
4. The Mamertine Prison
5. Piazza del Campidoglio
6. Santa Maria in Aracoeli
7. Monument to Vittorio Emanuel II
8. Trajan's Column (and Trajan's Forum)
9. San Marco
10. Piazza Venezia

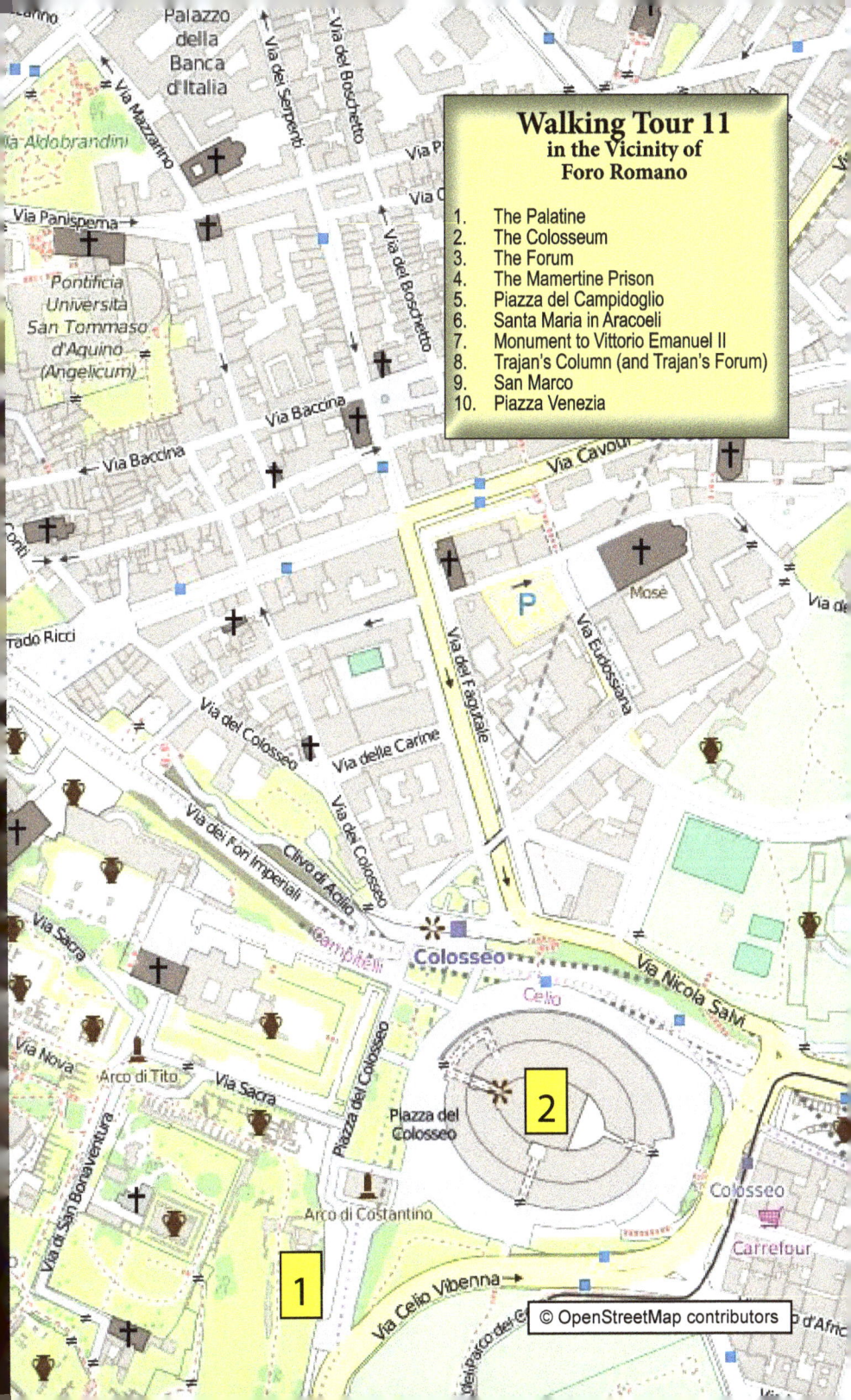

Palazzo della Banca d'Italia

Via Mazzarino
Via dei Serpenti
Via del Boschetto
Via P...
Via Panisperma
Via Aldobrandini
Pontificia Universita San Tommaso d'Aquino (Angelicum)
Via del Boschetto
Via Baccina
Via Baccina
Via Baccina
Via Cavour
Mosè
P
rado Ricci
conti
Via del...
Via del Fagutale
Via Eudossiana
Via del Colosseo
Via delle Carine
Via del Colosseo
Via dei Fori Imperiali
Clivo di Acilio
Campitelli
Via Sacra
Colosseo
Celio
Via Nicola Sal...
Via Nova
Arco di Tito
Via Sacra
Piazza del Colosseo
Colosseo
Carrefour
Via di San Bonaventura
Piazza del Colosseo
Arco di Costantino
Via Celio Vibenna
d'Afric...

1

2

PALATINO

Among the 7 hills of Rome, the Palatine is most centrally located and most historic. Here, in a cave, legendary infant twins Romulus and Remus were believed to have been nursed by a she-wolf. In fact, archeological excavations have shown that the first known Romans did live here, probably as early as 1,000 BC.

Upon Palatine Hill, Roman emperors established one of the grandest residences in the world, giving rise to the word "palace." From here, many of history's most powerful rulers enjoyed their enviable views of the Circus Maximus, to one side, and the Roman Forum, to the other. If only stones could talk we might learn more regarding the character of the Palatine's unique succession of occupants, from the intellectual heights of Augustus, to the decadent depths of Nero and Caligula.

COLOSSEO
THE COLOSSEUM
DAILY: 8:30 - 7:15 (TICKET BOOTH CLOSES 1 HOUR EARLY)

The Colosseum was begun under Emperor Vespasian and finished in 80 AD. It could hold 73,000 spectators who followed a precise entry, exit and seating procedure so that the arena could be emptied quickly. Its nickname came from the colossal statue of Nero that once stood nearby. The word "arena" derives its origin from the Latin word for sand, which covered the Colosseum floor. Though pampered spectators are believed to have enjoyed the shade provided by huge canvas awnings to protect them from Rome's blistering sun, performers had no such luxuries. Below the wooden floor of the arena, animals and gladiators sweated it out in darkened chambers until their bloody entertaining began.

Extravagant hunts, known as venationes, were held in the Colosseum from 80 to 523 AD. Some of the grandest were conducted during the inaugural celebrations of Titus, in which 9,000 wild beasts entered the arena. After Trajan's victory over the Dacians, 10,000 animals and 11,000 gladiators participated in the gruesome festivities.

In its days of splendor, the Colosseum was covered with marble and boasted larger-than-life sculptures in every alcove. It has survived fires, earthquakes, barbarian sackings, and the lengthy decline of Rome, at which time its facade and statues were routinely pilfered. Finally, in the 18th century, Pope Benedict XV consecrated the Colosseum in the belief that Christians had been martyred there. However, contrary to modern beliefs, Italian historians agree that no Christians were thrown to the lions in the Colosseum. Such "entertainments" were reserved for other venues, such as the nearby Roman Circus (See Circo Massimo, p. 114). Still, this iconic monument has been preserved ever since its consecration. Today, a cross has been erected on the grounds (right) and, since 1744, popes have lead moving and popular torch-lit processions during Good Friday Stations of the Cross.

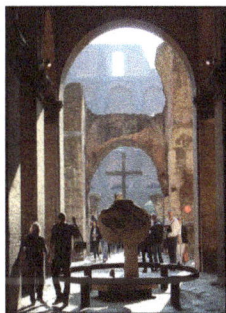

TIPS 4 PILGRIMS

Don't bring rolling luggage to the Colosseum, even if it is just a backpack with wheels. You won't be admitted. Also, watch for pickpockets, even during the Good Friday Stations of the Cross.

In ancient Rome, the Forum was the economic, political and social heart of the city. From the Arch of Titus (left) to the Arch of Septimius Severus (below), ancient throngs trod the Via Sacra amidst magnificent marble-clad buildings. Along the way, they admired the Senate House (known as the Curia), the Temple of Vesta and House of the Vestal Virgins, as well as cheering or mocking rousing speeches from the rostrum of the Forum's main square.

Generally, Rome succeeded at assimilating other cultures and religions into their empire because additional gods were always welcomed to the Roman club. However, Jews and a pesky new sect, called Christians, insisted on worshiping only their "one, true God." They refused to adore even the occassional Roman emperor who deemed himself worthy of such honor.

So, in 70 AD, tensions boiled over, Rome sacked Jerusalem, and Generals Titus and Vespasian fulfilled Jesus Christ's prophecy that the Temple would be destroyed. To celebrate their victory, Titus eventually built the Forum arch that bears his name, depicting soldiers carrying away the Temple's menorah (above, right). Ironically, the attack not only dispersed the Jews, (fulfilling another prophecy) but prompted the most prominent Christians – following the lead of Peter and Paul – to make their case in the midst of the enemy's encampment: Rome. Overcoming savage persecutions, the determined saints of Rome eventually won recognition, in 313 AD, in an imperial edict of toleration. As the years advanced, young Romans shifted their allegiance from Mars – the god of war – to Jesus Christ – the Prince of Peace. However, within a century, barbarians would begin savage sacks of Rome, and destruction of its empire. The last Roman emperor, Romulus Augustus, ended his reign on September 4, 476 AD. The chaos shattered the once-great Roman empire into a thousand regions, controlled by a thousand local rulers, for a thousand years. But the popes remained in Rome.

MAMERTINO
THE MAMERTINE PRISON
APR - SEP: 9 - 12:30 & 2:30 - 6; OCT - MAR: 9 - 12 & 2 - 5

Below the 16th century church known as San Giuseppe dei Falegnami is Rome's oldest prison, where Peter and Paul are said to have been incarcerated.

The ancient historian Livy dates the Mamertine to the 7th century BC and historical accounts recognize its continuing use at least until the 4th century. So, in this dungeon, terrorized and tortured prisoners were held for more than a millenium.

It was located 12 feet below ground in an old cistern, adjacent to the city's sewer. Historian Sallust wrote: "neglect, darkness and stench make it hideous and fearsome to behold."

Prisoners who were delivered to the lower cell usually died of starvation or strangulation. Then their bodies were dumped into the nearby sewer. A number of famous inmates lived and died here, including Vercingetorix, the tribal warrior who united the Gauls against Julius Caesar's Roman forces.

The prison consists of two underground cells. The upper room (left) was once at street level. It now contains an altar with the busts of Peter and Paul behind it. A well-tred staircase was later added, allowing more convenient access to the lower cell (below). At the top of the marble stairs is a stone that is said to bear an imprint of Peter's head. Nearby are plaques that display the names of many of this prison's most famous inmates.

This is not a museum with numerous artifacts but, instead, a site of important historical significance. A donation is expected, or pay for the audio tour (which can be a bit cheesy at times).

The lower cell has a modern platform extending into it (above). In its ceiling is a hole that served as each prisoner's only access to the outside world when, on rare occassions, food or water was supplied. A small column (left) is located under the hole. It is the one that both Peter and Paul were tied to during their imprisonment. While Peter was incarcerated, it is said that he caused a spring to penetrate the floor and then used that water to baptize his two guards.

PIAZZA DEL CAMPIDOGLIO
CAPITOL SQUARE

On Capitoline Hill, beside Santa Maria in Aracoeli, was the Roman version of the Greek Acropolis, where Roman gods were worshipped. Since then, Michelangelo designed the piazza that now welcomes tourists and Italy's government officials who operate out of these buildings. During the age when repurposing ancient bronze sculptures for contemporary churches was popular, the impressive equestrian statue at the piazza's center fortunately escaped the melting pot. It was believed to be depicting Constantine, the emperor who first recognized Christianity as an acceptable faith for Rome. This statue, however, is only a copy. It actually depicts the philosopher Emperor Marcus Aurelius – a Christian persecutor. The original statue is preserved in the Capitoline Museum.

SANTA MARIA IN ARACOELI
ST. MARY OF THE ALTAR OF HEAVEN
DAILY: 7 - 12 & 4 - 6 (6:30 IN SUMMER)

On the highest point of Capitoline Hill, this basilica is believed to date from the 500s. However, its name is derived from a story of an earlier time, even before Christ. A common belief in the Middle Ages was that Emperor Augustus (d. 14 AD) visited the Tiburtine Sibyl, here, who prophesied in Latin: "This is the altar of the first-born of God." The legend further said (a possible later embellishment) that the Virgin and Child also appeared to Augustus. The emperor then erected an altar on this site and a church was subsequently built over it. Many years later, it became known as *ara coeli* or "altar of heaven." The third column from the rear, left, is inscribed as coming from the room of Augustus.

TIPS 4 PILGRIMS

From street level, the steps leading to the front of the church number 124. But you'll be relieved to find that if you take the stairs to the right of the church, there are only 122!

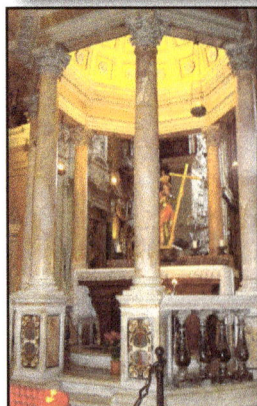

Since 1250, this church has been served by Franciscans, who renovated it at that time. In the 17th century, the Chapel of St. Helena (d. 330) was added (left). Under the white canopy, a porphyry urn contains the saint's relics. She was the mother of Constantine (emperor 306-337) who played a major role in converting her son and bringing many holy relics to Rome from the Holy Land. During the Napoleonic occupation of 1798, however, French troops severely damaged the Chapel of St. Helena. It had to be rebuilt in the 19th century.

MONUMENT TO VITTORIO EMANUEL II AND TRAJAN'S COLUMN

HISTORY 4 PILGRIMS

Vittorio Emanuele II was an ambitious man. In 1861 he reunited Italy for the first time since the 6th century, then declared himself King. His actions provoked anger from Italians and excommunication from the Church. On his deathbed, the king refused to accept the papal legates who had come, ready to rescind the excommunication. Today, his monument towers over Piazza Venezia, after having disrupted and destroyed some of the most archeologically sensitive land in the world.

For what is a man profited,
if he shall gain the whole world,
and lose his own soul?
Matthew 16:26

SAN MARCO
ST. MARK
SUN: 9 - 1 & 4 - 8; OTHERWISE, 8:30 - 12 & 4 - 6:30, EXCEPT CLOSED AM ON MON.

This basilica is believed to have been founded by Pope St. Mark in 336 because St. Mark the Evangelist lived on this site while in Rome. In fact, excavators have recovered fragments of wall paintings and floor mosaics from the 4th century structure.

The apse (below, right) dates from the first half of the ninth century. Beneath the altar is an ancient porphyry urn that contains the relics of Pope St. Mark. In the crypt below, two martyred saints from the 3rd century are buried.

A 9th century well is located in the rear of the church with an unusual 11th century inscription that invites all who are thirsty to drink, but curses anyone who charges for the water. The unusual facade (right) includes a two-tiered portico in which fragments from ancient Christian tombstones are attached to the walls of the lower level (below).

San Marco is one of Rome's oldest churches, but has faced many challenges through the centuries. It was destroyed and rebuilt in the 5th century. Goths, Lombrds and Byzantines repeatedly sacked it in the 6th and 7th centuries. Soon after being rebuilt, again, it was flooded when the Tiber broke its banks.

The gilded coffered ceiling (right) is one of the oldest in Rome (1474) dating from around the time of the execution of the ceiling in St. Mary Major.

Next door, in the 15th century, Pope Paul II built the Palazzo Venezia which became the residence of Venetian ambassadors. To this day, the popular town square nearby is known as Piazza Venezia and this is the national church for Venetians living in Rome.

FACTS 4 PILGRIMS

St. Mark's Gospel might just as well be called the Gospel of Peter because it was Simon Peter who dictated it to Mark. Still, Mark was one of the chosen 70 and the founder of the important Church of Alexandria, Egypt. It is believed that Mark fell away from Christ after hearing Him say that His followers must eat His flesh and drink His blood. But after Christ's Ascension, Peter brought Mark back to the faith.

Through the centuries, the relics of St. Mark have been subjected to deceptions worthy of a spy novel. In 828, Venetian merchants were eager to boost the image of their beloved homeland. So, they concocted one of history's greatest heists: stealing the body of St. Mark from Alexandria. Their scheme might have failed if they had not wisely prepared to deter Muslim ship inspectors by covering the saint's remains with pork. Today, St. Mark's scattered remains are in Venice, Alexandria and Cairo.

Piazza Venezia takes its name from the Venetian Cardinal, Pietro Barbo (later Pope Paul II) who built Palazzo Venezia (above) next to the church of Saint Mark, the patron saint of Venice. It became the embassy of the Republic of Venice in Rome and, in 1469, a papal residence. Later, Benito Mussolini maintained his offices there, delivering some of his most important speeches from its balcony, including his declaration of a new Italian empire on May 9, 1936. Today, this square seems to be at the heart of Rome's activity as everything from scooters to tour buses zip through the intersection amidst remnants of centuries past. This is Rome's seamless blending of old and new, from Trajan's Forum and Column (ca. 113 AD) to the dominating monument (below) to King Vittorio Emanuele II. Completed in 1925, Italians now disparagingly call it "the wedding cake," "the typewriter" or, worst of all, "English soup."

PAPAL TITLES
1. Bishop of Rome
2. Vicar of Christ
3. Holy See
4. Pontifex Maximus
5. Successor to the Prince of the Apostles
6. Sovereign Pontiff of the Universal Church
7. Archbishop and Metropolitan of the Province of Rome
8. Sovereign of the Vatican City-State
9. Servant of God's Servants
10. Patriarch of the West
11. Primate of Italy
12. Pope or Papa

Part Four: Pilgrim Walking Tour of Vatican City

View of
St. Peter's Basilica Dome
From Aventine Hill

Via Bernardino Telesio
Via Trionfale
Viale delle Milizie
Via Famagosta
Via Otranto
Ottaviano
Via Mocenigo
Via Toderache
Via Candia
Via Candia
Via Vespasiano
Via Germanico
Via Catone
Via Cipro
Via Cipro
Cipro
Via della Meloria
Via Ruggero Fiore
Via Francesco Sivori
Viale Vaticano
Via Luigi Rizzo
Via Sebastiano Ziani
Via Giorgio Scalia
Via Simoni

5

Horto Anglii
7

Stradone dei Giardini
Via Pius X
Via della Posta
Via della Tipografia
Via di Belvedere
Via del Mascherino

Civitas Vaticana
6

Via Fundatum
Via dell'Osservatorio

4 † **3**

Piazza San Pietro
2

Via Tunica
1

Via Paolo VI

Viale Vaticano
Città del Vaticano
Via Nicolò V
Via Aurelia

Galleria Principe Amedeo Savoia - Aosta
Via delle Fornaci

Via Paolo III
Via di villa Albercl
Santa Maria Mediatrice

Via Paolo II

Via Innocenzo III

Via delle Fornaci

Pon
Col
Ame
del

Via Gregori
Roma San Pietro

Map Labels

Luciano Manara
Viale Giulio Cesare
Lepanto
Via degli Scipioni
Via Giulio Cesare
Via degli Scipioni
Via Ezio
Via Pomp
Via Fabio Massimo
Via Paolo Emilio
Via dei Gracchi
Via Germanico
Prati
Via Cola di Rienzo
Via Pinio
Via Virginio
Via Boezio
Via Terenzio
Via Boezio
Via Boezio
Via Ovidio
Via Cassiodoro
Via Tacito
Via Crescenzio
Via Tacito
Via Albenico II
Piazza Adriana
Piazza Cavour
Ponte Cavo
Borgo Vittorio
Parco Adriano
Palazzo di Giustizia
Via Ulpiano
10
Borgo
Borgo Pio
Piazza Adriana
Battelli di Roma
Lungotevere Mar
8
9
Ponte Umberto
Via di Monte Brianzo
Via della Conciliazione
Ponte Sant'Angelo
Tevere
Via dell'Orso
Lungotevere Tor di Nona
Borgo Santo Spirito
Ponte Vittorio Emanuele
Via Paola
Via di Panico
Via dei Coronari
Ponte
Ponte Principe Amedeo

Walking Tour 12: The Grand Tour around Vatican City

1. Popular Vatican bus stop
2. Piazza di San Pietro
3. Basilica di San Pietro
4. Cupola di San Pietro
5. Entrance to Vatican Museums
6. Sistine Chapel
7. Vatican Gardens
8. Santa Maria in Traspontina
9. Castel Sant'Angelo
10. Sacro Cuore del Suffragio

Practical Tips 4 Pilgrims

1. The most popular transport for Vatican pilgrim's is Bus #64. (Notice, however, when heading back to your hotel, the returning bus stop is very near the tunnel's entrance.) Or, at Piazza Cavour, which is much closer to the 10th and final attraction on this tour, busses and taxis are plentiful. (Beware of pickpockets on Bus #64 and in the Sistine Chapel, especially when crowded.)

2. The best Metro stops are 10 minute walks from the Basilica. You can locate Cipro and Ottaviano (closest) on the left side of this map.

3. Museum lines can be extremely long, so it is very wise to purchase advance tickets, online. Prepaid ticket holders are granted access at the front of the line. Walk to the museum entrance (#5), outside the ancient wall, past those who are waiting without tickets.

4. Clearly, this is another tour that is not meant to be limited to a half day. Fortunately, shops and attractions, here, are not closed for the traditional mid-day riposo.

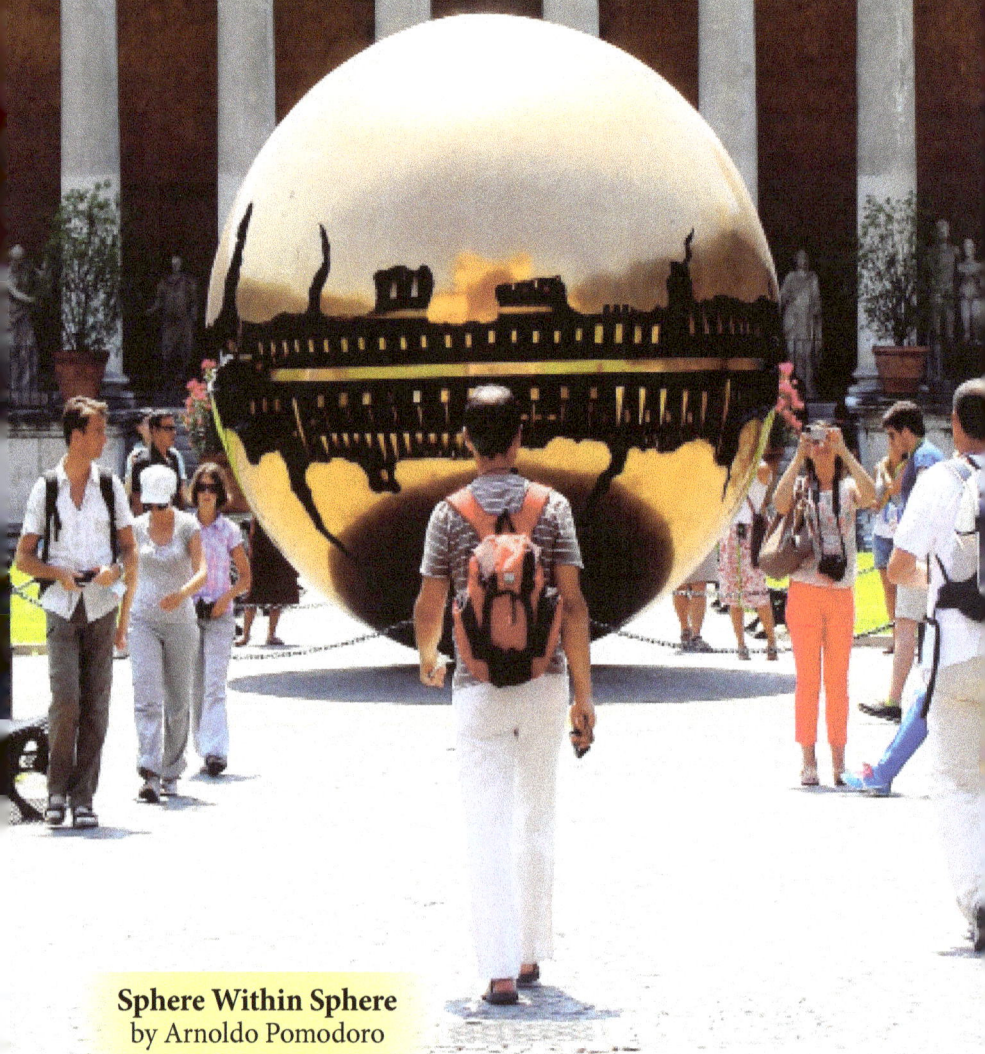

PIVS · VII · P · M · FECIT · AN · XXII ·

"THERE ARE THREE WAYS A MAN CAN RUIN HIMSELF: WOMEN, GAMBLING AND FARMING. MY FATHER CHOSE THE MOST BORING WAY." Pope John XXIII, musing on his family's impoverished roots

Sphere Within Sphere
by Arnoldo Pomodoro

STATO DELLA CITTÀ DEL VATICANO
STATE OF VATICAN CITY

VATICAN FAST FACTS
4 PILGRIMS

For countless reasons, the State of Vatican City is like no other sovereign nation. For the sake of brevity, however, we will attempt to identify just a few examples:

- The Vatican is the geographical headquarters for approximately 1.2 billion Catholics, worldwide, but is the smallest country on earth. It is only 70% the size of the Mall in Washington DC. Some golf courses are larger.
- From the 6th century to the latter half of the 19th, the pope was sovereign over the Papal States which, at their zenith, spanned the width of the Italian peninsula, at its mid-section.
- After the Italian peninsula became a unified kingdom in 1861, almost all papal lands were taken. It was not until the Lateran Treaty of 1929 that the tiny Vatican City State was formed with the protection of international law. (Many have argued that the Church's substantial loss of territory was actually a blessing, allowing the pope to eject many of the trappings and customs of temporal, territorial rulers for a more universal message.)
- Though the Vatican is relatively new, the Holy See was established early in the Christian era, representing the authority, jurisdiction, and sovereignty vested in the pope and his advisers to direct the faith and morals of the worldwide Roman Catholic Church.
- Technically, the Holy See, not the Vatican, maintains international relations and has diplomatic ties with 174 countries.
- At this time, approximately 1,000 residents and five dogs live within the walls of Vatican City and none of them are considered permanent residents. Every cardinal automatically gains Vatican citizenship, regardless of where he lives. The country has fewer citizens than the number of members of the U.S. Congress.
- Though women live in Vatican City, no baby has ever been born within the country's borders. It is the only nation with a birth rate of zero.
- Canon law requires that the altar of each Catholic church or chapel must enclose a relic. So, the Apostolic Palace holds one of the world's most unusual libraries. In shelves and cabinets, from floor to ceiling, relics of saints and martyrs, dating to the earliest Christian centuries, are preserved for inclusion into new altars.
- The Vatican is the only country in the world that closes every night. The gates are shut at 11:30 P.M., each evening. All non-residents must leave, by then, and residents must receive pre-approval to return home after closing.
- The Vatican maintains a fire department, with 20 firefighters on duty, continuously. However, not a single fire has needed to be extinguished for over a century.
- The Vatican railroad is the shortest in the world, traversing just 2,600 feet. It has no set departure schedule.
- The Vatican Post Office dates from the 1300s, when pontifical messages were delivered by horseback. Today, they handle millions of letters and post cards every year, and have earned a reputation of being more dependable than the Italian postal service.
- Only two industries operate in the State of Vatican City: making mosaics and issuing postage stamps.
- By 1886, the Vatican had installed the world's first central telephone system. It now has more telephones per capita than any other nation or city.
- Though a benevolent one, the pope is an absolute monarch, and citizens have no right to vote. He is transported in Mercedes Benzes with license plate SCV1.
- The Vatican is said to have the happiest citizens on earth because this country levies no taxes. Even the VAT tax that is so common around Europe does not apply because the Vatican does not belong to the European Union. Payroll deductions for workers are limited to those for pensions and insurance.
- Gas is sold at the country's two petrol stations for about 30% less than in the rest of Italy.
- The Vatican is the world's only nation that has no ethnic makeup.
- Vatican Museums employ just 450, compared to 2,000 employees at the Louvre. They receive no government subsidies, making them an extreme museum rarity in being able to cover expenses solely from admission ticket sales.
- The Vatican Library is arguably the most important one in the world because it houses many one-of-a-kind works. All totalled, it contains over a million books, almost 100,000 manuscripts, and over 100,000 historic maps and engravings. Its archives requires over 16 miles of shelves. This library is only open to accredited scholars.
- This is the world's only country with a border that can be walked within 60 minutes.

Piazza di San Pietro

St. Peter's Square

This piazza is one of Bernini's most appreciated master-pieces. At the lower end, it consists of two semi-circular colonnades, forming an ellipse that is 790 feet wide. Nearer to the basilica, the piazza forms into a rectangle, until three flights of stairs lead pilgrims to the basilica's entrance.

The striking design of the colonnades is meant to convey a sense of awe to incoming visitors, while symbolizing the church's outstretched arms, welcoming the world. It is said that the piazza can accomodate over 300,000.

Obelisk History 4 Pilgrims

This red granite obelisk (left) would have been one of the last things seen by St. Peter, before execution. In 37 AD, Caligula – one of Rome's most decadent emperors – had it brought from Hierapolis, Egypt, where it might have stood since 1800 BC. He placed it in the arena he was constructing that became known as Nero's Circus, where numerous Christians eventually would be slaughtered.

In 1586, Pope Sixtus V decided to have the monolith moved to its current location, some 825 feet away. The delicate procedure (below) took six months to plan and four to execute. On the day of its erection, 40 winches, 80 horses, and 800 workers were assigned to the task. During the raising of the unwieldy giant, Pope Sixtus issued strict orders for silence, under penalty of death. But when the lift proceeded with difficulty, the lines began to smoke from friction. An exasperated sailor could not restrain himself from screaming a solution: "Throw water on the ropes! Throw water on the ropes!" The suggestion worked, and his shouted guidance saved the obelisk from certain damage. So, instead of execution, he was given a papal reward: the right to supply the basilica with palms, every Palm Sunday. It is said that his descendants continue the practice to this day.

The small globe at the peak of the obelisk is believed to have once contained the ashes of Julius Caesar. However, Pope Alexander VII added a cross on top, with a relic of the True Cross inside it. A Latin inscription at the base of the obelisk translates into: "Christ conquers. Christ reigns. Christ commands."

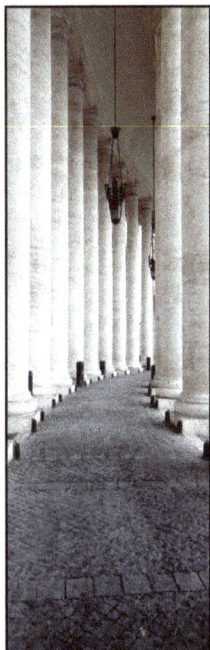

PIAZZA TRIVIA 4 PILGRIMS

Each colonnade has four rows of Doric columns, forming three corridors. The center lane (left) was wide enough to welcome the world's carriages, even up to the guarded door of the Papal Palace (right). The Piazza's colonnades consist of 284 columns and 88 pilasters. Overhead, 88 giant statues of saints look down upon the daily stream of tourists, but pilgrims can spot a total of 153 statues within view of the Piazza. The center of attention, however, is the 135 foot obelisk memorial that commemorates St. Peter's execution.

The piazza's sights and sounds are enhanced by two lovely fountains. They are 46 feet tall. This one (right) dates from at least 1492. It was later rebuilt by Bernini. On the opposite side of the obelisk, a duplicate of this fountain was consructed by Carlo Fontana.

In the background of the fountain (right) we see not only Bernini's colonnade, but the Apostolic Palace. From one of these windows, the pope traditionally addressed large crowds for his papal audiences.

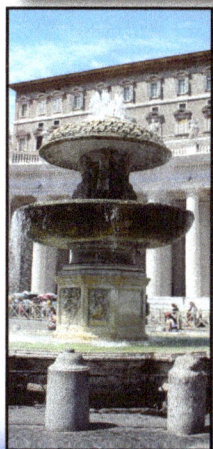

FUN 4 LITTLE PILGRIMS

Circling the St. Peter's obelisk, try to find the 16 stone markers (below, left) that identify wind direction from points on a compass. This monument can also serve as a sun dial. A stone marker (middle), identifies the exact spot where the shadow of the obelisk's cross will fall, at sunrise every June 22nd. (That is the longest day, each year, known as the summer solstice.) Finally, between each fountain and the monument, two *Centro del Colonnato* markers (right) identify where best to stand when viewing a colonnade. From here, all columns line up precisely behind each other so that only the front row is visible.

CUPOLA DI SAN PIETRO
DOME OF ST. PETER'S
DAILY: 8 - 6 (4:45, OCT - MAR) ADMISSION: 7€ W. ELEVATOR; 6€, W/O)

St. Peter's Basilica is so well proportioned that tourists often forget the immensity of its scale. For example, this arrow is not pointing at ants, but hundreds of people. ■■■>

Ascending to the top of the dome, tourists find a wide variety of stairs. However, as one reaches the higher levels, the passageway not only narrows (left and right), but the walls begin to conform to the curvature of the outer dome (left).

Along the way, a convenient rest stop is on the platform that encircles the lower portion of the inner dome (below). There, tourists have a bird's eye view of the basilica and an up-close view of the dome. We see, for example, the four Gospel Evangelists (below, right). Surprisingly, these mosaic medalions are 29 feet in diameter, and St. Matthew's pen is a whopping 8 feet long.

DOME TIPS 4 PILGRIMS

To control overcrowding, a 6€ admission fee is charged for stairway access to the top of the dome. Tickets can be purchased to the far right of the basilica's main entrance. For 1€ more, pilgrims may opt to use the elevator. That offer sounds great to those who seek an easy route to the top. However, by one calculation, the elevator only eliminates 171 steps, leaving 420 still to climb. Since sightseers are not allowed to turn around, only attempt the dome if you are ready for a moderately tiring ascent in exchange for a spectacular view.

BASILICA DI SAN PIETRO
ST. PETER'S BASILICA
DAILY: 7 - 7 (CLOSES AT 6, OCT - MAR)

Admission to St. Peter's Basilica is free of charge, just as with all Catholic churches around Rome. So, every year, more than 10 million tourists – of every religious persuasion – become invited guests, welcome to enjoy some of the world's greatest art and architecture. With that in mind, guests should remember that to Catholics this basilica is not just a tourist attraction. It is sacred ground. Therefore, proper dress (see below) and behavior are expected.

On their way to the basilica, pilgrims might notice the central balcony of the facade (right). This is the spot where every new pope is introduced to the world. As he approaches the elevated window, he first sees the cross, perched atop St. Peter's obelisk. Then, moving closer to the window, the cheering faithful.

Before entering the basilica, tourists pass through a wide portico (left) that was completed in 1612. This portico, alone, is larger than some of the world's cathedrals. At one end, to the right, sits Bernini's equestrian statue depicting Constantine at the moment he saw the Sign of the Cross in the sky and heard, "In this Sign, you will conquer." To the far left is another equestrian statue of Charlemagne, the first emperor to be crowned in the Old St. Peter's Basilica.

Though visitors enter the basilica (right) through the center doors, the front of the church has five ornate doors, symbolizing the five most grievous wounds of Christ's passion. The beautifully panelled door farthest to the right is the Holy Door (left) that is only opened by the Pope each Holy Year. Behind, it is sealed with bricks and mortar until the ceremony that begins each Holy Year. The central bronze doors – along with the pilasters at the sides of the first, third and fifth doors – are from the earlier basilica.

In the first century, over the pauper's grave of St. Peter, Pope Anacletus built an oratory. In the fourth century, however, Constantine replaced the humble memorial with the first grand basilica dedicated to the martyred apostle. Twelve centuries later, that church had fallen into a state of disrepair, prompting Julius II to do the unthinkable: level the structure in which numerous popes, saints and martyrs had been buried, to make room for the largest church in Christendom. Eventually, the audacious project consumed 120 years, 18 popes and 12 master architects. This basilica contains 10 domes, 11 chapels, 45 altars, nearly 500 columns, and over 430 large statues. The church floorplan covers nearly 430,000 square feet – roughly the size of six football fields – and can accomodate up to 80,000 congregants for the offering of Holy Mass.

BALDACCHIN TRIVIA
4 PILGRIMS

The spiral bronze columns are a grand imitation of the ones that surrounded St. Peter's tomb in the old basilica. However, their four marble bases conceal a bit of humor. Each one displays a feminine face with increasing expressions of pain until, finally, a look of excitement. They represent the pain of labor and the joy of birth. Bernini had not only honored his patron, Pope Urban VIII, by incorporating his coat of arms into the design, but also honored the pope's neice who was nearing childbirth at the time of the *baldacchin's* completion.

BALDACCHIN TRIVIA 4 PILGRIMS

Bernini's magnificent *baldacchin* – 96 feet tall – is undoubtedly a masterpiece, but it was not produced without criticism. When the artist requested 200,000 pounds of bronze for its construction, Pope Urban VIII (from the Barberini family) ordered the metal be taken from the ceiling of the Pantheon's portico. After centuries of enduring barbarian invasions and pillaging, disapproving Romans quipped, "What the barbarians didn't do, the Barberini did!"

BASILICA TRIVIA 4 PILGRIMS

Referring to the massive support structures of St. Peter's dome (above, left and right), and eager to find his first independent commission, master architect Francesco Borromini once boasted, "Give me just the area of one of these pilasters, and I shall create a sizable church." The offer was accepted in 1634 by the Spanish Trinitarians, a shoeless (discalced) order of monks that worked to free Christians who had been kidnapped by Muslim pirates. The result was Rome's charming little church known as San Carlino in Quattro Fontane (see p. 110), said to have been built to the precise dimensions of one of this dome's supporting piers.

BASILICA DI SAN PIETRO

Inside the basilica's main entrance, a large prophyry disk has been inserted into the pavement. It was once located in front of the main altar in the old basilica. On Christmas day, in the year 800, Charlemagne knelt on it as he was anointed and crowned Holy Roman Emperor.

The papal altar is not directly under the dome (right) but exactly over the tomb of St. Peter (left), as it was in the old basilica. On this altar, only the pope can offer Mass or, in rare circumstances, a cardinal he deputes.

St. Peter's famous dome was not a part of the basilica's original design. Its dominance causes tourists to forget that this church has 9 more beautiful domes (left and right).

Donato Bramante, the first architect, chose a Greek cross floorplan, with four arms of equal length. Raphael, his successor, introduced a major change, designing a Latin cross with an extended nave. He eventually won in the end. However, over its 120 years of construction, the basilica's 12 architects vacillated 6 times between the 2 designs.

The interior length of the basilica is 611 feet, and the height of the nave (left) is 145 feet. In the floor of the nave, bronze markers indicate the length of other world-famous churches. The shortest is St. Patrick's Cathedral in New York, barely more than half the length of this basilica.

The four massive pilasters that support the basilica's dome were decorated by Bernini with the intent of highlighting some of the holiest relics possessed by the Church. The 16' 6" statues (from left to right, above) depict Longinus (by Bernini) holding the Holy Lance, St. Helena (by Andrea Bolgi) supporting the True Cross, St. Veronica (by Francesco Mochi) displaying the veil with Christ's image, and St. Andrew (by Francois Duquesnoy) gripping the cross upon which he was crucified. Of these, only Andrew's relic is not obvious. His head was preserved here until 1964, when it was returned to the Greek Orthodox Church. In addition to their structural purpose, the piers serve as repositories for the relics. In 1506, Julius II laid the basilica's cornerstone, under the Veronica pilaster.

A TALE OF TWO TOMBS

If any single man deserves credit for igniting the Roman Renaissance and initiating construction of the greatest church in Christendom, it would be the doggedly determined Pope Julius II (see p. 28). Once constructed, he planned that the basilica would hold one of the world's most spectacular tombs: his own. So Julius engaged Michelangelo to design and sculpt a magnificent sepulcher, along with 40 large statues. Michelangelo knew that that one project could consume an artist's entire lifetime, but Julius left the obedient sculptor no choice in the matter.

Today, the tomb includes the famous *Moses* masterpiece, but no Julius. Pilgrims who visit the monument, at San Pietro in Vincoli (see p. 104), see that it is undoubtedly grand, but significantly less than the one Julius had envisioned. That is because Michelangelo was released from further work on it after the pope's death.

So, where was the body of the demanding pontiff laid to rest? Far forward, near the right corner of St. Peter's Basilica, is evidence of a grand irony. In the pavement, a simple stone marks the buried sarcophagus of Pope Sixtus IV. It is shared with his nephew, Pope Julius II. Among the 148 former popes buried here, the tomb of Julius is one of the least noticed.

One of the access points to the Vatican Grottoes is near the pilaster statue of St. Andrew (pictured left, far right). There, under the basilica, is an extensive network of tombs, chapels, statues and artworks. A red wall identifies the ancient burial site of St. Peter. The grottoes also include columns and a wall from the 4th century basilica as well as a 3rd century statue of St. Peter, seated. All totalled, 148 former popes are buried in this area.

The basilica's many works of art, such as the one pictured (left), are not fragile oil paintings or even frescoes. They are all mosaics, designed to endure the ages. Though this church is packed with outstanding statuary, two of the most popular are Michangelo's marble *Pietà* (below) and Arnolfo di Cambio's 13th century bronze *St. Peter* (right). As an act of veneration, pilgrims traditionally touch the foot of the great apostle. Now, after millions of such contacts, St. Peter has the shiniest toes in Rome!

Pietà Trivia 4 Pilgrims

Michelangelo Buonarroti was just 24 when he completed his moving masterpiece called *Pietà*. After spending two years on the project, the young sculptor was justifiably proud of his extraordinary artistic accomplishment. Soon after its unveiling, however, he overheard a conversation between admiring spectators who credited another artist, one Michelangelo considered an inferior. That night, he returned to his masterpiece and sculpted a sash across the Madonna's chest, proclaiming in Latin, "Michelangelo Buonarroti, Florentine, made this." He regretted his prideful outburst, and the *Pietà* remains his only signed work.

On at least two occasions, the priceless *Pietà* has sustained damage. In 1736, four fingers on the Virgin Mary's hand were broken during a move. Scholars are divided on whether the restoration by Giuseppe Lirioni precisely recreated the original gesture. The worst damage, however, occurred in 1972. It was on Pentecost Sunday when a disturbed geologist walked up to the unprotected statue and began attacking it with a geologist's hammer while shouting, "I am Jesus Christ!" Horrified onlookers gathered up the hammered chunks of historic marble. Some were returned to the Church; many were not. In the painstaking restoration, Blessed Mother's fingers, nose and chin were reconstructed, partly from stone cut out of the back of the statue. Today, bullet-proof acrylic panels protect the *Pietà*.

THE PONTIFICAL SWISS GUARD
OF THE HOLY SEE

The Pontifical Swiss Guard was formed by Pope Julius II, who was also known as "The Warrior Pope." He hired 150 Swiss soldiers in January of 1506, the year construction of the new St. Peter's Basilica began. The Guard is responsible for the safety of the Pope, as well as the security of the Papal Palace. It is the oldest military corps in existence.

On May 6, 1527, the Swiss Guard was nearly wiped out when, under orders from the Spanish Emperor Charles V, 10,000 German and Spanish mercenaries stormed the Vatican at the beginning of the infamous sack of Rome. On that day, 147 out of 189 Guards defended and died, while Pope Clement VII escaped to the *Castel Sant'Angelo* with his surviving Guardsmen. The site of the battle is memorialized to the left of St. Peter's Basilica in the area called *Campo Santo Teutonico* (The German Graveyard). In modern times, May 6 continues to be the day of initiation for new Guardsmen.

Another famous conflict occurred near the close of the 18th century. When Napoleon Bonaparte invaded the Papal States and occupied Ancona and Loreto, Pope Pius VI successfully negotiated a peace agreement with him. But within months, Napoleon found a pretext to invade Rome. Rather than witness a slaughter of the Swiss Guards against a superior military force, the pope ordered the Guard to lay down their arms. Victory, however, was not enough for Napoleon and he demanded that the pope renounce all temporal power over the region. When the pope refused, he was taken prisoner and confined until his death, six months later. Napoleon left the body unburied for five months, until he saw advantage in ordering a funeral.

In 1804, Pope Pius VII attempted to mend fences by attending Napoleon's coronation. However, among other humiliations, Napoleon's crown was found to be ornamented with large emeralds, previously looted from the papal tiara. Eventually, relations grew even worse and when Pius excommunicated Napoleon, troops imprisoned the pope. For six years, the sickly Pius was shuttled from one place of confinement to another.

When Napoleon finally fell, the Papal States were largely restored. Turning the other cheek, Pius offered refuge in Rome to Napoleon's family. His mother, two brothers and an uncle accepted. The pope also wrote the British government, requesting better treatment of the former emperor in captivity: "He can no longer be a danger to anybody. We would not wish him to become a cause for remorse."

The Guardsman directing traffic (above) is in regular duty uniform. Contrary to popular myth, the extravagant dress uniforms were not designed by Michelangelo or Raphael. Instead, they are the product of the imagination of an early 20th century Vatican seamstress.

The corps of the Swiss Guards consists of roughly 135 men between the ages of 18 and 25. The pay is low, the hours are long, the work can be monotonous, and the restrictions on personal freedoms are greater than in any other army. Thus, these outstanding young men are truly sacrificing their comfort and convenience for the service of God and His Church on earth. In the spirit of good will, they occasionally offer to pose for pictures with children (below).

SWISS GUARD TRIVIA

Throughout the long history of the Guard, popes have differed greatly in their manner and style. Sometimes, the transitions have not been easy to predict. In 1758, for example, the Swiss Guards turned away a humble friar from the coronation of Clement XIII. Eleven years later, upon his ascent to become Pope Clement XIV, the Franciscan quipped, "I fully enjoyed the coronation. This time the Swiss Guards let me in!"

SISTINE TIPS 4 PILGRIMS

Pilgrims who are short on time can take a little-known shortcut into the Sistine Chapel. After passing through the Gallery of Maps, then the Gallery of Tapestries, do not turn left with the crowds. Instead, go straight, heading into and through an undecorated hallway that takes you to the front of the line, at the entrance to the Sistine Chapel. By taking this route, you will miss the excellent Raphael Rooms, but save a lot of time for the crown jewel of Vatican art. While inside, however, watch out for pickpockets.

MUSEI VATICANI
VATICAN MUSEUMS
MON - SAT: 9 - 6; LAST MON OF EVERY MONTH: 9 - 2

The Catholic Church is history's greatest patron of art. The Church also has served humanity by being at the forefront of artistic preservation and restoration. Even modern archeology owes a great debt to the Church's role in developing its field of exploration.

So, it is not surprising that the Vatican Museums encompass the largest museum complex in the world, with over 1,400 rooms, and arguably the greatest collection. It is said that one will walk 9 miles to see it all. By one calculation, viewing the collection item by item, one minute at a time, would require 14 years. That may be an exaggeration – others claim only 4 – however, it might be a worthwhile endeavor, considering the collection spans 3,000 years of the world's greatest art and architecture.

The Vatican Museums include the following famous art collections:
- Egyptian and Assyrian;
- Etruscan and other pre-Roman;
- Greek and Roman;
- Early Christian and Medieval;
- Renaissance;
- Modern religious;
- The Sistine Chapel;
- The Raphael rooms.

It may be the only museum in the world in which the gift shop (left) looks this magnificent!

Ornate barrel vault
in the Geographic Chart Hall

TIP 4 PILGRIMS
Advance ticket purchases or guided tours are highly recommended because lines for same-day purchases range from long to excruciatingly long. Usually, lines are shorter in the afternoon. Additional tourist information can be found at the following two websites:
- http://saintpetersbasilica.org/touristinfo.htm
- http://mv.vatican.va/3_EN/pages/MV_Home.html

The Vatican collections not only span three millennia, but seemingly every medium of artistic expression. The Raphael tapestries (opposite page, below) were the rage of Rome in their day. Caravaggio's paintings, on the other hand (right), did not receive their deserved praise until modern times. Though only dating from 1932, even the museum's double spiral staircase by Giuseppe Momo (see page 167) becomes a classic work of art. Frescoed cherubs (below) were painstakingly relocated from a Roman church. Finally, could it be that this sculpture (left) depicts an average ancient Roman waiting for the bus?

The greatest works of art have great stories to back them up. *Laocoön and His Sons* (below), is a good example. In Greek and Roman mythology, Laocoön was the priest of Troy who warned against accepting the Trojan Horse from enemy Greeks. He insisted that they burn the wooden gift. However, neither the Trojans nor the gods listened to him anymore. In fact, the gods resented that Laocoön had insulted them. So, they not only blinded him, but dispatched two sea serpents to destroy Laocoön and his two sons. This famous 1st century sculpture is the work of three Rhodian artists. It is just one example that, even outside the realm of Christian art, the Vatican Museums are some of the best in the world.

"DO NOT TRUST THE HORSE, TROJANS. WHATEVER IT IS, I FEAR THE GREEKS, EVEN BEARING GIFTS."

Laocoön

At the dawn of the 16th century, Pope Julius II planted in Rome the Renaissance that had flowered in Florence. However, Julius was no gardener. The "Warrior Pope" planned to engage the arts as if conducting a war. This Spiritual batttle would be fought with new weapons: architecture and Biblical images.

Julius possessed a talent for identifying artistic genius and motivating productivity. So, after directing Bramante to design the greatest church in Christendom, he pitted Raphael and Michelangelo against each other in a not-so-friendly competition at different ends of the papal property. Young Raphael eagerly accepted his task to create images in four papal apartments (bottom of page) that would convey the continuity of classical philosophy and Christianity in their common goal of finding Truth. However, the more temperamental Michelangelo balked at his Sistine assignment. The famed sculptor complained that he was not a painter. But Julius left him no choice, suggesting that the ceiling be covered with twelve images of the apostles. Perhaps the simplicity of the papal suggestion invigorated Michelangelo's competitive instincts. He returned to Julius with drawings and ideas that foreshadowed the immense masterpiece we see today (opposite page).

Michelangelo spent four years on his back, alone, painting the barrel vaulted ceiling. He was invited back 24 years later to paint the altar wall. So, from Creation to Last Judgment, the great artist's work spanned the entire human drama in this life. Raphael and his associates spent 16 years on the papal apartments, finishing after the mentor's death.

The most iconic hands ever painted (above): the drooping finger of Adam accepts God's purposeful touch. The Creator, powerful and fatherly, while exchanging embraces with His loving creatures, is wrapped in a maroon shroud that forms the shape of man's brain. Adam, in his nakedness before God, is handsome and strong, but indifferent and perhaps even lazy. It is just one of the Sistine's many unforgettable images.

SISTINE TIPS 4 PILGRIMS

On the ceiling, all subjects are from the Old Testament except the Sibyls (left), who were said to have prophesied the birth of Christ. Here is a basic key to Sistine art:
Front wall:
>   The Last Judgment.
The right wall, beginning at front:
>   Scenes from Christ's life.
The left wall, beginning at front:
>   Scenes from the life of Moses.
Center ceiling, beginning at front:
>   Three stories of Noah;
>   Three stories of the Downfall;
>   Three stories of Creation.
Surrounding panels:
>   Prophets and Sibyls.
Lower surrounding panels:
>   Ancestors of Jesus.

SISTINE TRIVIA
4 PILGRIMS

The wall on which the Last Judgment was frescoed had two windows in it. Not only did Michelangelo fill the windows, but he had the wall modified to slope a few inches inward so dust would not settle on his fresco, over time, diminishing its pristine appearance.

SISTINE TRIVIA 4
PILGRIMS

Michelangelo was focused and driven. During the four years it took him to paint the Sistine ceiling, he often slept in his boots and sustained himself on a diet of stale bread and onions. In a letter to his father, he wrote, "I have no friends and don't want any."

Botanico Giardini Vaticano

Vatican Gardens

Guided Tours Only, Arranged Through Vatican Museums

No other nation can boast that almost half its land is dedicated to gardens. The Vatican Gardens originated in the Middle Ages. Filled with fountains, trees and shady natural settings this is a restful place to restore serenity after a hectic day queuing with tourists.

It began under Pope Boniface VIII at the beginning of the 14th century, when medicinal herbs were cultivated here. By the end of that century, though, enthusiastic papal successors expanded the gardens, making them among the most important in Europe.

In 1559, Pope Pius IV built in the gardens his summer house, or *casina*. It is a lovely, beige stucco gem in an idyllic setting, once called "a perfect image of an ancient Roman country house." There, Pius would conduct *Notti Vaticane* – Vatican Evenings – with discussions of art, poetry, philosophy and theology.

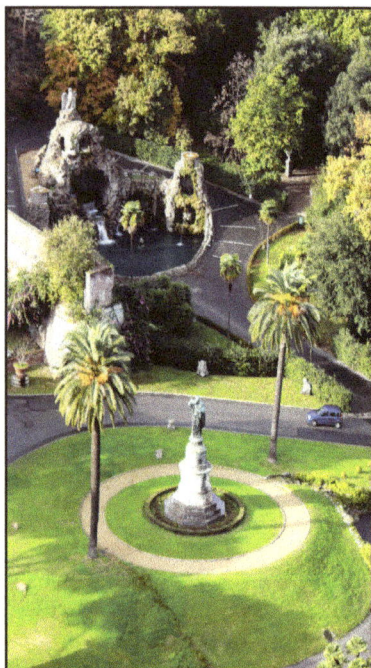

Tips 4 Pilgrims

If you wish to walk in the footsteps of popes past, the Vatican Gardens are only seen through guided tours, arranged through the Vatican Museums. For more information, visit: www.MuseiVaticani.va and click the Guided Tours/Vatican Gardens link. Tours are not available Wednesdays and Sundays.

Through the centuries, popes have strolled these grounds, reciting the rosary, saying prayers or practicing their speeches. However, not all popes were interested in the gardens, and some let them deteriorate. After Pope Leo XIII died, in 1903, the gardens experienced a decade of decline. But by 1914, Benedict XV reestablished their former beauty.

Vatican History 4 Pilgrims

Among the historic documents preserved in the Vatican archives is a parchment petition from King Henry VIII. The manuscript is roughly two feet by three feet, in size, and contains the ribbons and wax seals of its 75 signatories. In it, the love-sick king requests papal approval for a divorce from his wife, Catherine of Aragon. Pope Clement VII, however, denied the petition. So, Henry demonstrated his fury by declaring himself the head of a new Church of England, paving the way for his Archbishop of Canterbury to declare the king's marriage unlawful and, thus, illegitimate from the beginning. By then, however, Henry already had married Anne Boleyn who was pregnant with the future Queen Elizabeth I. Unfortunately, though, the honeymoon did not last long. Within 39 months, Anne had been charged, convicted and beheaded for treason, witchcraft, adultery and incest. Not surprisingly, this marriage also was annulled.

SANTA MARIA IN TRASPONTINA

In the shadow of St. Peter's Basilica is a lovely church that many pilgrims hurry past. *Traspontina* probably refers to the church's location, on the other side of the bridge from Rome. The first church that used that name, here, was built by Pope Hadrian I in the 8th century.

Santa Maria in Traspontina is situated on the former site of an ancient Roman pyramid that was said to enclose the tomb of Romulus, Rome's founder. However, during the Sack of Rome in 1527, cannon fire from the *Castel Sant'Angelo* severely damaged the church. Construction of a new one was not initiated until 1566. This time, it was designed without an elevated dome, so that it would never again interfere with defensive bombardments. Its facade was constructed from travertine that came, mostly, from the Colosseum. In 1484, Pope Innocent VIII gave the church to the Carmelite Order, and Calced Carmelites continue to serve this church.

The main altar (left) is both unusual and beautiful. Eight red marble columns support a large marble crown that serves as a *baldacchino*. Over the altar is an image of the Virgin Mary that is especially venerated by the Carmelites. At the beginning of the 13th century, when the Order was forced to leave the Holy Land, the Carmilites carried this image with them on their long, difficult journey back to Europe. The altar was designed by Carlo Fontana and built in 1674.

The 3rd chapel on the left (below) contains an altar painting called *Saints Peter and Paul Bound to Columns*, by Giovanni Battista Ricci. Easy to miss, however, are the less obvious pair of partial columns that stand on each side of the altar. They are said to be columns that Peter and Paul were bound to before scourging and martyrdom.

CASTEL SANT'ANGELO
HOLY ANGEL CASTLE
TUES - SUN: 9 - 7:30; TICKET OFFICE CLOSES AT 6:30

Castel Sant'Angelo was built around 123 AD as a tomb for Emperor Hadrian and his family. Throughout its long life, however, this impressive landmark has evolved from funerary monument, to fortified outpost, to feared prison, to opulent Renaissance residence. Few structures in Rome can attest to the history that this structure has endured. This picture (left) was taken from the top of St. Peter's dome, and includes the famous *Ponte Sant'Angelo,* the bridge that Hadrian completed in 134 AD. Later, in one of Bernini's last large projects, he was commissioned to provide 10 angels, for the bridge, who carry the instruments of Christ's passion (one puctured, below).

In the year 590, a terrible plague was decimating Rome. So, Pope Gregory the Great led a procession of prayer to plead for God's intervention. As they advanced past the enormous tomb of Emperor Hadrian, the pope saw a vision of an angel hovering over it, with sword drawn. Inspired by faith, the pope declared that their prayers had been answered and the epidemic had ended. Indeed, no new cases occurred. In the eighteenth century, a colossal bronze angel, brandishing a sword, was placed on the roof of the *Castel Sant'Angelo* to commemorate the end of the plague.

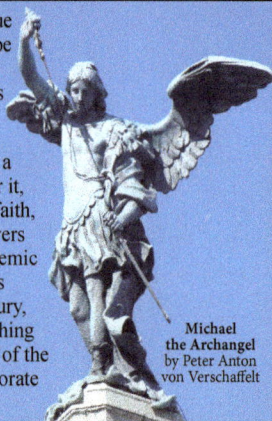

**Michael
the Archangel**
by Peter Anton
von Verschaffelt

In 1527, Pope Clement VII was a man with few powerful friends. He had alienated King Henry VIII by refusing to grant him an annulment of his 18 year marriage. More dangerously, however, he had vacillated between support for military powers, Spain and France, who were competing for dominance in Europe. Closer to home, the Medici pope had roused the hostility of an enemy from within, Cardinal Pompeo Colonna. Now, his defenses against Muslim invasions into Europe from the east and Martin Luther's outrageous propaganda from the north seemed less pressing. Clement feared an imminent attack from predominantly German mercenaries, under the direction of Emperor Charles V.

On May 6, while his Swiss Guard was being wiped out on the steps of St. Peter's Basilica, Clement raced toward the *Castel* via the escape route known as the *Pasetto di Borgo* (left and right, above). Then Rome was sacked worse than any barbarian horde had ever accomplished. Unspeakable rape, slaughter, and sacrilege reigned supreme for 80 days while the pope and 3,000 Romans cowered in the *Castel's* quarters (left, right and below.).

Oblivious to the terrors of 1527, tourists today enjoy a lovely rooftop restaurant (below and right), as they scan exceptional vews of St. Peter's Basilica.

SACRO CUORE DEL SUFFRAGIO
SACRED HEART OF SUFFRAGE
EVERY DAY: 7:30 TO 11 & 2:30 TO 17:30

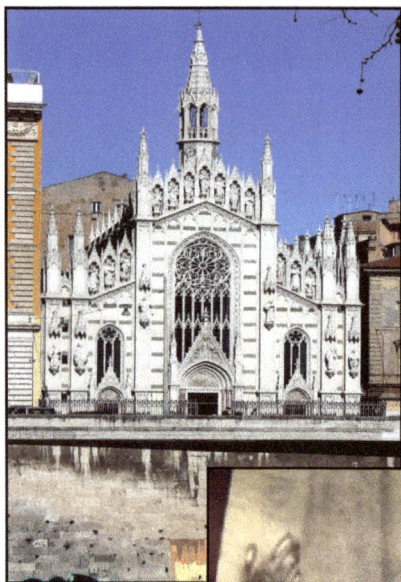

Rising above the banks of the Tiber River, this unusual church stands out in both mission and appearance. *Sacro Cuore del Suffragio* is dedicated not only to the Sacred Heart of Jesus, but to intercessory prayers for souls in Purgatory. Its ornate neo-Gothic facade—more French than Roman in style—is populated by the statues of nineteen saints who were specifically chosen by St. Pius X. Because of its miniaturized similarity to Milan's famous Cathedral, this church is sometimes called *Il Piccolo Duomo di Milano*.

In 1893, Père Victor Jouet, a Missionary of the Sacred Heart, founded in Rome the Association of the Sacred Heart of the Suffrage of Purgatory Souls. Soon after, on this site, a small chapel burned down, leaving behind a scorch mark that some claimed revealed the image of a soul in Purgatory. A new church was then initiated by Pope St. Pius X and, eventually, the new association was officially recognized.

Father Jouet became dedicated to collecting physical evidence (such as the scorched handprint above) as well as witness testimony from seemingly supernatural events that appeared to prove the existence of Purgatory. Now, displaying the result of his efforts, an interesting, small Museum of Purgatory has been established that can be viewed, free of charge, in an area next to the church sacristy. (But it's always nice to leave change for the sacristan.)

Though prayers, here, for the souls of our departed loved ones, feel particularly poignant, the Funeral monument of Monsignor Pietro Benedetti (below) brings us into an even deeper meditation. As a shadowed Blessed Mother tends to her Son's lifeless body, while angels weep, we can not only see, but touch, the sacrificial wounds that prove Christ's unfathomable love.

PART FIVE:
ROME'S PILGRIM SITES, FARTHER AFIELD

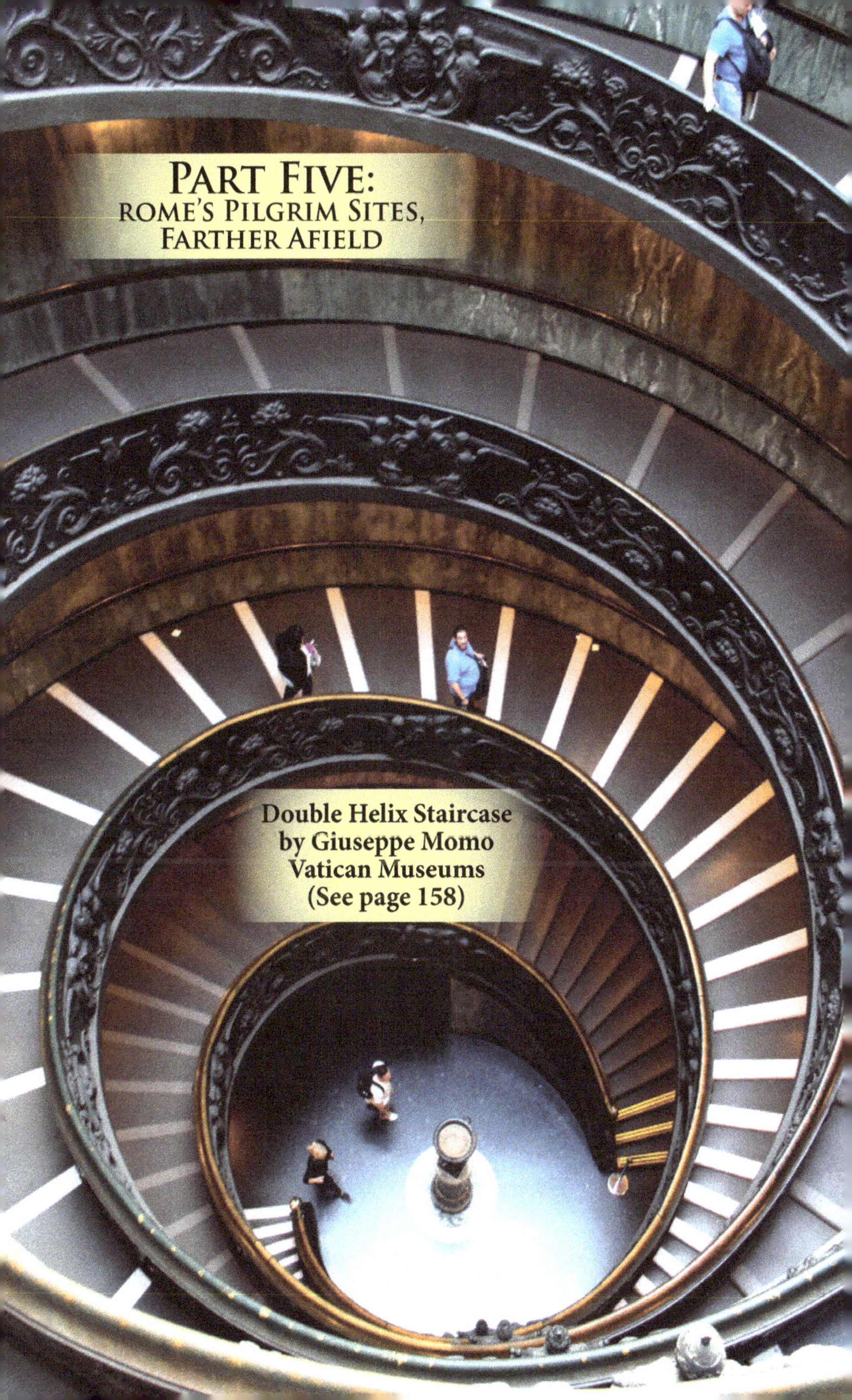

Double Helix Staircase
by Giuseppe Momo
Vatican Museums
(See page 158)

SAN PAOLO FUORI LE MURA

St. Paul's Outside the Walls

DAILY: 7:30 - 6:45

One of Rome's four 'Patriarchal' Churches.
Take Metro Line B to San Paolo stop, then
a 10 minute walk.

In 324, Emperor Constantine ordered construction of a basilica over the hallowed grave of St. Paul. However, an increasing flood of pilgrims soon necessitated a larger church, which was built in 386. This shrine to the great saint survived every challenge for 14 centuries. Neither invasions, sackings, storms, floods, nor malaria stopped the flow of prayerful pilgrims. Then, on the morning of July 15, 1823, fire consumed the sacred shrine.

The tragedy shocked the faithful, but was not revealed to Pope Pius VII because of his declining health. The night before the fire, the pontiff had been disturbed by a nightmare in which a Roman Catholic Church was struck by misfortune. He died four days later, never knowing that his dream had come true.

The faithful were so moved that donations for reconstruction began pouring in from everywhere. Czar Nicholas I of Russia even sent malachite and lapis lazuli for the tabernacle. So, from the generosity of believers around the globe, the basilica we see today was rebuilt, even more beautiful than before. It remains Rome's second largest church.

This magnificent church is a must-see, even though it is a bit farther afield than most pilgrim sites.

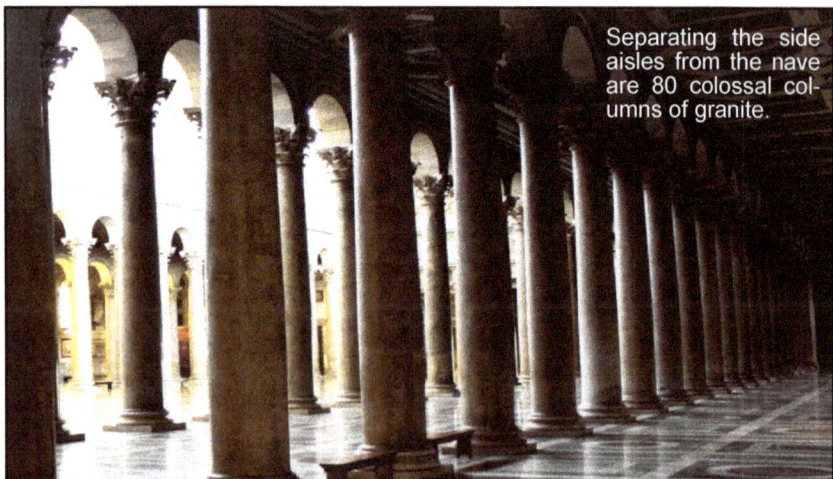

Separating the side aisles from the nave are 80 colossal columns of granite.

ST. PAUL AND EMPEROR NERO

By the time of his latter years, St. Paul's evangelizing had provoked so many accusations and charges in Jerusalem that he, as a Roman citizen, appealed to Rome for justice and protection. Escorted to Rome in a long journey that included a shipwreck, Paul finally arrived in the city of Nero to face Roman justice. There, under military arrest, he wrote some of his epistles and began to play a major role in Rome's early Christian development. However, after two years of restraint, he was acquitted of all charges when his accusers did not appear for his trial. Still, his freedom did not last long. After the great fire of Rome, in 64 AD, Nero identified Paul as a leader of the strange movement he found threatening. Paul was arrested, again, and imprisoned in the filth of the Mamertine (See p. 133) The saint was beheaded outside the gates of Rome in the year 67. An account by St. Clement, the fourth pope, suggests Nero actually watched the execution in which, another tradition says, Paul's dismembered head bounced three times, where three springs instantly emerged. Today, it is the site of the Three Fountains Abbey. Paul's body was moved three kilometers and buried on the property of a Roman matron named Lucina. The grave became a revered destination for early pilgrims, prompting popes and emperors to mark the site with ever-greater monuments to one of the most determined saints. The famously vicious emperor, however, was assassinated a year later and died at the age of 30.

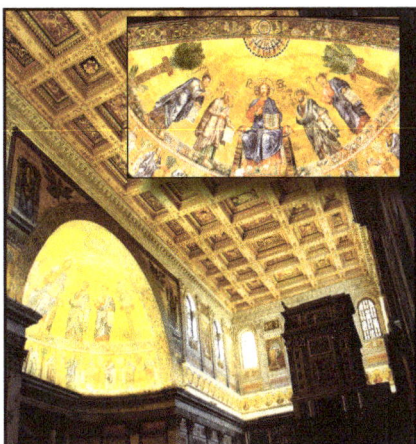

The apse mosaic (above) survived the great fire. It dates from around 1220. To the right of the apse, a famous series of mosaic roundels begins, displaying the image of every pope since Peter. Forty two of the original papal portraits, in fresco, survived the fire. They are now preserved in the adjacent monastery.

Below, is the magnificent nave, the main aisle as it appears today and, inset, as it appeared after the ruinous fire of 1823. (Engraving by Luigi Rossini.) The overall design of the church resembles the shape of a T, with the nave intersecting, at the main altar, with left and right aisles. Exiting through the left doors reveals the north portico, where fire-damaged columns from the ancient basilica were preserved. One of them bears the inscription *"Siricius Episcopus..."* from the pope who consecrated the basilica in 390.

SAN PAOLO LE FUORI MURA

St. Paul's Outside the Walls
Continued

Punctuating the upper walls are 36 frescoes (above) of major points of St. Paul's life. Below them, circular mosaic portraits of every pope line the basilica. The canonized saints, among them, are identified by subtle halos.

From behind the main altar (below), we view a gothic *baldacchin* that dates from 1285, supported by four porphyry columns. Plentiful windows brighten the church, its finely coffered ceiling and colonnaded nave. Under the beautiful baldacchin lies the remains of St. Paul and, nearby, the remains of St. Timothy.

The mosaic of Pope Francis (left) is now highlighted. One legend says that when there is no more space for papal portraits, the end of the age will be near. After the portrait of Pope Francis, only 6 slots remain.

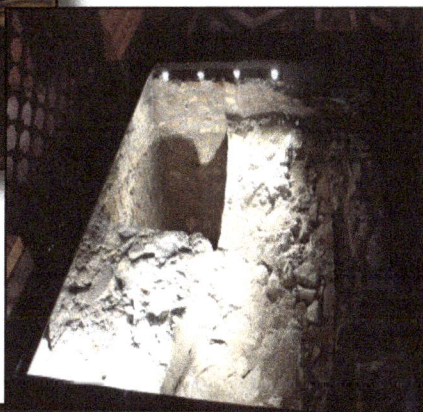

On display are the prison chains (left) that restrained St. Paul in Rome during the last days of his life. They are encased over the saint's sarcophagus that has has been available for viewing since 2006. This grave rests below the main altar, under a marble tombstone bearing the Latin words "*Paulo Apostolo Mart*" meaning "Apostle Paul, Martyr."

In June 2009, Pope Benedict announced excavation results concerning the tomb of Paul at the basilica. The sarcophagus was not opened but was examined by means of a probe, which revealed pieces of incense, purple and blue linen, and small bone fragments. The bone was radiocarbon dated to the 1st or 2nd century. The investigation results were consistent with belief that the remains were, indeed, from St. Paul.

SOME OF ST. PAUL'S PERSECUTIONS

Five times I received from the Jews the forty lashes minus one. Three times I was beaten with rods, once I was pelted with stones, three times I was shipwrecked, I spent a night and a day in the open sea, I have been constantly on the move. I have been in danger from rivers, in danger from bandits, in danger from my fellow Jews, in danger from Gentiles; in danger in the city, in danger in the country, in danger at sea; and in danger from false believers. I have labored and toiled and have often gone without sleep; I have known hunger and thirst and have often gone without food; I have been cold and naked. Besides everything else, I face daily the pressure of my concern for all the churches.

2 Corinthians 11:24-28

Below: An enlarged view of the chains that restrained St. Paul.

Grotta della Madonna della Tre Fontane
Grotto of the Madonna of the Three Fountains
Daily: 10 - 6

Bruno Cornacchiola was a struggling, troubled tram conductor in Rome. By 1947, he had defiantly converted from Catholicism, embraced communism, and fought on the side of anti-Catholic forces in the Spanish Civil war. Years earlier, he had divorced his wife but, by now, had returned to the marriage. Yet, he had become adulterous and abusive to her, and demanded that she forsake the practice of her Catholic faith. His anti-Catholic animus was so extreme that he had even plotted to assassinate Pope Pius XII on the Feast of the Nativity of the Blessed Virgin Mary, later that year.

CHURCH JUDGMENT REGARDING PRAYER AND VENERATION: APPROVED; REGARDING AUTHENTICITY: NO DECISION.

On April 12th, Bruno took his three children to a picnic near Tre Fontane, where St. Paul had been martyred. As he relaxed in a cove, while the children played, he prepared notes for a presentation in which he would ridicule the Immaculate Conception. He even wrote on a nearby statue of the Virgin Mother, "... you are neither virgin nor mother."

When Bruno looked for his children, he saw one of them joyfully kneeling near the entrance of a cave, saying "Beautiful lady!" Then the other two knelt in awe. Bruno saw nothing, but tried to snatch them up and run. However, he could not budge them. Then Bruno saw a flash and felt weightless as if his soul were leaving his body. When his sight returned, Bruno saw a woman of dazzling beauty, wearing a luminous white dress, a rose sash, and a long green mantle.

She identifed herself as the "Daughter of the of the Father, Mother of the Son, and Spouse and Temple of the Holy Spirit. I am the the Virgin of Revelation". Then she admonished Bruno, "You persecute me. Enough of it now. Enter into God's kingdom on earth. The nine first Fridays of the Sacred Heart have saved you. You must be like flowers picked by your daughter Istola – they make no protest, they are silent and do not rebel." (In fact, early in his marriage, at the insistence of his wife, Bruno had attended the nine First Fridays prescribed by St. Margaret Mary Alacoque.)

In a vision that lasted 80 minutes, the Mother of God added, "In this place of sin, I will perform miracles for the conversion of unbelievers.... Return to the pure source of the Gospel. Pray much and recite the rosary for conversion of sinners, of unbelievers, and of all Christians." Then, anticipating the 1950 proclamation of the Dogma of the Assumption, she explained "My body would not be allowed to decay. My son came for me with his angels."

Indeed, Bruno reversed his anti-Catholic, rebellious nature. Eventually, he claimed an additional 28 apparitions. Today, pilgrims pray at the grotto and then make their way through a tunnel that is covered with many hundreds of marble plaques that thank the Virgin of Revelation for miraculous answers to prayers (pictured above). When they emerge from the tunnel (below), they find a less permanent tribute but, perhaps, even more moving. In addition to many notes regarding miraculous healings, it includes a hodge-podge of dangling braces and crutches that are no longer needed.

Information 4 Pilgrims
- Closest Metro station: Laurentina
- Preplan transportation options because Metro is a considerable walk away from both Tre Fontane sites.
- Website: divinarivelazione.org

SAN PAOLO ALLE TRE FONTANE

ST. PAUL'S AT THE THREE FOUNTAINS
WINTER: 9 - 1 & 3 - 6; SUMMER: 8 - 1 & 3 - 7

Within the Abbey of Tre Fontane, this is the oldest of the three churches, constructed on the site of St. Paul's martyrdom. It is said that when the saint was decapitated, his head bounced across the ground three times. From those spots, springs began to flow.

Approaching the church, pilgrims notice that the ancient stone pavers, upon which St. Paul would have walked his last steps, are preserved (left). Inside, one end of the small church displays a moving image of St. Peter's crucifixion (right).

The longer wall displays three marble monuments (left) that each include a lower grate through which pilgrims can observe each fountain. The column from the martyrdom of St. Paul is also preserved and displayed (right).

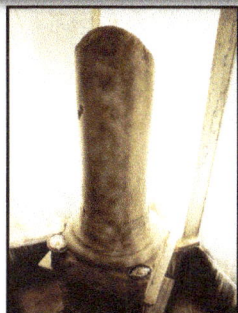

INFORMATION 4 PILGRIMS

- Closest Metro station: Laurentina
- Preplan transportation options because Metro is a considerable walk away from both Tre Fontane sites.
- Website: sanpaolotrefontane.org

SAN LORENZO FUORI LE MURA
ST. LAWRENCE OUTSIDE THE WALLS
MON - SAT: 7:30 - 12:30 & 3:30 - 7; SUN: 7:30 - 1:30 & 4 - 8

St. Lawrence Outside the Walls is one of Rome's five Patriarchal Basilicas. It is formed from two two adjacent churches, that faced in opposite directions. The earliest one was first built in 330 by Emperor Constantine, on the site of an oratory for St. Stephen, who had been buried here. That church was rebuilt on this site in 578. The newer church, nearer the entrance, was built in the 13th century. However, the church was severely damaged by aerial bombardment during World War II. It was closed for six years during the reconstruction work.

The portico's walls have frescoes (above) that date from the first half of the 13th century. They were restored in the 19th. However, we see signs of modern dangers (left) as sandbags are piled around the portico to prevent flooding of the church. The cosmatesque pavement of the nave (below) is exceptional, and dates from the 13th century. Near the altar, cosmatesque benches and a throne also date from 1254. The main altar, with its porphyry columns and white marble *baldacchino* (below, left), is 106 years older.

This basilica is particularly fitting for the veneration of martyrs. Eight steps lead down to the *confessio* (left) where relics of Saints Lawrence, Stephen and Justin are preserved, as well as remains of St. Cyriaca, the Roman matron who buried St. Lawrence here. The main altar's triumphal arch depicts them.

Stephen is the protomartyr mentioned in the Book of Acts. Lawrence was a deacon of the early Church, martyred on August 10, 258 during the persecutions of Emperor Valerian. Justin Martyr was a Father of the Church, a voluminous author of many early Church works, after earlier subscribing to Plato's philosophy. For his faith, he was executed around 165.

TIPS 4 PILGRIMS

Barely outside the ancient walls, San Lorenzo is a little harder to find than most of Rome's churches. It is a 20 minute walk east of Termini Station or a 10 minute walk (south on Viale Regina Elena) from Policlinico metro stop (line B). This site is also serviced by trams, which may be your best chance to try that form of transportation. They operate much like the buses and accept the same multi-day transportation passes.

Beyond the altar is the golden Funerary Chapel of Pius IX (below). Highlighted in a level under the main altar (left), is a marble slab (right) upon which Lawrence's body was carried after his martyrdom from roasting. It is said that an image of his body remained on the slab for many years after his death and that this stain will never leave it. Not without some degree of stoic acceptance of every ordeal, if not outright humor, the Church named St. Lawrence the patron of cooks and chefs.

From the triumphal arch rearward (left), more indications of this church's antiquity are evident. The upper galleries (far left) were designed for women, in the tradition of the ancient orthodox Jewish community that segregated worshippers by gender. This feature is found in a number of Rome's oldest churches.

HISTORY 4 PILGRIMS

Todays pilgrims might become skeptical when they encounter multiple locations that claim a particular saint's relics. However, regardless of our modern-day sensitivities to this practice, early Christians sometimes distributed the remains of important saints for veneration in multiple communities.

VIA APPIA ANTICA
The Old Appian Road

The Appian Way is called "Old" because it really is. Construction began in 312 BC! So, if you want to escape Rome's hectic congestion, try this tour on a Sunday, when street traffic is mostly restricted to walkers, joggers and cyclists. Then, step back into history as you wander the street that ancient troops and travelers trod. The atmosphere was not always this pleasant. Around 71 BC, General Marcus Licinius Crassus was eyeing political office while dealing with a slave revolt. So, along this road, Crassus solved his problem by crucifying Spartacus and 6,000 of his cohorts.

Rome's Appian Way is now a nature and archeological park that spans over 30 kilometers. The most popular short stretch for tourists is from the visitor's center to Cecilia Metella (second from bottom), an ancient mausoleum dedicated to the daughter-in-law of Crassus. After his slave revolt solution, he went on to become a member of Rome's ruling triumvirate and one of history's richest men.

Today, pilgrims with other priorities can enjoy the natural beauty of Appia Antica and even pause to thank God at each Station of the Cross that is placed along the way (below, right).

APPIAN WAY
TIPS 4 PILGRIMS

These are some of the highlights for an unstructured tour of the Old Appian Way. There is no map because it is just a straight stretch of road, where most pilgrims venture. Be sure to check out the following three important sites for pilgrims:
*   San Sebastiano Fuori le Mura
*   Catacombe di San Callisto
*   Chieasa di Quo Vadis
However, walking amidst the rich history of the Appian Way is, itself, a treat.

+S.P.Q.R.
VILLA E CIRCO DI MASSENZIO
MAUSOLEO DI ROMOLO

INGRESSO AL N

DIRECTIONS TO APPIAN WAY:

*   From Circo Massimo Metro stop, take Bus 118 to a variety of Appian stops;
*   Or, from Coli Albani Metro stop, take Bus 660 to a stop near Cecilia Metela;
*   Or, from San Giovanni Metro stop, take Bus 218 to Domine Quo Vadis;
*   Or try the Archeobus tour (see p. 201), or reserve taxis.
*   Note: Though traffic is lessened and the ambiance more enjoyable on Sundays, transportation options are also lessened. Plan accordingly.

In 257, Emperor Valerian forbade Christians from assembling for religious purposes in Rome. So, unable to venerate the tombs of Peter (on Vatican Hill) or Paul (on the Ostian Way), Christians secretly arranged to move their relics to this site, outside the Aurelian Walls. Here, they could venerate the saints and conduct the Sacraments in relative safety. Eventually, Constantine lifted the restrictions and the remains of the two saints were returned to their former sites. So, though smaller than the nearby Catacombs of San Callisto, below this church is the first of the roughly 40 Christian catacombs around Rome.

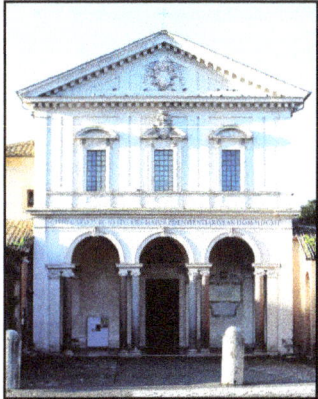

Prior to 350, a church was built on this site, dedicated to Saints Peter and Paul. A door to the right of the facade leads to the catacombs. There, in addition to the remains of early Christians, many 3rd century graffiti etchings have been discovered, expressing sentiments like, "Peter and Paul, pray for...". These inscriptions not only document that the bodies of those saints had been here, but also that the earliest Christians prayed for the intercession of saints, just as Catholics do today.

This major basilica was one of the seven Pilgrim Churches visited during each jubilee year. In 2000, however, Pope John Paul II removed this church from the list in order to add the Sanctuary of the Madonna of Divine Love. The carved wood ceiling (left) dates from 1612, at the construction of the present church. The chapel of relics (below) includes an arrow that wounded St. Sebastian, as well as a fragment of the column to which he was bound. Preserved also, are said to be Jesus Christ's footprints in stone from when He appeared at the site of the Church of Quo Vadis, described on page 179.

St. Sebastian (below) was an officer in the Praetorian Guard when he was denounced as a Christian. So, Diocletian ordered his archers to execute Sebastian. An eyewitness report said "...the archers shot at him 'till he was as full of arrows as an urchin." Then they left him for dead. However, a kind widow nursed Sebastian back to health, allowing him to continue fearlessly preaching, converting and healing the sick and blind.

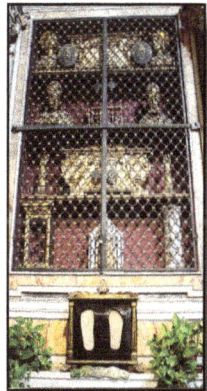

Then one day, as Diocletian paraded past, Sebastian publicly rebuked him. The enraged emperor ordered his men to club the saint to death (ca. 300). For that reason, he is sometimes known as the saint who was martyred twice. Because the courageous Christian is buried here, the church became known as the Basilica of the Apostles and St. Sebastian. By the 9th century, however, this church and its catacombs were commonly referred to simply by the name of the martyred saint.

CATACOMBE DI SAN CALLISTO
CATACOMBS OF ST. CALLIXTUS
DAILY: 9 - 12 & 2 - 5 (CLOSED EVERY WED & ALL OF FEB)

The Catacombs of San Callisto are the biggest attraction on Via Appia Antica. The Christian community owned this property in the early 3rd century and it became the Church's principal cemetery. More than 50 martyrs and 16 popes were buried here. This is where St. Cecilia was found in an incorrupt state, the image of which Carlo Maderno sculpted (See p. 78). A copy of the famous sculpture is on display where St. Cecilia was entombed, next to the crypt of the popes.

The grounds of San Callisto are quite lovely, offering a stark contrast to the tunnels below ground (lower right). A small gift shop (right) is on site and tours are guided in a wide variety of languages. There is a charge for admission.

TIPS 4 PILGRIMS

Since food and drink are not widely available on this tour, bring a backpack with liquid refreshments. Better yet, tour the Appian Way on a lovely day and bring a picnic lunch. For the more adventurous, bicycles can be rented at the visitors center, allowing the tour to stretch out for most of a day. For the more wealthy, the Cecilia Metella Restaurant and Bar is located across from San Sebastian, offering fine dining with a very pricey tab.

In ancient times, Romans preferred to cremate the dead since burial within the walls was forbidden for health reasons. Christians, however, preferred burial, and this site became one of the most congested, housing a half million bodies. The soft volcanic *tufa* rock, below ground (right), was highly suitable for the tunnelling work that was necessary for underground catacombs. In fact, San Callisto's tunnels span about 12 miles, over 4 levels. The niches (right) are known as *loculi*.

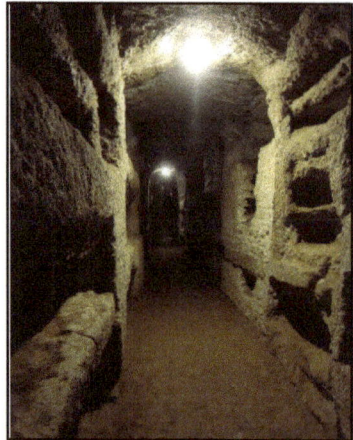

The most revered rooms were decorated with stucco and frescoes. Particularly important are the Crypt of St. Cecilia and the nearby Crypt of the Popes. Various paintings have survived that remind us that this was a place for Sacramental gathering, including Baptism and distribution of the Holy Eucharist (left).

TIPS 4 PILGRIMS

Always travel with some small bills and extra change. It is not uncommon to find access to toilets restricted by coin-operated turnstyles. At other times, for a very "technical reason," a 6€ admission charge may actually cost you 10.

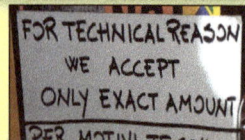

FOR TECHNICAL REASON
WE ACCEPT
ONLY EXACT AMOUNT
PER MOTIN...

SANTA MARIA IN PALMIS aka Quo Vadis

The church of *Santa Maria in Palmis* is best known as *Domine Quo Vadis?*. Located at the foot of the Appian Way, this site has an interesting tradition behind it, giving rise to its unusual name.

When fellow Christians convinced Peter to leave Rome because of Nero's intensifying persecutions, the apostle encountered the Ascended Christ here, on his way out of town. The startled Peter asked, "Domine quo vadis?' or "Lord, where are you going?" Jesus answered, "To Rome, where I will be crucified again."

Peter—the man to whom Jesus had entrusted the Keys to the Kingdom— understood the gentle instruction: He was to lead Christ's Church from Rome, whatever the consequences. Indeed, Peter returned to Rome, and Nero's evil designs eventually overcame him. But, today, Nero is dead, yet Christ's Church lives on, led by a continuing succession of popes who are willing to live and die for Christ.

A church existed on this site from at least the 9th century but this humble structure dates from 1637. Inside, the altar image displays the Madonna and Child while they are flanked by frescoes of the crucifixions of Jesus and Peter (above). Also displayed nearby is a fresco depicting Peter clutching the Keys to the Kingdom..

It is said that when Jesus Christ appeared to Peter on this site, He left behind lasting evidence of His visit. Today, footprints in stone (right) are placed near the front doors of this church. This is a copy of what are believed to be the Lord's footprints that were left on the stones upon which He stood. The original stone footprints are preserved and displayed a short distance up the Appian Way at St. Sebastian Outside the Walls.

There, we find evidence that Peter and Paul actually lived in this area. In the catacombs of San Sebastiano is an epigraph that reads "Domus Petri" or "House of Peter." Also, there, is an epigram by Pope Damasus I (366-384) stating, "You that are looking for the names of Peter and Paul, you must know that the saints have lived here."

HISTORY 4 PILGRIMS

The word Sarcophagus means "flesh eater" in Greek. It was believed that these burial boxes somehow caused the deterioration of the corpses that were placed in them. Consequently, a common ornamentation developed in which wavy lines were often carved into stone sarcophagi. However, these were not just for decorative purposes. They symbolized the curved *strigiles*

(left) that Romans used to scrape oil and dirt off their bodies in the public baths. So, these symbols (right) reminded grieving Romans that losing flesh was as harmless as scraping away the dirt from a body.

PART SIX:
ROMAN CURIOSITIES

RUINS: THE PALATINE PALACE
OVERLOOKING THE ROMAN FORUM

Rome's impressive monoliths once proclaimed the conquering grandeur of emperors and pharoahs. Now, adorned with Christian symbols and statuary, they punctuate the Eternal City's streets with the message that kings will be swept away by the passage of time, but God never will.

- Rome has more obelisks than any other city, including 8 from ancient Egypt, 5 from ancient Rome, and others of more recent origin.
- Rome also contains at least 4 grand monumental columns, 3 of which are of ancient origin.
- An ancient Ethiopian obelisk left Rome in 2005.

The most revered of obelisks (right) was made from a single block of pink granite and is situated at the center of *Piazza San Pietro.* It was constructed, in Egypt, in 1835 BC and brought to Rome by one of its most decadent emperors – Caligula. It once marked where St. Peter was crucified, upside down, during Nero's persecutions. At that time, the monolith was located nearby, within view of Peter, at the time of his execution. Today, it provides witness to the victory of Peter's faith. The former pagan monument to the sun is now not only topped with a bronze cross, but with a fragment of the True Cross. (See p. 144 for the story of the raising of this obelisk.)

At the heart of Piazza Navona is Bernini's famous Fountain of Four Rivers (above) with an ancient obelisk rising from its center. (See p. 48.)

A bronze statue of St. Paul tops the Triumphal Column of Marcus Aurelius (lower left) in the *Piazza Colonna.* The structure that was completed in the late 2nd century, has a shaft that consists of 28 hollowed blocks of Carerra marble, more than 12' in diameter. An intricately sculpted spiral relief (inset left) tells the story of the Emperor's military conquests in a manner similar to the earlier column of Trajan (right), which now supports a bronze statue of St. Peter in Trajan's Forum. The column and pedestal are 125' tall and were erected in 115 AD. The intricate relief carved into the column shows the story of the emperor's miliary conquests with a 625' spiral that wraps the column 23 times to the top. Inside the column's 20 Carrara marble drums, a spiral staircase consists of 185 stairs. Roman engineers topped the column with a capital block that weighs 53 tons.

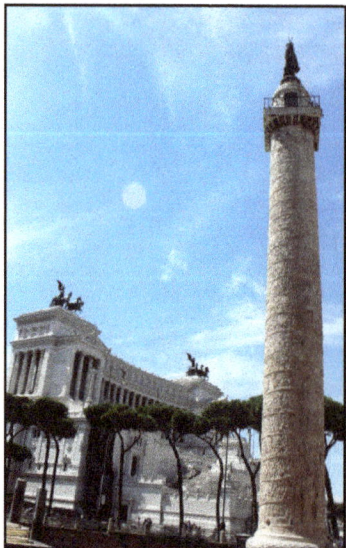

Bernini's whimsical *Elefantino* (below) appears undaunted as he transports an ancient Egyptian obelisk through *Piazza della Minerva.* The obelisk dates from the 6th century BC.

The Column of the Immaculate Conception (left) (*Colonna dell' Immacolata*) is a 19th century monument, located near *Piazza di Spagna.*

Madonna and Child (below) gaze upon *Santa Maria Maggiore* from the Column of Peace (*Colonna della Pace),* a marble, fluted column that was originally placed in the Forum's basilica of Maxentius.

Piazza del Popolo (right) holds an Egyptian obelisk of Ramasses II that was brought to Rome by Augustus in 10 BC.

The world's largest, standing, ancient Egyptian obelisk (right) is at the Lateran basilica. It weighs almost a half million pounds.

Italians and tourists scurry past the Pantheon's obelisk. Della Porta's amusing fountain ornaments its base.

DRINKING FOUNTAINS

Rome has an abundance of centuries old drinking fountains from which cool, clean water flows continually, even on scorching summer days. Many of the fountains are ornately decorated, such as the one pictured left. Others, however, are more utilitarian in design (right). Rome's abundant water supply was made available by a sophisticated system of aqueducts (below), transporting water from surrounding highlands. However, Goth besiegers cut off the aqueducts, beginning in 537, forcing Romans to draw from polluted water sources. This began a long period of city flight and aqueduct deterioration. Eventually Rome's population decreased to 30,000, in Medieval times, from an ancient population peak of 1 million.

ROMAN HISTORY 4 PILGRIMS

Ancient Rome enjoyed a good supply of water from springs, wells and the Tiber, but the area's growing population eventually made more sophisticated options desireable. So, even before the reign of Roman emperors – in 312 BC – Consul Appius Claudius built the first of the great aqueducts. It spanned 11 miles, most of which was underground. Over the next 200 years, 10 more aqueducts were built around Rome. These products of engineering genius eventually supplied water to not only Rome but to many other parts of Europe, as in the case of France's Pont du gard (right). Though the aqueducts eventually declined into disrepair and disuse, modern pilgrims can thank the popes who, beginning in 1570, restored the ancient water supply systems.

Rome's aqueducts supplied not only the city's drinking requirements, but also its latrine sanitation needs, as well as it famous public baths. The inflow of abundant water even assisted Rome's milling industry.

On a hot summer day, this young pilgrim (left) is filling a container with cold, fresh water to take with her, just as ancient Roman girls did many centuries ago. The only difference is that they didn't have any pink, plastic squirt bottles.

TIPS 4 PILGRIMS

When in Rome, do as the Romans do. To drink from a fountain, place a finger under the running water spout, plugging the flow. Then a stream of water will fly through the air, allowing thirsty pilgrims to slurp to their heart's content.

PUBLIC FOUNTAINS

Historian Pliny the Elder called Rome's aqueducts "The greatest wonder the world has ever seen." So, it may not be surprising that such a proud accomplishment would eventually be trumpeted with more than just practical applications. Over time, beautifully decorated, and even artistically excellent, public fountains sprang up simply for the visual enjoyment of Romans and their visitors.

In addition to other well-known public fountains that are highlighted elsewhere in this book, some of Rome's more interesting ones can be found at Chiesa Nuova (right), Piazza Republica (above), Piazza del Popolo (top right), Piazza Barberini (far right), and at the base of the typically crowded Spanish Steps (right). The fountain statuary shown at the bottom of the page are from the very popular fountains at Piazza Navona and the Pantheon's piazza. Pictured, left, is the fountain at the Temple of Hercules Victor.

In Rome, no tourists appreciate the public fountains more than the pilgrim pigeons.

Stunning Ceilings

ROME'S PILGRIMS ARE DAZZLED BY SO MANY SPIRITUAL, ARTISTIC AND ARCHITECTURAL WONDERS, AT GROUND LEVEL, THAT THEY MAY RUSH ALONG WITHOUT NOTICING THAT MUCH OF THE WORLD'S GREATEST ART IS ABOVE THEIR HEADS. HERE ARE JUST A FEW OF ROME'S MANY DAZZLING CEILINGS.

WALKING ON ART

IN THE 12TH AND 13TH CENTURIES, THE COSMATI FAMILY OF ITALY POPULARIZED A DECORATIVE STYLE OF GEOMETRIC STONE INLAY. THIS ORNAMENTAL ART BECAME POPULAR IN PRESTIGIOUS CHURCHES THROUGHOUT EUROPE, BUT ESPECIALLY IN ROME WHERE THE DISTINCTIVE DESIGN BECAME KNOWN AS COSMATESQUE. THOUGH THE TECHNIQUE WAS MOSTLY APPLIED TO PAVEMENT, – REPLACING TRADITIONAL STYLE FLOORING (LEFT) – IT IS ALSO FOUND ON ORNATE PULPITS, THRONES AND COLUMNS (RIGHT).

MANY OF ROME'S CHURCH FLOORS ALSO HAVE MONUMENTS IMBEDDED IN THE PAVEMENT. EVEN THOUGH OUR EYES ARE NOT ALWAYS DRAWN TO THE FLOOR, PILGRIMS SHOULD REMAIN AWARE OF WHERE THEY WALK. AVOIDING THESE MEMORIALS NOT ONLY SHOWS DUE RESPECT FOR THESE SAINTS, BUT ALSO PRESERVES FOR FUTURE GENERATIONS OF PILGRIMS TO APPRECIATE THEIR TOMBSTONES, SUCH AS THE WELL-WORN ONE AT THE RIGHT.

AROUND TOWN: MADONNELLE

It seems *Madonnelle* (Little Madonnas) are everywhere in Rome, reminding Romans of the protections she offers to the buildings she decorates, the streets she watches over, and even the occasional line of drying laundry that hangs by her side. They are presented in almost every form of artistic tribute, and many of these frescoes, paintings, mosaics and statues display Baby Jesus in His mother's arms. A form of this Roman tradition dates from the pre-Christian era but, centuries later, *Madonnelle* oil lamps were Rome's only public street lighting.

Because these images tend to be mounted on street corners, they hang at first floor ceiling height. This was once thought wise in order to protect against damage from wayward carriages.

In 1853, one researcher listed 2739 sacred images for public viewing on Rome's streets. However, when some of these were associated with miracles, many were moved into churches.

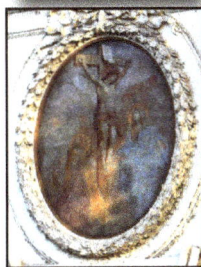

MADONNELLE

Remnants of Ancient Rome

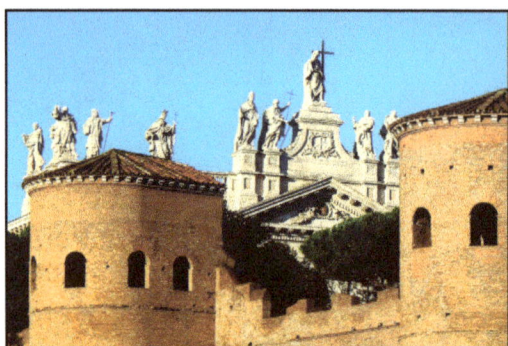

In addition to Rome's famous tourist and pilgrim attractions, the Eternal City is packed with so many surprising but lesser known remnants of ancient history that they are far too numerous to cover in this book. Often, the remains of one century stack over or under the vestiges of a completely different era. For example, the 3rd century Aurelian Wall winds through Rome to this very day. At its *Porta San Giovanni*, the Lateran Basilica rises above the ancient wall (left), while modern sports cars zip through its gates (below).

PART SIX: ROMAN CURIOSITIES

THE PALATINE PALACE

CIRCUS MAXIMUS,
SITE OF CHRISTIAN SLAUGHTER
FOR ENTERTAINMENT

REMNANTS OF ANCIENT ROME

(Right) Where else will one find excellent window shopping for the best dressed bishop?

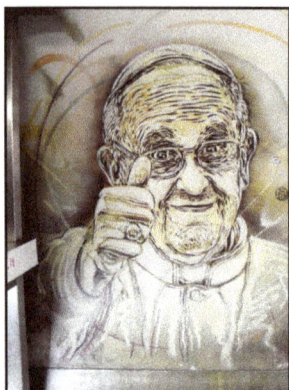

(Above) In Rome, subway graffiti can be amusing. (Inside the Spagna Metro station.)

During Advent, Roman streets become a festival of lights.

Enjoy a lovely stroll along the tree-lined Tiber River (left), or try one of Rome's other forms of unusual transportation. Just remember to leave the driving to the Romans!

Rome is notorious for tight parking spaces except, perhaps, for dogs (above and right).

(Left) Watching Roman police officers direct traffic can be entertaining. Still, there is probably no truth to the rumor that this statue (right) depicts an ancient Roman traffic cop.

No trip to Rome is complete without gelato (below). If your knees don't buckle when you taste it, you're not in one of their best gelaterias.

This statue (above) resides in the gardens of the Villa Borghese. Should we be horrified or amused?

Rome's version of street gangs.

TRIVIA 4 PILGRIMS

In Rome, it is not unusual to come across well behaved dogs. Some of them bring to mind an interesting interpretation of a charming Bible story.

The Old Testament Book of Tobit is included in Roman Catholic as well as Greek and Russian Orthodox Bibles. In that Book, righteous Tobit is losing his sight and nearing death. So, he sends his son, Tobias, on a dangerous mission to recover money that he had entrusted to a relative. The son will be accompanied on the trip by a man who no one realizes is actually the Archangel Raphael.

However, before they leave, Tobit offers a blessing in which he asks God to send an angel to accompany *both* men on the trip, there and back. (In the original Aramaic, the word 'you' is plural.) Then, without explanation and like nowhere else in the Bible, a dog becomes important enough to mention in the story. The loyal pup joins the pair on both legs of the blessed journey in which Tobias returns with riches and a bride.

Interesting...So, could it be that this Roman Pug (right) is actually an angel in disguise? Isn't it obvious? Of course, he is!

PART SEVEN:
RESOURCES 4 PILGRIMS

REMNANTS OF
TWENTY-SIX CENTURIES

WHY ROME?
A BRIEF SCRIPTURAL AND HISTORICAL GUIDE
TO THE ESTABLISHMENT OF THE PAPACY AND THE CATHOLIC CHURCH

Recently, a friend asked what book I was working on, and I told her the title of this one. Her response was almost as negative as if I had said, "A pilgrim's guide to the moon." I know she is a devout Christian, but her "Why Rome?" befuddlement indicated to me that her faith is completely divorced from the Christian history of Rome.

That, in a nutshell, is why I believe this book is so important. Even among Christians, Rome is a touchy subject. Why? Because for many Christians the history of Rome prompts the uncomfortable question, "What is the Church?"

St. Paul proclaimed that the Church is "the pillar and foundation of the truth" (1 Timothy 3:15), and he repeatedly returned to the theme that the Church is the mystical Body of Christ:
- "Now I rejoice in what I am suffering for you, and I fill up in my flesh what is still lacking in regard to Christ's afflictions, for the sake of His body, which is the Church." (Colossians 1:24)
- "For the husband is the head of the wife as Christ is the head of the Church, His body, of which He is the Savior." (Ephesians 5:23)
- "And He is the head of the body, the Church; He is the beginning and the firstborn from among the dead, so that in everything He might have the supremacy." (Colossians 1:18
- "His [God's] intent was that now, through the Church, the manifold wisdom of God should be made known to the rulers and authorities in the heavenly realms..." (Ephesians 3:10)

More significantly, Jesus Christ established the hierarchy of His Church even during His lifetime. Regarding sinners, He taught the apostles: "...if they refuse to listen even to the church, treat them as you would a pagan or a tax collector." (Matthew 18:17) By the time of the Book of Acts, the apostles knew what Jesus wanted for the hierarchy of His Church, so they established bishops, deacons and elders according to the tradition they were taught. But Christ, Himself, established an even higher authority in His Church that many find hard to accept. To the Apostle Simon, The Lord proclaimed: "...you are Peter [which means 'rock'], and on this rock I will build my church; and the gates of hell shall not prevail against it." (Matthew 16:18)

Consequently, Peter became a prime target for today's fact-challenged historians. The cynics believe that Peter's and the Catholic Church's authority are inextricably intertwined. (On this point, they are right.) So, if they can discredit Peter's authority, they would discredit his every successor and, indeed, the authority of the Catholic Church itself.

So, modern skeptics quibble with Matthew's translation, written in Greek, saying he used *petros* – a masculine noun that means "small rock" – for the apostle's name, while using *petra* – a feminine noun that means "large stone" – for the word "rock." From the Greek translation they claim Christ was referring to Peter as a pebble and Christ, Himself, as the stone upon which His Church would be built.

However, the truth is that Our Lord did not speak Greek when he made this pronouncement; He spoke ancient Aramaic. In both cases – referring to "Peter" and to "rock" – Jesus Christ used the word *kepha*. St. Matthew was simply constrained, in his Greek translation, from giving a feminine name to a man.

More absurdly, however, modern skeptics have sold many books that claim Peter never even made it to Rome. The counter-evidence is more than abundant, including the following:
- Clement of Rome, around 70 AD, wrote that Peter and Paul had died there. (Some Protestants recognize Paul was martyred in Rome, but not Peter.)
- In 110, Ignatius of Antioch wrote that he could not command the Roman Christians the way Peter and Paul once did.
- In 170, Dionysius of Corinth wrote to the 12th pope: "You have also, by your very admonition, brought together the planting that was made by Peter and Paul in Rome."
- A generation later Tertulian wrote: "How happy is that Church ... where Peter endured a passion like that of the Lord, where Paul was crowned in a death like John's [the Baptist]."
- Before 200, Irenaeus reflected on when "...Peter and Paul were evangelizing in Rome, laying the foundation of the Church."
- Near that time, Clement of Alexandria wrote about "When Peter preached the Word publicly in Rome..."
- Around 311, Bishop Peter of Alexandria wrote, "Peter, the first chosen of the apostles, having been apprehended often and thrown into prison and treated with ignominy, at last was crucified in Rome."
- By 318, Lactantius noted, "...when Nero was already reigning Peter came to Rome."
- About 303, Eusebius Pamphilius wrote that Peter's first epistle was written in Rome, but that he had referred to it as Babylon – no longer a city that could be called 'great' by any standard. Why? Because of the persecutions, of course.

The list could go on, but the point is made.

Others have wrongly argued that Peter's tomb under the basilica has no markings to prove it was his. A nearby inscription, however, translates, "Peter is here." That would be less convincing if the apostle's given name had been Jude or Joshua. But this carving more precisely reads: "Rock is here," making the reference clear.

More critics claim that even if Peter had made it to Rome, he was never the leader of the Church. After all, he was always messing up: thrice denying the Lord, losing faith while walking on water, even provoking Christ enough for Him to scold, "Get behind me, Satan!"

But Scripture validates that Peter was, in fact, the leader of the apostles. He was almost always listed first. (See Matthew 10:1-4; Mark 3:16-19; Luke 6:14-16; Acts 1:13) In Luke 9:32, they were called "Peter and his companions." Peter often spoke for the apostles. (See Matthew 18:21; Mark 8:29; Luke 12:41; John 6:69) He was the first to preach to the crowds on Pentecost. (Acts 2:14-40) He was one of three apostles at the Transfiguration, and the first to speak. (Matthew 17:1-4) Ironically, Peter was the one who received the revelation that Gentiles were to be baptized, even though many Gentile Christians today want to discredit him. (Acts 10:46-48)

Jesus Christ declared to Peter: "Whatever you bind on earth I will bind in heaven; whatever you loose on earth I will loose in heaven." (Matthew 16:19) The Lord also said: "I will give you [singular] the keys to the kingdom of heaven." (Matthew 16:19) To the modern ear, that gift may not sound as significant as it really was. In ancient times, one great gate, with one great lock, sometimes protected the entire castle. Giving control over what was usually the only key was a supreme act of trust. (See also Isaiah 22:22 and Revelation 1:18) At His Last Supper, Christ said to Peter, "...I have prayed for you [singular], that your faith may not fail; when, after a while, you have come back to me [after the denials], it is for you to be the support of your brothers." (Luke 22:31-32)

So, even if Peter was in Rome, and was named by Christ to lead his global Church, who is to say that the Bishop of Rome retained that primary role? To find the answer, we should ask more questions. Through the centuries, could every bishop assemble councils (synods)? Could any bishop embrace heresy with the full authority of the Church? If so, today's Christianity would have evolved into a mishmash of disjointed beliefs. Surely, this would not have reflected the unity Jesus Christ prayed for shortly before His arrest. (See John 17)

Fortunately, however, the historical record is clear. Around the world, the early Christians relied on Rome to lead the Church, through the pronouncements of Peter and his successors. Here are a few of the many examples:
- "Rome has spoken; the case is closed." (St. Augustine, citing Rome's authority to declare Pelagianism heresy, Sermon 131:10)
- "… set sail...to the chair of Peter and the principal Church [at Rome], in which sacerdotal unity has its source...whose faith was praised by the preaching Apostle, and among whom it is not possible for perfidy [errors of faith] to have entrance." (St. Cyprian on the Church and the papacy. Epistle 59:14)
- "...to the head, that is to the See of Peter the Apostle, the bishops of the Lord shall refer from all provinces..." (St. Athanasius on papal authority, Council of Sardica, c. 343 AD
- "If the primacy of St. Peter is so unimportant a fact – if it gave him no prerogatives, no duties, no successors – why on earth is it so extraordinarily prominent in Holy Writ?" (St. John Chrysostom on papal primacy, ca. 400)
- "The refutation has been so often repeated, and is so easy, that one feels almost the need to blush in reiterating it. I wish to give the answer here with all painstaking exactness, so that there may be no room for any other reply than misrepresentation or abuse; but one feels as though one were using a steamhammer to kill a flea...." (St. Jerome, defending papal authority, ca. 400.)

The primacy of the papacy, among others, is an Apostolic Tradition the Catholic Church refuses to discard. All Christians – even Fundamentalists – should recognize that Sacred Scripture, itself, requests that we not lose these Traditions. St. Paul taught, "...brothers, stand firm and hold to the traditions that you were taught by us, either by our spoken word or by our letter." (2 Thessalonians 2:15) He wrote, "I praise you for remembering me in everything and for holding to the traditions just as I passed them on to you." (1 Corinthians 11:2) Yet, today, many Christians ignore or even deny the extraordinary role of Peter and his papal successors. These critics embrace the Bible, but reject the Church that compiled it. They reject the Apostolic Traditions of the Church that were established before the Bible, but embrace any one of thousands of Christian faiths that surfaced sixteen centuries after Christ. Almost as if the centuries of vicious Christian persecutions were 'the good old days,' many have claimed that the Catholic Church may have been inspired in the beginning but corrupted some time after Emperor Constantine embraced the faith. In order to advance that argument, however, they must first answer one question: Exactly when did the gates of hell prevail against Christ's Church?

Just as every Christian owes a debt of gratitude to many generations of Jews who preserved the faith of the Old Testament, each Christian should respect the heroic virtue of the early Christians in Rome, and the faithful dedication to the earliest Christian teachings that continues to this day. To fully appreciate the grandeur of Christian history and faith, after visiting the Holy Land, there's no place like Rome.

Relics And Revelations
A Catholic Perspective

The remains of saints (first class relics) are found throughout Rome. However, many non-Catholics misunderstand the Church's practice of venerating these relics. They incorrectly assume it is akin to believing in magic: assigning supernatural power to natural objects (a heresy that the Church, itself, long ago condemned.)

The truth, however, is that the practice is rooted in Scripture. In the Old Testament, for example, when a dead man's body touched the bones of the Prophet Elisha, the deceased man revived immediately (2 Kings 13:20-21). In Matthew 9:22, a woman was cured of a hemorrage, simply by touching the hem of Christ's cloak (a second class relic). The sick were healed when Peter's shadow cast upon them (Acts 5:14-16). In fact, all Christians should be aware of Acts 19:11-12: "And God did extraordinary miracles by the hands of Paul, so that handkerchiefs or aprons were carried away from his body to the sick, and diseases left them and the evil spirits came out of them."

The practice of venerating the relics of saints became so popular with the earliest Christians that it enmeshed itself in Christian tradition. Among other accounts, we read that in 156 AD Christians gathered up the burned bones of martyred Polycarp, before writing that they considered them "...more valuable than precious stones and finer than refined gold..." The biblical scholar and saint, Jerome, may have described the practice best, in the 4th century: "We do not worship, we do not adore, for fear that we should bow down to the creature rather than to the Creator, but we venerate the relics of martyrs in order to better adore Him whose martyrs they are."(*Ad Riparium*, i, P.L., XXII 907)

That many miracles have been attributed to the veneration of relics of Christian saints is indisputable. Yet critics remain skeptical. Another relic phenomenon, however, is harder for cynics to dismiss. Over the course of Christian history, the bodies of a few hundred saints have been found to remain incorrupt for an unnaturally long period of time – sometimes even indefinitely – without the benefit of any natural means of preservation (ie. human intervention, chemicals, or environmental factors). Cases have been documented as far back as St. Cecilia (177 AD) and St. Agatha (251 AD). In the catacombs, their bodies remained lifelike, while being credited with miraculous cures for Christians.

In many cases, defying natural laws, the bodies of Incorruptibles not only remain free of the stench of bodily decay, but they actually maintain the "Odor of Sanctity," a pleasing floral aroma. For some saints, however, only parts of their bodies were preserved. For example, St. Anthony of Padua died in the 13th century, but his tongue is still intact. St. Padre Pio's face is preserved, while other parts of his body have decomposed. Still other saints have remained entirely incorrupt, until some mysterious time in which God seems to let the natural order resume.

Though incorruptibility is not a requirement for canonization, and its mysterious discovery is not proof of saintliness, it adds to confirming that seemingly miraculous phenomena were gifts from God. With that in mind, the faithful are likely to give greater credence to Church-approved apparitions, such as is the case with the preservation of Jacinta Marto (Fatima), St. Bernadette Soubirous (Lourdes), and St. Margaret Mary Alacoque (Sacred Heart of Jesus devotions). So, since Sacred Scripture is filled with Revelations to Biblical saints, what about these, and other, Private Revelations that have been communicated through saints since that time? After all, St. Paul wrote, "I keep asking that the God of our Lord Jesus Christ, the glorious Father, may give you the Spirit of wisdom and revelation, so that you may know Him better." (Ephesians 1:17)

The Church is rightly slow and methodical in rendering judgment on Private Revelations and, even when one is eventually judged worthy of belief, does not require all Catholics to put their faith in it. Only belief in Public Revelation (the Bible) is required of Catholics. The Church teaches: "Christian faith cannot accept 'revelations' that claim to surpass or correct the Revelation of which Christ is the fulfillment..." (Catechism of the Catholic Church 67).

Still, detailed investigations into Private Revelations are regularly conducted by the Church for those ostensibly miraculous phenomena that reveal messages that are consistent with Sacred Scripture. Scientists – of every faith and no faith – are invited to evaluate whether a seeming miracle can be explained as resulting from natural causes. The event can only be declared worthy of belief if investigators conclude that the circumstances are scientifically inexplicable. Then, at least two approved miracles must be attributed to a holy person before canonization. (Still, the Church recognizes that heaven holds far more saints than just those who have been canonized.)

So, if we, as Christians, accept that "we were all baptized by one Spirit so as to form one body" (1 Corinthians 12:13), and that Christ is "...the head of the body, the Church...", then just as Christ is still the head of the Church – even after His death on the cross – shouldn't we recognize that deceased saints continue with us as members of the Body of Christ? The holy on earth and the holiest in heaven share in the Communion of Saints. Therefore, whenever we encounter difficult or desperate circumstances, Catholics pray for the intercession of these, the holiest of saints, just as we request, from our faithful friends on earth, prayers for our intentions.

The church of San Crisogono displays the tomb of Blessed Anna Maria Taigi (below). She was born in Siena, but by the age of five her father's apothecary shop was failing. So he moved the family to Rome. (She frequented many Roman churches that pilgrims visit today.)

There, she later married Dominico Taigi who worked for the wealthy and powerful Chigi family. For three years, she aspired to a life of luxury and, though she maintained her moral standards, she learned to enjoy the frivolities that she experienced with the nobility of Rome.

One day, however, as she clung tightly to her husband's lead while he plowed through a massive throng in St. Peter's Square, she accidentally bumped into a Servite priest named Angelo. He had never met the beautifully adorned young woman, but heard an inner voice say: "Notice that woman, for I will one day confide her to your care and you will work for her transformation. She shall sanctify herself, for I have chosen her to become a saint."

Indeed, Anna Maria soon experienced a profound conversion in which she became determined to reject her worldly pursuits. But she was also a committed wife and would become a mother of seven children, over a dozen years. So, her journey to Spiritual favor could not include the convent. Also, on her initial attempts, she experienced a variety of humiliations as she clumsily sought her path. Finally, Anna Maria was moved to confess her sins at the church where she had been married: San Marcello (see p. 62). Inside the confessional, the delighted priest responded, "So you have come at last, my daughter. Our Lord loves you and wants you to be wholly His."

Father Angelo Verandi became Anna Maria's Spiritual Director guiding her prayers, penances, miracles and ecstasies within the constraints of her station in life. Her husband was no St. Joseph, but accepted her saintly aspirations. So, eventually, she was received into the Third Order of Trinitarians and served at the Church of San Carlo alle Quattro Fontane (see page 110) for further Spiritual development. She also humbly ministered to the sick at San Giacomo of the Incurables (see p. 69).

Then, one day, while praying before the crucifix at Sant'Andrea della Valle (see p. 65), she heard a voice: "What is your wish: to follow Jesus, poor and naked and stripped of all, or to follow Him in His triumph and glory?" She responded, " I embrace the Cross of my Jesus. I will carry it, like Him, in pain and ignominy. At His Hands, I await triumph and glory in the hereafter."

Blessed Anna Maria Taigi died in 1837, after 47 years of mystical experiences and prophetic utterances. Since then, her tomb was inspected repeatedly, proving that even though the other contents of the coffin had deteriorated, her body remained incorrupt. Then, in 1920, her remains were inspected again, finally revealing a condition of decomposition. Wax, today, preserves the face of a servant of God: beautiful, calm and at peace.

LENTEN CHURCH STATIONS

During Lent, pilgrims to Rome can participate in a tradition that dates to the 4th century. At that time, the Roman faithful honored the martyred saints each year by assembling for a prayerful procession to a certain church each day of Lent. There, the Pope would then conduct Mass. St. Pope Gregory the Great (d. 604) formalized this tradition by establishing the specific order of churches to be visited. For a time, however, this practice was interrupted, during and after the papal Avignon years (1309 - 1378).

Week of Ash Wednesday
Ash Wednesday – Santa Sabina
Thursday – San Giorgio al Velabro
Friday – Santi Giovanni e Paolo al Celio
Saturday – Sant'Agostino

First Week of Lent
Sunday – San Giovanni in Laterano
Monday – San Pietro in Vincoli
Tuesday – Sant'Anastasia al Palatino
Wednesday – Santa Maria Maggiore
Thursday – San Lorenzo in Panisperna
Friday – Santi Apostoli
Saturday – Basilica di San Pietro (Part 1)

Second Week of Lent
Sunday – Santa Maria in Domenica alla Navicella
Monday – San Clemente
Tuesday – Santa Balbina all'Aventino
Wednesday – Santa Cecilia in Trastevere
Thursday – Santa Maria in Trastevere
Friday – San Vitale
Saturday – Santi Marcellino e Pietro

Third Week of Lent
Sunday – San Lorenzo Fuori le Mura
Monday – San Marco al Campidoglio
Tuesday – Santa Pudenziana
Wednesday – San Sisto
Thursday – Santi Cosma e Damiano in Via Sacra
Friday – San Lorenzo in Lucina
Saturday – Santa Susanna

Fourth Week of Lent
Sunday – Santa Croce in Gerusalemme (first)
Monday – Santi Quattro Coronati al Celio
Tuesday – San Lorenzo in Damaso
Wednesday – San Paolo Fuori le Mura
Thursday – Santi Silvestro e Martino ai Monti
Friday – San Eusebio all'Esquilino
Saturday – San Nicola in Carcere

Fifth Week of Lent
Sunday – Basilica di San Pietro (second)
Monday – San Crisogono in Trastevere
Tuesday – Santa Maria in via Lata
Wednesday – San Marcello al Corso
Thursday – San Apollinare
Friday – San Stefano al Celio
Saturday – San Giovanni a Porta Latina

Holy Week
Palm Sunday – San Giovanni in Laterano (second)
Monday – Santa Prassede all'Esquilino
Tuesday – Santa Prisca all'Aventino
Wednesday – Santa Maria Maggiore (second)
Thursday – San Giovanni in Laterano (third)
Good Friday – Santa Croce in Gerusalemme (second)
Holy Saturday – San Giovanni in Laterano (fourth)
Easter Sunday – Santa Maria Maggiore (third)

PRACTICAL TOURIST INFORMATION FOR ROME
(click on English version, where necessary):
- www.RomeToolKit.com
- www.EnjoyRome.com
- www.Rome.info
- www.RomeExplorer.com
- www.ItalianTourism.com
- www.enit.it
- www.RomeGuide.it

TICKETS FOR VARIOUS SITES:
- www.tosc.it
- www.ItalyTickets.it

REVIEWS AND RECOMMENDATIONS:
- www.TripAdvisor.com (Use appropriate keywords)

CATHOLIC SITES:
- www.Vatican.va (primary Vatican site)
- www.VaticanState.va (especially "Practical Information" found at bottom)
- www.MuseiVaticani.va (Vatican Museums)
- www.SantaSusanna.org (American Catholic church in Rome)

APARTMENT RENTALS:
- www.WantedInRome.com

PUBLIC TRANSPORTATION:
- www.atac.roma.it (in Rome)
- www.EuroLines.com (buses outside Rome)
- www.ItaliaRail.com (rail outside Rome)

FREE TICKETS FOR PAPAL AUDIENCE OR PAPAL MASS
(PLUS OTHER PAID TOURS):
- www.VaticanTour.com

HOP ON, HOP OFF TOUR BUSES IN ROME:
(HOHO buses are a great way to see a lot of Rome in a little time. For reviews and tickets, search the internet using the following key words, depending on the focus you prefer. Comparison shopping is a good idea, but any of these bus tours would be enjoyable.)
- Yellow Christian buses: "Rome Cristiana bus tours"
- Green Archeo buses: "Rome tram bus open"
- Red general tourist buses: "Rome hop on hop off viator"

OMNIA CARD FOR DISCOUNTS ON MULTIPLE SITES:
- www.OmniaVaticanRome.org/en/the-card/index.html

MONASTERY HOTELS:
- www.Hospites.it
- www.MonasteryStays.com

RELIGIOUS ITINERARIES:
- www.emmeti.it

TRIVIA 4 PILGRIMS

The four steps to sainthood include:
- "Servant of God:" title after candidate is nominated, usually by local bishop;
- "Venerable:" after investigation establishes "heroic virtue;"
- "Blessed:" after Church investigation concludes candidate's sainthood is "worthy of belief;"
- "Saint:" after establishing at least two miracles, accomplished through saint's intercession, the Church then canonizes, assured that the candidate shares the Beatific Vision.

Glossary

Church & Architecture Terms

- apse - rounded end of a church, behind the altar
- baldacchino - a canopy over an altar, shrine or throne in a Christian church
- *baroque* - a style in art and architecture, highly ornamented and flamboyant
- basilica - a Roman Catholic church given ceremonial privileges by the pope
- bas-relief - sculpture in which the image projects from a flat background
- campanile - a bell tower
- cappella - a chapel
- catacomba - underground tomb complex
- cattedrale - cathedral, where the seat (cathedra) of the local bishop is kept
- chiesa - church
- chiostro - cloister
- colonna - column
- confessio - before an altar, a sunken area, often holding relics, for confessing faith
- cosmatesque - style of mosaic flooring and other surfaces, originating from the 12th century Cosmati family
- cupola - dome
- facade - the ornamented front of a church
- fresco - combining colors with mortar on walls, adding permanence to the artwork
- Gothic - architectural style using pointed arches, flying buttresses, and high curved ceilings
- Greek cross - church floorplan with aisles of equal length intersecting at the altar
- icon - a venerated image
- Latin cross - church floorplan with a longer aisle in front of the altar
- le mura - city wall
- Madonelle - Madonna images (often with Child) used to decorate and protect buildings
- Mosaic - an arrangement of small cut stone or glass of various colors, forming an image
- Nave - the main aisle of a church
- Neo-classical - revival of art and architecture in the style of the eras of ancient Rome and Greece
- portico - the covered front porch, oftentimes on a church
- reliquary - a sacred container for holy relics
- rococo - a style of art and architecture, very ornate and popular in the 18th century
- Romanesque - style of 11th and 12th century European architecture, esp. with rounded arches and barrel vaults
- stucco - decorative work molded from wall plaster
- titulus - a private house once used for clandestine Christian worship
- tondo - art work in the round
- transept - church aisles that intersect right and left of the altar
- travertine - stonelike in appearance
- trompe l'oeil - painted architectural details that look three dimensional
- Vault - the ceiling over the nave

Everyday Italian

- aeroporto - airport
- albergo - hotel (up to 5 stars)
- autostazione -bus station
- autostrada - highway
- biglietteria - ticket counter
- biglietto - ticket
- bottega - shop
- carabinieri - police
- casa - house
- castello - castle
- centro storico - historic city center
- circo - circus, chariot race-track
- enoteca - specialty wine shop
- EUR - a Fascist-era complex south of Rome
- ferragosto - Feast of the Assumption but usually refers to August vacation after that day
- ferrovia - train station
- festa - holiday
- fiume - river
- fontana - fountain
- fornaio - bakery
- forum - public square
- gabinetto - public toilet (WC)
- gasolio - diesel fuel
- gelateria - gelato parlor
- Ghetto - popular "Jewish quarter" of Rome
- isola - island
- lago - lake
- largo - small square
- lido - beach
- locanda - small hotel
- loggia - covered porch
- mercato - market
- Metropolitana - metro
- monte - mountain
- museo - museum
- orto botanico - botanical gardens
- ostello - hostel
- palazzo - palace or very large building of any kind
- panneteria - bakery
- parco - park
- passeggiata - evening stroll
- pescheria - fish shop
- piazza - a public square
- saldi - sale (prices reduced)
- servizio - restaurant service charge
- stazione - station
- via - street or road

Index of Sites and Churches

IMAGE CREDITS

PHOTOGRAPHS
p. 24 Nero by shako
p. 24 Domitian by Jastrow 2006
p. 25 Marcus Aurelius by Bibi Saint-Pol
p. 25 Decius by Mary Harrsch
p. 25 Diocletian by G.dallorto
p. 41 Sancta Sanctorum by croberto68
p. 45 Mithraic Temple by Ice Boy Tell
p. 48 Piazza Navona by Tango7174
p. 77 S.M. dell'Orto nave by Lalupa
p. 80 San Benedetto exterior by LPLT
p. 80 San Benedetto interior by Lalupa;
p. 84 Tempieto by MarkusMark:
P. 89 Baths of Diocletian by Joris
p. 91 Santa Susanna interior by Tango7174
p. 106 San Martino crypt picture by Attilios
p. 108 Capuchin crypt by stanthe

p. 119 San Nicola interior by Paname-IV
p. 122 Baths of Caracalla by Chris 73
p. 122 Santi Nereo interior by LPLT
p. 123 San Cesareo interior by LPLT
p. 145 St. Peter's Square by Wknight94
p. 153 St. Peter's Basilica at night by Beatrice
p. 162 Vatican Garden maze & steps by Gugganij

PORTRAITS:
P. 28 Pope Julius II by Rafaello Sanzio
p. 29 Pope Alexander VI by Cristofano dell'Altissimo
p. 30 Michelangelo by Jacopino del Conte
p. 30 Raphael self-portrait
p. 30 Borromini self-portrait
p. 31 Bernini self-portrait
p. 31 Caravaggio by Ottavio Leoni

www.ingramcontent.com/pod-product-compliance
Lightning Source LLC
Chambersburg PA
CBHW051212090426
42742CB00021B/3426